CRITICAL ACCLAIM
FOR TRAVELERS' TALES

"This is travel writing at its glorious best."

—*Chicago Tribune*

"The Travelers' Tales series is altogether remarkable."
   —Jan Morris, author of *Trieste and the Meaning of Nowhere*

"For the thoughtful traveler, these books are invaluable."
                —Pico Iyer, author of *The Global Soul*

"Nightstand reading of the first order."

—*Los Angeles Times*

"…the popular Travelers' Tales collections offer a perfect fit
for just about anyone, with themes of geography, women's
travel, and a passel of special-interest titles on topics including shopping, pets, diners, and toilets around the world."
                —*Chicago Sun-Times*

"These well-edited anthologies of first-person travel narratives are like mosaics: Each piece may add only a single
note of color, but combine them and step back, and a rich
and multifaceted portrait emerges."

—*San Francisco Chronicle*

"The Travelers' Tales series should become required reading
for anyone visiting a foreign country who wants to truly
step off the tourist track and experience another culture,
another place, firsthand."

—*St. Petersburg Times*

"This is the stuff that memories can be duplicated from."
                —*Foreign Service Journal*

Antarctica
Life on the Ice

Antarctica
Life on the Ice

Edited by
SUSAN FOX ROGERS

TRAVELERS' TALES, AN IMPRINT OF
SOLAS HOUSE
PALO ALTO

Credits and copyright notices for the individual articles in this collection are given starting on page 297.

We have made every effort to trace the ownership of all copyrighted material and to secure permission from copyright holders. In the event of any question arising as to the ownership of any material, we will be pleased to make the necessary correction in future printings. Contact Solas House, Inc., 853 Alma Street, Palo Alto, California, 94301. www.travelerstales.com

Art Direction: Stefan Gutermuth
Cover Photographs: © Michael Graber/Peter Arnold, Inc.
Map: Keith Granger
Page Layout: Cynthia Lamb

Library of Congress Cataloging-in-Publication Data

Antarctica: life on the ice / edited by Susan Fox Rogers. —1st ed.
    p. cm.
  Includes bibliographical references and index.
  ISBN 1-932361-53-7 (pbk.: alk. paper)
  1. Antarctica—Description and travel. 2. Antarctica—Social life and customs.
I. Rogers, Susan Fox.
G860.A558 2007
919.8'9—dc22

                    2007024080

First Edition
Printed in the United States
10 9 8 7 6 5 4 3 2 1

For my father, Thomas H. Rogers,
who first turned my imagination to the South Pole

Table of Contents

Introduction

In the austral summer of 2005, I made a day trip by helicopter to Robert Falcon Scott's hut at Cape Evans on Ross Island. This was Scott's base in 1910 on the journey that ended with his death and the death of four of his crew. The story of this expedition is one of the saddest in Antarctic history and is my favorite. As a young girl, my father filled my head with stories of the South Pole (at one point I imagined Scott was a distant cousin and was angry with him for killing both dogs and ponies), so to visit the hut where they lived was a sort of pilgrimage. The hut was busy with a crew of New Zealand men digging out ice from its south side. I knew how the ice piled up there as I had read about it in Scott's journals and in Apsley Cherry-Garrard's marvelous account of Scott's final expedition, *The Worst Journey in the World*. The men handed me a pickax and for a while I chipped away with them with the great sense that this small gesture connected me to the past, even to heroism. Soon enough, though, this heroic traveler was tired, so I gave up my digging and wandered into the hut.

Once my eyes adjusted to the dim light I stood, overwhelmed by what had been left there: cans of collard greens and bottles of medical supplies above Dr. Wilson's bed; reindeer sleeping bags and *finneskos* (the Norwegian-style boots). When I looked closely I could see that the leather soles were peeling away. The daily lives of these explorers I so admired became clear to me as I looked at Cherry-Garrard's bunk bed, and noted where Ponting processed his photos. When I saw toothbrushes propped in glasses at the head of some of the men's beds I wanted to weep. For me, their lives were contained in those toothbrushes.

Daily details allow me to imagine a place, and the bigger the place, the more I need those details. Lucky for me, Scott's narratives are filled with passages like this from his 1901 expedition: "The first task of the day is to fetch the ice for the daily consumption of water for cooking, drinking and washing. In the latter respect we begin to realize that many circumstances are against habits of excessive cleanliness, but although we use water very sparingly, an astonishing amount of washing is done with it, and at present the fashion is for all to have a bath once a week."

A bath a week in melted ice water—for almost two years. With this sort of detail the "heroic age" of Antarctic exploration is brought down to the basics. What they ate, how they slept, and other facts of daily life make up much of the 1,200 pages of Scott's narrative of his 1901 expedition. Readers are dragged through days of manhauling; along with Scott and his men we suffer great cold and eat a lot of hoosh and biscuits. It is these details that are the foundation of their great feats.

What is remembered, however, is the tragic manner in which Scott and his men died in 1911, eleven miles from a food supply on their return from the Pole. A cross rests at the top of Observation Hill above McMurdo marking the deaths of Scott, Bowers, Wilson, Evans, and Oates. On it is inscribed Tennyson's great line: To strive, to seek, to find and not to yield. When I arrived at the top of Observation Hill, breathless in the thin clear air, tears emerged spontaneously and unexpectedly. I realized that the cross told the same story as that contained in their toothbrushes. I looked at the Ross Sea, made sure no one else was nearby, and kissed the cross.

The stories of Robert Falcon Scott, Earnest Shackleton, and especially Apsley Cherry-Garrard lured first my imagination and then me to the white continent. I am not alone; most people who venture south have these narratives as their framework, imagining that they, too, will experience blizzards and extreme temperatures, see penguins, and stand in awe of Mount Erebus.

I wanted to know what sort of tent I would sleep in at a remote camp, and if I would feel lonely waking in that tent—or if I would even be able to sleep with that endless sun. I wanted to experience an Antarctic wind on my face and understand what deep cold did to my bones. To understand a place I break it down into the simplest of human needs of sleep, warmth, food. But also: How do you keep communication with loved ones back home? How often does mail arrive? Are there showers? How do people travel around? Where do people pee? And what about love?

Through the narratives of early explorers I could gather some answers, but my two final questions remained unanswered. It wasn't until I visited Cape Evans that I saw that Scott and his men had outhouses, three for officers and one for enlisted men. (Modern visitors to the Antarctic do not use these outhouses.) But love, that remained the great mystery. Cherry-Garrard, in about six hundred pages, once thinks of "girls, or a girl…" That's a meager fantasy in two and a half years living in an all-male world on the most desolate continent on earth. I can forgive his omission only because these were, after all, British gentleman.

But the early accounts only gave me a sense of life in

Antarctica long before permanent bases, heated and with running water, and long before helicopters and LC130 cargo planes. I wanted to know what it was like for modern travelers on the continent. Some modern narratives gave me an idea of life on the Ice, but I wanted more; I needed to track down the stories I wanted to read, which meant I had to go to Antarctica.

No one ends up in Antarctica by accident. Flying there on your own dime is expensive and the other most commonly used route—getting a grant or a job on the Ice—is difficult. You have to be qualified for specialized jobs such as fixing snowmobiles in below zero temperatures or loading helicopters or pushing snow in a D8 Caterpillar bulldozer. Then there are those people who have learned a skill just to go south. In their real lives they are a park ranger or a dentist who wanted an adventure. In addition all workers and grantees have to be physically and mentally qualified for life on the Ice. So all of these healthy workers have landed in a place they want to be, and despite complaints about work (a six day/sixty hour a week schedule), a buoyant optimism reigns. I fell into that atmosphere with great joy when I arrived in McMurdo just before Christmas in 2004.

It had taken me years to get to the Ice. I applied for a Writers & Artists grant from the National Science Foundation in July of 2002. The proposal I sent them—to edit this collection—followed in the footsteps of other anthologies I had edited, especially one on Alaska, but I worried they would think I could put together the collection just as easily sitting in an office in the U.S. But that summer, a tentative "yes" arrived and over the course of the next year I attended meetings, had a rigorous physical, contacted dozens of scientists who might help me to see and experience the continent, and read as much as I could. The preparation was spectacular—lists of clothing I would need, plus all of my daily necessities for six weeks, which could not exceed forty-five pounds. I would like to say that after a six-hour flight from New Zealand, I stumbled out of the cargo plane and onto the Ross Ice Shelf and bent down and kissed the ice, head turned to honor Mount Erebus. But I did not. I was deaf from the plane ride, slightly nauseated, and a migraine was mounting an attack. I staggered to an orientation meeting in the galley, then to my overheated dorm (my roommate had the window propped wide open) and slept.

Since my goal while in Antarctica was to experience daily life and to find people in different fields of work who could describe that life for me, I was open to just about any experience that came my way. I worked with Solar Joe installing solar panels at a camp at New Harbor at the mouth of Taylor Valley, and there learned how to make Antarctic concrete: take sandy soil, hand carry a bucket of water from the Ross Sea, add to the sand, and within twenty-four hours it will be a frozen block. I helped penguinologist David Ainley count Adélie penguins and then inject pit tags in nesting penguins. I got to cup that football-shaped creature under my arm, as its flipper faintly beat me. I assisted Phil Allen as he hand drilled for ice cores in Garwood Valley and I chopped garlic for Rae Spain at Lake Hoare. When in McMurdo I wrote in my office overlooking the Ross Sea and then would take a shuttle out to Williams (Willy) Field and skate-ski the several miles back to town. These were some of the happiest weeks of my life.

From these experiences I wrote dramatic emails filled with tales of forty-five-mile-an-hour winds and the charm of penguins. Still, what fascinated me most was how people lived their lives, how our very human needs of food, work, play, sleep, and love fit in such a big place.

These essays will offer travelers a sense of those human needs—plus some. And yet I know that all of these writers and travelers are trying to describe the indescribable. You just cannot know what it is like to crave Ritz crackers slathered with butter until you've lived in a camp for several months in temperatures hovering near and below zero. Still, these essays reveal with great intimacy and detail moments of life in Antarctica, from the late '70s to the present. We have the voices of GAs (General Assistants) and scientists, of writers and those who have never written for publication. Through these vivid experiences, we are taken onto the Ice, and are offered the richness of daily life: there are essays here about food and loneliness, about riding snowmobiles and finding love. The essays that follow are set in the three U.S. bases—McMurdo, South Pole, and Palmer—and in camps in the Dry Valleys or on Ross Island and at remote camps on the polar plateau. There is one essay describing the thrill of flying in with the only independent company on the continent. The range of experiences here cannot cover life on the Ice, but they do offer some heroism, and much insight and humor from a big and beautiful place.

I can also promise that the writers here are not proper British gentleman—these essays reveal the ways of love on the Ice. But if you want to know how to pee in Antarctica, you will have to go there.

—Susan Fox Rogers

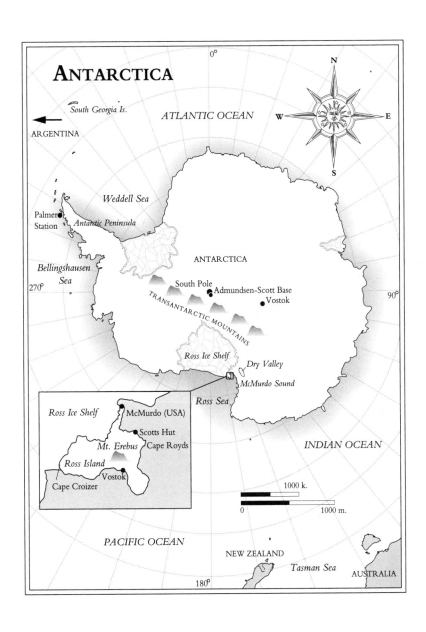

ANTARCTICA

South Georgia Is.

ARGENTINA

ATLANTIC OCEAN

Weddell Sea

Palmer
Station

Antarctic Peninsula

Bellingshausen
Sea

270°

ANTARCTICA

South Pole
● Admundsen-Scott Base
● Vostok

TRANSANTARCTIC MOUNTAINS

90°

Ross Ice Shelf

Dry Valley

McMurdo Sound

Ross Sea

INDIAN OCEAN

Ross Ice Shelf
● McMurdo (USA)
● Scotts Hut
Mt. Erebus Cape Royds

Ross Island

● Vostok

Cape Croizer

1000 k.

0   1000 m.

PACIFIC OCEAN

NEW ZEALAND

Tasman Sea

AUSTRALIA

180°

The Dry Valleys of Antarctica lie just across McMurdo Sound from Ross Island. It is in these valleys that many scientists conduct their work—search for nematodes, or measure the levels of the many small lakes and ponds that dot the valley. It's an impressive landscape, and in the Taylor Valley, where Joe Mastroianni is walking, sand and gravel meet the impressive Commonwealth, Canada, then Suess glaciers. They are called the Dry Valleys for a reason—they have almost never seen any precipitation, but there is plenty of wind, which has carved the rocks into ventifacts and shaved the fur off of seals that lie, freeze-dried, almost fifty miles inland.

It is amidst this surreal landscape that Joe finds himself with another contributor to this anthology, William Fox (whose own story "Leaving the Ice" appears on page 264 of this book). Their rambling conversation reveals the way the mind and the emotions move in such a landscape.

Joe has worked in Silicon Valley as a high-level engineering executive for twenty years. He's also a novelist, screenwriter, poet, musician, entrepreneur, programmer, engineer, technologist, father, and friend. He has tried almost everything once, and always winds up home.

In This Dream

* * *

JOE MASTROIANNI

THERE ARE PLACES IN ANTARCTICA WHERE YOUR FOOT-prints will outlive you.

On a long walk in the Taylor Valley, you can hear every grain of scratching dust compressed beneath your boot.

You can stand on a hilltop paved with red stones that extend to the mesa's edge, and see to one side the Kukri Hills, to the other the Matterhorn and the 7,000-foot-tall crags of Hill 1882, dripping glacier ice. At the center of the red mesa stands a house-sized boulder, wind-carved with swirls and patterns. Nature's hieroglyphics.

When confronted with something infinite, the mind invents stories to frame everything in well-bounded familiarity. Even a man of science and numbers, trained to ignore the nagging influence of imagination, must remind himself this place is not strewn with the ruins of a temple built by an extinct race. But rather, that non-linear equations and physics of laminar flow explain the spirals and serpentine shapes on the ground and in stone. That the depressions and passageways through the rock do not lead to chambers of worship, but are only regions of erosion where vortices spawned by the katabatics collected sand grains with regularity. That the wonder that has filled his chest has not killed him, but rather, in one blow has destroyed the intricate construction of pedestrian, suburban logic upon which he has based his self-image.

When men returned to this place in the 1950s they saw footprints and campsites they presumed were the remnants of recent explorations. Then in the detritus at the campsites they found the cast-offs from Scott's party, all appearing as if Scott and his men had left only a short while before. And they knew that time meant something different here.

The mind invents stories.

You walk through the valley as a mouse in a giant's house. Occasionally one of you mutters something absolutely trite, how gorgeous it is, how there are no words. The way the glaciers fall over the mountains like the head on an overfull glass of beer. The way the frost heave cracks in the ground in straight-sided polygonal structures. You point out the way millions of years of wind-blown sand turns boulders to pentagonal pyramids. You wonder at the age of the mummified seal carcasses. How a creature with no arms or legs could have traveled so many miles inland, crawling on its belly like a giant slug.

In awe of titanic beauty, you know why the ancients told stories. And now you need one, too.

I'm trying to keep my mind on the hike. My job—insinuating technology into this most holy geography. Putting up wireless networks so scientists studying the dry valleys can e-mail their home institutions, send instant messages, and order replacement hats and gloves online from the farthest place on earth. I'm trying to keep my mind on the twelve miles I was elected to traverse with the camp's professional writer. The perk people back in town would give up body parts for. Guide the writer between camps, on foot. Experience in-your-face

Antarctica. Towering blue ice and an ozone-free atmosphere guaranteed to cause cancer and cataracts. Trying to keep my mind on the landscape, and away from a simple human problem people bring with them wherever they go. What would Scott think? What would Nansen do in this situation?

I say—"Annie Haslan is mad at me," after one long stretch of nothing going by but the scribbles and doodles God left on a mountainside during a particularly boring hour of creation.

My travel companion, Bill Fox, stops in his tracks and stares at me as if I've just burst into flames.

"Say what?"

"The singer. She was online answering e-mails on a fan site and I posted a note about how I thought Renaissance had shown up drunk for a performance in Miami in 1977. Her producer assured me no such thing had happened. She sent me an email and chewed me out. They never drank before a performance."

It comes out and I have no idea why, or how I can control it.

Bill furrows his brow, considers what I've said, and looks back at the glaciers. "I see."

"You don't know who she is," I say. "I'm getting punchy."

We're walking between Lake Bonney camp and Lake Hoare camp. It's a trip of roughly eight miles across reasonably level ground. On the way we'll pass three glaciers and two frozen lakes. Lots of seal carcasses, freeze-dried and mummified by the atmosphere. Though they're hard as rock, some look like they died a few weeks ago. One of the biologists told us they're only between nine hundred and a couple thousand years old. Eternity to us is a mere eye-blink to the ice.

"How do you think these seals got here?" Bill asks. He's writing a book about the way humans interact with infinitely remote landscapes. Will my answer wind up on his pages? I need to set the record straight, then. Something else is in my mind besides the sundogs and rocks that seem to have been carved by the very mythical beings UFO-aficionados believe built the temples at Machu Picchu.

"I didn't sleep with her last night."

"Annie Haslan?" Bill says.

"No. The biology lady. I didn't. I swear, when I didn't expect it, she kissed me and threw me into severe, life-threatening cognitive dissonance."

"Life-threatening cognitive dissonance," Bill says, seeming as convinced as if I was trying to sell him a purple sky. "An unexpected kiss. I've heard that can happen."

"Totally, I mean, I'm married, O.K.?"

"So are a lot of other people down here. What do they say? 'What happens on the Ice stays on the Ice?'"

"Puts Antarctica on the same plane as Mardi Gras. There's something fundamentally sick about that. Like on a religious level."

Bill starts walking and I follow, but my mind keeps rolling back to the night before at the Bonney camp. In the Jamesway.

Last night there was a circle around the sun. A half-dreamed halo. The air turned translucent with ice fog. The clouds muffled the thumps to nothing when the final helicopter crossed the Commonwealth glacier. The radio chirped in the background one last time, then squelched dead for the weekend. She and I maneuvered in the Korean-war era tent like submariners. Always touching and bumping. Smiling.

On the Ice the territory is nearly infinite. In this landscape humans are nearly as rare as unicorns. But where there is one of us, there is almost certainly another. For safety. The buddy system. Or because habitation is sparse and so we must huddle for warmth. So there is no privacy on the Ice.

Until it finds you, unexpectedly.

The mind needs a story.

She and I in Bonney camp, alone. Bone and blood, imbued with the infinite mystery of biological chemistry that causes inanimate molecules to animate flesh. She did not know how to define the force that became locked within carbon, oxygen, and nitrogen at the Big Bang, and demands certain molecules reproduce and give rise to sentience.

"Nobody knows that," she said, handing me a mason jar filled with a greenish liquid.

She turned her back, resuming to her preparation at the counter. Outside a mild wind began. It rattled the sides of the Jamesway, raising in me questions about the fragility of the half cylinder upon the ground. A bubble of warmth that seemed it would collapse in the next big gust.

We could have been astronauts on an alien planet. We were surrounded by 10,000-foot-high peaks and blue-ice glaciers. Standing on land that hadn't changed since DNA emerged from the primordial soup, and would remember every step we took. The only sound for miles was the wind and our breath.

Then she started bashing blue lake ice with a hammer. And I wondered if somewhere, the great cosmic whomever who had decided to grant me consciousness was laughing and heading to the fridge for another beer.

The mind tells a story.

She decanted the last lime juice that existed for thousands of miles, but I couldn't stop thinking about the boulder we walked to, sides inscribed with the wind's handwriting, the plane of red and the Paleolithic swirls in the mountain's flesh.

"What's written on those rocks?" I asked her.

"What rocks?" She capped the Nalgene bottle and shook it.

"The ones up there, the red mesa."

"Oh, you mean up at the Rock Garden. They're ventifacts. The wind wears them down like that."

"I know. I've seen the ventifacts up by the Hughes Glacier. They're just smooth rocks with holes. Those ones up there are different though. It's like—what the hell is that plane of red rock? It's like being on Mars."

"Wild, isn't it?" she said. Poured herself a margarita. Set it down on a folding table that could have been borrowed from the thrift shop of the nearest Catholic Church, 6,000 miles to the north somewhere. She turned backward a beat up folding chair and sat, knees wide and almost touching mine. She rested her elbows on the chair back, chin on her forearms.

"So, what do you think?" she asked, and I sipped my margarita.

"Not bad," I said, tipping my jar toward her. "Good job."

"Not the drink. About the rocks."

There was a lot going on in my head. Stories rumbling through the gyri of my cortex. She'd think I was crazy if I told them. Maybe I was.

I said, "Did you know that half the people on the Ice are left-handed or blue-eyed? Statistically that's…"

"Cut the bullshit."

"O.K., then. You really want to know?"

"You worried someone's going to hear? You can trust me. I won't tell." She kicked my boot. Smiled. Sipped without breaking eye contact. "It stays on the Ice."

I knew that back home this would be something. Was it the same out here in Antarctica? What would Shackleton do in this situation?

Then I noticed. Couldn't help. Her eyes were blue-gray.

Her hair was blonde with streaks of strawberry. She held her jar in her left hand. She took a gulp. Wiped at her mouth with the back of a hand then rested her chin in the palm, elbow on the chair back and I could hear the words in my mind that one of us would have to say.

What are we going to do now?

She took another sip of her drink.

I said, "Thomas says the ice in these margaritas is as old as Jesus," figuring I could obscure the facts with more facts.

Outside the wind kicked up. Outside, the same sun that burned the Sahara flared impotently above the fruitless land. All that existed was the motion of the inanimate and prehistoric germs she'd come to study in the frozen lakes.

And us. All the other scientists were out at the west lobe drilling holes in the ice to take samples. They wouldn't be back for hours. Infinite solitude flooded two souls. Mine was drowning.

Find anything. Yesterday the camp manager took me to the Rock Garden.

"What's the deal with pictures up there?" I asked, fumbling, sorry I left my camera in my tent when the others in the camp requested I record nothing of the hike up the mountainside. Looking for any subject to take the place of the one she was pushing toward.

"Because it's our place. It's special. It's private. It belongs to the people who come here. There's no reason for anyone else to see it."

She took the jar out of my hand and put it on the table behind her.

"It's so beautiful," I said, something warm stirring in my chest, thinking if I said enough quickly enough we could just think about something else. Let's just think about something else. Tell her the story. I said, "It's like a fairy tale. If you told me it was a movie set, I'd believe you. It looked like—it made me feel things. Like…"

Her chair squeaked against the plywood floor as she skootched closer.

I said, "Like it was—like it was built by somebody for a reason. Like you could turn around and see the spirit of the ice, the Lady of the Frozen Lakes, rise from the ice and hand you Excalibur. Like we're blessed. Right on top of that hill is Shangri La and only we have ever seen it."

I remember her lips were cold from the blue ice; her tongue tasted of tequila and lime that used to be, and I never perceived her crossing the distance between us, but only saw her drifting from me, back into her chair, eyes closed, like someone who drowned and was carried away by the current.

"What happens now?" she said without opening her eyes.

I was trying to understand. Why. Couple things to consider. Workload. Lack of sleep. Incoherence. How to erase a memory that lived beside a geographic miracle.

Seconds, maybe a minute later I found my voice and said, "The rest of our lives, I suppose."

By the time I finish the story Bill and I reach Mummy Pond. We strap our stabilicers onto our boots. They're modified beach sandals with machine screws protruding from the soles that bite into the ice. We venture out onto the deep blue ice and despite everything the experts have said to me about the ice thickness, the insecure child in my mind assures me I'm going to fall through.

I'm staring at my feet waiting for the ice to break when Bill says, "It's thirty feet thick, you know." Strolling casually, turning occasionally to observe me. "They land airplanes on ice thinner than this."

I heard myself say, "I really mean it, I didn't sleep with her," as if that was as important as the fact the ground we were traversing had been crossed by a hand-counted number of people. Everyone who had ever been in this spot had their name in a ledger somewhere, either logged in the NSF's helo records, or Robert F. Scott's diary. It's a historic, isolated area, one of the most unattainable and gorgeous on earth.

But I feel as if Antarctica has taken a sandblaster to my mind and abraded years of learning and expectation. Nothing was the way I thought it would be. It was all bigger, colder, more beautiful, and more intense than I expected. And it was changing me. I could feel it. It was as if I'd sold my soul for a glimpse of Atlantis, and when I returned to the real world everyone would see me as a madman, babbling about imaginary cities of blue ice, about having touched the hand of a newly discovered god, about being damned forever for the arrogance of the deal.

I say, "She told me she slept in the Scott tent. I knew that was an invitation, but I just ignored it. I came back to the polar haven. Didn't you hear me come in?"

"O.K.," Bill says. "Enough." I follow him to the shore of the frozen lake. He pulls off his pack and I do the same. Snap a few photos. He takes out some food I didn't see him pack in the Jamesway at Bonney. We sit next to a large ventifact and he hands me a piece of cheese and a Cadbury bar.

We munch our snacks in silence. And after a good long time, when the cold has had the chance to still my mind, Bill says, "This is pretty wonderful, isn't it?"

At last, words don't come to me.

"You O.K.?" he asks, and I nod automatically. Bill says, "You gotta take it slowly. Integrate. Get some perspective. You're not the first person to be blown away by the ice."

"This isn't hell, then?"

Bill laughs. Sighs. Stares out toward the Suess Glacier. He says, "When you get home, read some of the stuff you've written in your blog. You don't realize how important it is to you. You can't until you get back and you come back to yourself."

"Come back to myself?"

"You started to tell me but you never finished—how did it feel, the moment you stepped on the ice?"

How do I feel? I'd just spent a lifetime worrying about where I had been and where I would go. Was I positioned well for the next career move? Had all the bills been paid? Did I have enough insurance so I could die responsibly? Could I be forgiven for tossing away so many precious heartbeats that way? And from whom would I ask forgiveness?

The sun streams upon us from an ozone-free sky that's almost black. Ice clouds high above divide the light into rainbows of yellow, magenta, and cyan. The glacier creaks. A chunk of blue-green ice calves from its face. It sounds like a case of drinking glasses falling from a warehouse shelf.

I say, "There's the one thing that defines you to yourself in your own head. You can tell other people, 'Well, I'm an engineer, or a plumber, or a mechanic.' But this is it for me. No matter what I ever told anyone else, I have always been in my mind someone who lives on the Ice. I can remember being a kid in the grammar school library reading about Scott and Shackleton and wishing as hard as I could to go. I have had no greater wish in my life."

Bill crumples his candy bar wrapper, careful not to get the slightest crumb on the ground.

I say, "It feels like being in love."

He smiles and I see myself reflected small and abstract in his dark glacier glasses. Bill says, "Rae Spain, the camp manager for the Taylor Valley told me she thought our life here was as close to a utopian society as you could get on earth. We're clothed, fed, kept healthy, surrounded by nature; we work on interesting things and are continuously accompanied by interesting people. We just have to realize how lucky we are, and be appropriately thankful."

When he stops speaking, and there is no voice to fill my ears, my heart is as loud as the wind.

"Strange things happen to people in your state of mind," he says, gathering his backpack, reseating his stabilicers. "But I think—well what I think is that if it feels like love, it probably is."

We get back onto the ice and make our way toward the Suess Glacier defile, and Lake Hoare camp beyond.

And as we walk I wonder how I will explain it to my family at home. What story I can invent to make them accept that I have betrayed the normal, everyday life of which they have been a part these many years, and fallen in love with a dream.

Those who tell stories of the old days in McMurdo are the most renowned—and funniest—storytellers on the Ice. Karen Joyce is in that league. After sixteen seasons of Antarctic work Karen seems to know everything about what happened then, and what happens now. Karen defies the image of the polar traveler: "It's strange how much I love this place, even though I am absolutely the wrong body type for Antarctica. Cold places select for gigantism, for a ratio of surface area to interior space that maximizes the latter, and I am a wee peanut of a woman. I have been frozen hard and thawed out so many times, I ought to be a quaking gelatinous mess by now." She knows that Scott never would have picked her to pull a sled to the South Pole, and yet she did once try and reenact Scott's manhauling feats.

Karen was born in New Castle, Pennsylvania, and lived in San Francisco for fifteen years before heading to Antarctica, where she first worked as a General Assistant (GA) and now serves as the Information Technology Manager for the science community. Through the long Antarctic night, she writes her second novel, "The Winter of My Discount Tent."

The Day It Rained Chickens

＊ ＊ ＊

KAREN JOYCE

IT'S BEEN ALMOST FIFTEEN YEARS, BUT EVEN NOW THE construction guys find the occasional chicken bone lodged deep in the eaves and gutters of McMurdo Station. And quite possibly I'm the last person still around who remembers how they got there.

McMurdo was a different place back then, my first year on the Ice. I had leapt at the job the Antarctic company had offered me: a General Assistant, a jack-of-no-trades grunt. Minimum wage for fifty-four hours a week, but so what? It was a free ticket to Antarctica! When the contract showed up in the mail at my apartment in San Francisco, I was doing backflips down the hallway like a Lotto winner.

Not everyone got my glee. The reaction from my co-workers at the marble-floored law firm where I was temping was digital, ones and zeroes: "What're you, nuts?" or "Wow, how can I get a job down there?" Either you got it, or you didn't.

This whole Antarctic thing had come around for me almost as fast as I'd conjured up the aspiration for it. A couple of weeks earlier, our little group of temp workers had spent a dispirited Friday afternoon crystallizing in a single sentence what our perfect jobs would be in an ideal world. It took some mental gnashing but what I finally came up with was anything that took me to the far ends of the Earth, with the transport on somebody else's nickel.

Two months later I was standing on an ice shelf the size of Texas, my heart pounding under five layers of company-issue clothing as I took it all in. A drab-colored military aircraft squatted behind me on scenery straight off the cover of a science-fiction novel: an unbroken plain of ice, stretching without boundary to the east, rimmed in by a massive mountain range to the south and west. Even after I'd fished out my inky sunglasses, the ice dazzled my eyes in the wild sunlight. It seemed lit from within and without, a neon stage for the Japanese woodcut of a volcano to the north: Mt. Erebus, with a plume of steam flowing away from its perfect cone like an aviator's scarf. At its base there appeared to be a town spread out across a brown hillside spackled with dirty snow. McMurdo?

As I stood there, a sharp wind came up and slapped me hard across the face, zinging my cheeks into saddle leather. Like a herd of musk ox, the group of us spun away from it and faced east. I leaned back into the wind as far as it would allow and suddenly the air felt bracing, joyous, full of unprecedented adventure. With the next big gust I fell forward, staggering like Heidi taking her first steps into Grandfather's arms. *Whee-haw!* I yelled into my balaclava. *This is great!*

But my numinous moment of polar ecstasy was brief. The station itself was not at all what I'd expected, more overheated Navy base than REI camp. It looked and felt like a down-on-its-luck Club Med on Mars, an anachronism squatting on a depleted pile of mining slag, the sad sheetmetal buildings of the town slung out across the landscape in strict military rows. The whole place left me feeling betrayed, somehow. Those

PBS specials on Antarctica I'd been watching for the past ten years must have conveniently passed over this depressing metropolis of a thousand people, a town that was by far the largest (and most likely the ugliest) human settlement on the entire continent.

Right from the start, my new life was taken over by the bureaucracy: I was told I needed to report for orientation in the Chalet, get the keys to my rundown Motel 6 dorm room, run up to Hill Cargo for my bags, and then quickly head over to the Galley for dinner before it buttoned its blouse for the night. And when I finally got to dinner, the food did not look promising. The guy in front of me was glopping some orange mush onto his prison tray as he read the sign out loud, Sloppy Joe's. Turning to me, he whispered, *More Slop than Joe, hey?* It turned out to be the first of many meals that leveled hunger but left another kind of longing in their wake. At least it was all free and unlimited. And somebody even lower on the food chain than I had to clean it all up.

That same night I joined a couple of other new arrivals making the rounds at the four frontier bars, each strictly segregated by Navy rank: Chief with Chief, enlisted with enlisted. I was beginning to realize that for most of the people who worked here, the place was thoroughly drenched in the syrup of American comfort. Sheltered by the overheated buildings, they dressed for shopping-mall climes, suffering only when they stepped outdoors. I watched as a pair of dainty women, bolstered on the arms of their stalwart dates, demurely held up their hoods to protect their hairstyles against the wind as they passed from the Erebus to the Chief's. Not one little bit what I had been envisioning.

The next day, my first day of work, I found out that we GAs were different. Not only did the eight of us struggle against the elements for ten hours a day, our jobs were guaranteed to be the station's worst of the worst, filthy stuff that nobody else wanted. But from the start we shared a pride in our exceptionalism, flaunting our leprous, grease-covered coats when we hung them outside the Galley. We ate and drank like pink-cheeked peasants. I didn't have enough guts to tell the others that I was wretched with cold most of the time, yearning for my sweetly carpeted cubicle back in the city. After my first long day of frozen struggle at −40°F, against a wind that instantly turned my exposed flesh into agonized wax, I began to reflect on how my tiny body might not be ideally suited to the job and climate I'd signed on for. Five months of this looked to be an eternity of pain, when taken moment by moment.

October and November went by at the speed of geology. But a day finally came when the cold retreated like a time-lapse shadow and the sun hit us square in the face, hot as a sauna rock. We burst out of our cold weather gear like snakes shedding skin.

The day had started off up at the dump. We'd spent the last week wading knee-deep in garbage, looking for the lost crates of windows that Rusty, the famous drunk, might have accidentally "delivered" to the landfill instead of the Carpentry Shop. I hated the dump: the squishiness of half-frozen rot underfoot, the boards with their rusty nails sticking up, and who knew what worse horrors with every step. But there was no point in complaining.

We were already three hours into the morning's trudge when a giant forklift pulled up with two enormous cardboard boxes riding on its forks. The driver opened the window and yelled down at us, "Hey, where do you guys want this?" The wind blew the sickly-sweet smell of rotting meat across us, overlaying the fruity vinegar of the dump.

Jason, our self-appointed spokesman, glanced back at the rest of us. "Ha! Where do *we* want it? Anywhere but here, dude! Thanks for playing!" He waved a cupped hand and turned away.

Just then Guster, our wizened little cowboy of a boss, materialized from behind the forklift. "So what you got in there?" he yelled up at the driver, setting his enormous bunny boots at acute angles to each other.

"Chickens from the Galley. Got left out a little too long on the back deck. Got a little ripe."

Guster walked over and flipped the lid of one of the boxes open before spinning away. "Hoo, *daddy*! He held a gloved hand over his nose and looked over it at us, half-buried as we were in the station's detritus.

"Just leave them boxes over there by them folks, they'll take care of it," he said, gesturing at a spot a few feet away. The forklift driver dutifully dropped his load and bounded away down the hill, empty forks crashing violently with every bump in the road. By then we'd managed to pull ourselves out of the dump and were circling the boxes warily.

Jason pulled up in front of Guster, leaned on his shovel and asked, "So what exactly do you suggest we do with this pestilential bullshit?"

Jason had made it abundantly clear that he had no intention of returning to McMurdo next season, a decision that had considerably swelled his balls in the authority-challenging department. Most of the time we appreciated his insouciance, united as we were against Guster and his shriveled Little Hitler act.

Guster jerked a pack of Marlboros out of his jacket, tapped one out and cupped it against the wind. He gave the match a cursory shake before tossing its tiny fire behind him. "Well," he replied as strings of smoke traced an arc from his mouth to the barren hills in the distance, "let's just let nature's scavengers have their way!"

None of us were exactly sure what he meant by that, but it was just about time for lunch so we all nodded vaguely and headed down the hill to the Galley.

As we sat bunched together eating cardboard pizza, we debated what Guster meant. Should we just let the skuas, those mean-ass Antarctic scavengers that hovered in great swirling packs above the dump, take the chickens away? Howie said that wasn't kosher: didn't the Antarctic Treaty make that totally illegal? We'd been lectured on the Treaty at the Chalet when we'd first arrived—how any interference with the native wildlife (and feeding the skuas in particular) would drop a $10,000 fine on your head. But on the other hand if we didn't just leave the boxes open to be raided, *we* would have to deal with 500 pounds of stinking rotten full-body fryers. And who wanted to get anywhere near that?

As we spooned the day's soggy dessert into our mouths, we gradually came to consensus in favor of "following orders." Choose your battles, Jason kept repeating. And this one just ain't worth it.

We emerged from the Galley a half an hour later and were remarking for the tenth time that day on the miracle of the sun, when Snackbar stopped dead like he'd walked into a dump truck.

"Ho-ly shit, look at that! Are they burning the dump?" We followed his gaze up to a dark, undulating shadow that was moving across the sky above the landfill.

The wonder of it shut us up, heads cocked. I was getting used to things in Antarctica verging so far off the norm you had to suspend the usual set of assumptions about the Earth.

There were the fata morgana mirages across the ice shelf, for one. Anyone seeing them for the first time would assume that the Royal Society Mountains sprouted out of the great white plain from a series of spectacularly sheer ice cliffs. An optical illusion, it turned out, light bending across a cold surface. So who knew what kind of trick the atmosphere was playing on our eyes with this writhing black mass above the dump? It was way too early for the monthly burn. And that definitely did *not* look like smoke.

Jason broke the silence. "Oh God. What do you want to bet those are skuas?"

Sure enough, when we were halfway up the hill we could make them out, a seething, protean mass of avian fury, fascinating and sickening as a mass of spiders.

"Jesus!" came from Chris as he sheltered his eyes with a glove. "Wow, that's like...like straight out of that movie, what was it called? The one with all the birds...?"

"*The Birds*," we chorused.

"Yeah, that's it!"

Strong like ox, smart like tractor, Jason was fond of saying about Chris.

When we got within a hundred yards of the boxes, the sky darkened above us with skuas dive-bombing from all directions, descending in whirling vectors. All of them were squabbling violently over the only chicken that they had managed to wrangle out so far, when the boxes held enough chickens to last a lifetime for every skua on the continent. We watched as one bird made a quick grab and tried to fly away with it, but the three-pound carcass weighed almost as much as its new owner and dropped with a wet plop onto the rocks right next to us. Suddenly we found ourselves in the middle of the fierce commotion, wind from flapping wings whooshing our cheeks, surrounded by a deafening cacophony of squawks. Each bird was desperate to wrest the fallen chicken away from its fellows, oblivious to the 501 uncontested fowl that lay, heaped and reeking, a few feet away.

We took a couple of steps backwards as every skua within a half-mile radius hurtled towards us like kamikazes. But in less than a minute, these new arrivals discovered the bounty in the boxes. A giant atomic feather-ball rose up, every skua fighting to extract a slippery chicken from the box. But for every chicken that was airlifted away, another fell to the ground at the feet of some lucky dope, who defended it valiantly against all rivals with a great show of wingspan and beak.

None of us had ever seen anything even remotely like this before, up close or otherwise. "Wow!" said Chris, the youngest of our gang. "It's like Animal Planet!"

Jason began expounding on how far off balance the human race had gotten if reality brought nothing more to mind than a TV show, when Guster suddenly snuck up on us from behind.

"Whay-hale, look-y that!" he grinned, showing off his yellowish teeth. Sometimes I wondered whether Guster put on the South Texas accent extra-thick just for the recoil he got out of us.

We turned to face him, hoping he might feel a certain measure of shame and responsibility for the scene erupting around us. Maybe he'd somehow be able call a halt to it, seeing as it had gotten so obviously out of hand.

"Whale, things seem to be taking care of 'emselves just fine up here, so let's just git out of the way here now. Let's head on back to the fuel bladders till this here is...all finished up!"

He took a few steps down the hill before he turned

around to see that none of us were following him. We'd spent the entire month of November up at the Retro Yard, cutting enormous fuel bladders into eight-inch squares, completely covered in the black, stinking fuel oil that had gelled inside of them. All of us would have gladly given up our end-of-contract bonuses than return to that pox of a job. Jason and Snackbar exchanged glances, each waiting for the other to lead the rebellion.

But as usual, after a few blank moments we silently shrugged and avoided each other's eyes as we trailed our splay-footed little boss down the hill. Reluctantly picking up the tools we had thrown down a month before, we shuffled back to the field of bladders, kicking violently at the first ones we passed. They shuddered like beached whales as the fat layer of wet snow fell off of them in sheets. We kept on going, kicking and stabbing half-heartedly till Guster disappeared. Then we headed back up to the dump.

By the time we got there, the scene had escalated into a skin-crawling horror, a wreathing mass of annihilation. Feathers, birdshit, and chicken parts carpeted the area within a hundred yards of the boxes. Naked, headless chickens held none too securely in the flimsy beaks of skuas, were being dropped again and again within a few feet of lift-off. These were instantly swooped down upon by other birds who bullied all rivals in great contests of squawk and wing. The less dominant birds took hold of whatever body parts had been scattered onto the surrounding rocks and beat a hasty retreat with a piece of pink flesh dangling from their beaks. I tried to focus my eyes from the chaos to individual birds, who appeared to be moving their spoils to secluded spots in the protected invaginations of boulders, or spiriting them off to God knows where.

It seemed to me that, amusing as it was, the whole thing boded ill for us. My law-firm training kept dredging up the terms "legally culpable" and "accessory to the crime." Everything about this bizarre fracas of birds beak-deep in a largesse unprecedented in the history of Antarctica, nose-diving in the egregious waste of McMurdo and hardwired to fight for their lives on the raw edge of starvation, spelled trouble for us—the complicit GAs.

The morning of the following day we woke up to find the entire town festooned with swinging chickens. They were hanging by their wings from power lines, strewn in parts and wholes across the parking lots, and decorating the hoods of pickup trucks and the buckets of loaders plugged in at Derelict Junction. They fell from the sky next to pedestrians on their way to breakfast, who stood with their hands shielding their eyes, looking up in wonder at the bodies swinging from telephone wires and stepping carefully over the torn-up pieces on the ground. It looked like a war zone, the scatterings of a misguided airdrop—as if the heavens had opened up and rained chickens upon the town.

Heading out of my dorm toward the Galley, I fell in behind a couple of electricians who were trying to make sense of the scene.

"Ho man, what the hell kind of prank is this?" Shades asked Eddy as he watched a half-chicken slip off the sheet-metal roof of Dorm 208 and land with a splat to his left. "Man, somebody's gonna get their ass kicked for this one!"

"Yeah, no shit! Whoever did this is one fired son-of-a-bitch!" Eddie agreed with a crooked grin.

"Probably took at least a couple of guys to cover this much area," Shades figured.

"But how the hell did they manage to get all this crap all the way up there and everywhere?" Eddie gestured broadly across the utility poles strung out across town.

Shades theorized that some drunks must have gotten it into their heads to "decorate" the town last night, most likely using the Linemen's bucket truck. Both of them started speculating about the culprits: Who would have had access to the Linemen's truck? Suddenly it came to them: *Mike Bates and Mickey Quinn! Who else but the Linemen themselves? Oh my God,* they laughed, *they are going to get so fired for this!*

By the time I made it in to breakfast, I realized that the whole town had come alive with the magic of a witch-hunt. And only nine of us knew the truth.

Later on we heard that Guster had panicked when he'd seen the carnage outside his dorm door and made a beeline for the dump. Vaguely aware that there would be hell to pay if the source of the diaspora was traced to him, he decided to call a pre-emptive powwow.

"O.K!" he said, rubbing his palms together as we gathered up at the dump that morning. "We've...uh, kind of opened what you might call Pandora's Triwall Boxes up here, heh heh!"

We avoided his eyes, focusing instead on the birds that swirled above us in loops and figure eights, an elaborately choreographed aggro-ballet.

"If you know what I mean, these boxes here, I mean," he waved a hand toward them, ignored by his audience. "What I'm trying to say is, well, we're...."

He got stuck. What *was* he trying to say?

"Now listen up! Let me ask a big favor of you all, a real big favor now. If you all don't mention anything about these here triwalls, I'll make sure you never have to get anywhere near that dump ever again!"

Suddenly he had our full attention.

"Whoa, whoa, whoa, hang on a second!" came from Jason. "Are you saying you want to *buy* our silence on this 'potential issue'?" His fingers sketched quotes in the air. "Like, we agree to hush this thing up in return for not having to dive into this putrid slop anymore, is that it?"

Guster turned his desiccated face toward each of us, his dry eyes blinking.

"Sounds like a deal to me," said Snackbar. "Trading silence for a reprieve from hell? I'm in. Or maybe we should hold out for the fuel bladders, too, what do you guys think?" The rest of us shrugged and lifted our eyebrows. It sounded good to me till Jason spoke up again.

"Now wait a second!" he said, raising a scabrous glove. "I don't see any reason why we should buy in on this. For one thing, if the truth ever comes out about what happened, our asses would be on the line, too, and we had nothing to do with this decision, right? He's just trying to buy us off. And do any of you guys trust him not to sell us down the river if it comes down to that?"

Guster suddenly realized he'd walked into a box canyon, and the only way out was fight.

"O.K. hold on there, hold on there!" He turned a gloved palm at Jason. "You are not...you are misunderstanding what I'm sayin' right here, I didn't say nothin' about anything bein' wrong up here! Everything is just *fine* up here, just..."

As if on cue, a skua with a grayish swatch of flesh in its beak swept down across his face. He swatted at it like a gnat before continuing.

"Now do I need to remind you all that your job is whatever and where ever I tell you to go and do? And they ain't nothin' up here requires your attention at the moment. So you best git yourselves back up to them fuel bladders, till I tell you elsewise!" He flung a hand at us, shooing us away.

We needed no further encouragement to spin around on our boot heels and head back down the hill toward the Retro Yard. But as soon as we got out of earshot of Guster, we turned on Jason and started debating the relative merits of what had just gone down. Most of us agreed that we might have had some leverage with the guy, some room for negotiation, and now here we were being sent back up to wallow in the veritable La Brea Tar Pits.

The sound of tires slogging axle-deep in water turned our heads. An unusually clean double-cab pickup truck was heading our way, careening wildly back and forth as it crossed the deep erosion gullies on the road.

"Hey look, it's the NSF!" said Jason.

Snackbar stood out of the road to make room. "Wonder what they're doing up here?"

"Overseeing the new poultry operations, perhaps?"

The truck pulled up next to us and stopped. Four immaculately groomed men and a woman sat inside, each decked out in a spotless red parka. The driver rolled his window down and nodded sharply at us. Jerking his head slightly uphill, he asked if we had seen any open boxes full of…. He glanced nervously at the Senatorial gentleman sitting next to him, seemingly at a loss for the proper terminology.

"Chickens?" Jason volunteered.

He swung back around toward Jason and replied, "Why, yes, in fact. Chickens. Exactly. Have any of you seen an open box up here full of chickens?"

Jason and Snackbar pointed up the hill like a couple of tattling school kids. "Up there! And there's *two* boxes, not one!" they yelled. "See all those skuas? Right up there!"

"And the man responsible for the whole debacle is sitting right next to them, picking the birdshit out of his hair!" Jason added.

The three bureaucrats in the back seat burst into giggles that were quashed instantly by a sharp Senatorial glance.

"Alright then, thanks! Appreciate the information!" the driver said as he hit the gas, splattering us with mud as the truck lurched forward towards the dump.

We turned uphill to watch the truck disgorge its passengers next to Guster, who was shaking hands with one arm while straining the guano out of his hair with the other. Unfortunately we were a couple of hundred feet too far away to be able to hear anything.

"We should go back up there and find out what lame-ass excuses he's giving them," suggested Jason.

Snackbar shifted backwards on his boot heels. "Yeah, and what do you want to bet he's telling them the whole thing was all our fault?"

Howie turned on Jason. "I wonder if your little outburst is going to wind up making us spend the rest of the season sawing fuel bladders into pointless geometric shapes."

"Eet bodes veddy veddy eel, por chore," commented Aaron, finger in the air.

Jason just shrugged and focused on the scene up the hill. Not knowing what else to do, we slowly drifted back to our headquarters, the GA Shack, for want of a better destination. Crumpling into our homeless-shelter couches and chairs, we sat quietly awaiting the next chapter of our fate.

"And it's not even eight-thirty yet," observed Snackbar. "Almost two hours till break and I'm already goddamned starving."

Just then Guster blew in the door like a Texas windstorm.

He scowled across us, mouthbreathing. I sunk deeper into my cold-weather gear, hoping to vanish.

"Who.... Which one of you?..." His pinched eyes landed on Jason. "Oh don't think I don't know. Don't think I don't know what you done." He pulled his workman's gloves off and stood wheezing heavily over him, his wrinkled eyes disappearing even further into their folds.

"You know what? I believe I have a special assignment just for you. Something you gonna enjoy. All by yourself."

Jason drilled himself backwards into the couch, squirming right and left like a dog being threatened by a newspaper.

"You come on ouside here with me, and let's have ourselves a little talk."

Jason pulled himself up and looked around at us, his eyes desperate. But there was nothing we could do, so we kept quiet. The two of them went outside into the wind, which was just starting to pick up like it did every morning.

After a moment of stunned silence, Ben, our Zen-master GA, shocked us all by springing to his feet with a fist in the air. "That is totally bullshit! He didn't do anything wrong!" Ben paced back and forth in the twelve feet it took to get across the tiny shed, wild-eyed and panting.

I certainly couldn't see any way any of us could help Jason. American labor law has a long tradition of being suspended down here: for starters, we worked fifty-four hours a week, meaning a guaranteed fourteen extra hours with no overtime. Making an issue out of that or any of the rules could run you right up against the "My Way or the Fly Way" maxim that had been hammered into us when we first got to McMurdo. It was no lame threat: we'd seen several of our friends get the boot when they'd taken up some cause or offered a glib editorial comment to an upper management type in the lunch line. Just about anything could get you fired, and "lawsuit" wasn't part of the Antarctic lexicon. For all we knew, Jason was being drawn and quartered at the Chalet even as the rest of us sat paralyzed, deep in our crumbling furniture.

Except for Ben. He was on some kind of a tear, about to fly outside and reign holy jihad on the town when the door flew open again, revealing a solitary Jason.

"Whoa!" we chorused, springing to life. "What the hell, man?"

Jason raised a palm at us, smiling. "You are not even going to believe what just went down!"

He paused, his thin lips frozen in a fox grin till I couldn't stand it anymore.

"Ha!" he said, throwing both hands in the air. "So, get this! We were walking back down the hill towards the Chalet, right? And Guster isn't talking, isn't saying a word, so I'm wondering whether he's marching my ass off to fire it, right? When, get this—that same truck full of NSF guys that we ran into on our way to the dump pulls up, but this time Guster's boss and the Station Manager are with them!"

Jason twirled neatly around and dropped to one knee, punching his fist in the air. His eyes were burning with triumph. "And so guess what happens then?"

All of us sat wordless with anticipation.

"They freakin' told him to get in the freakin' truck! WHOO!"

My eyebrows pulled together as I looked around at the others for their reaction.

"I don't get it," said Snackbar. "So they told him to get in the truck. So what?"

Jason scanned the room. "Don't you guys *see*? Man, there was no love in that truck, I'm telling you! I mean it was freakin' *grim*, the way they were looking at him! And then he just got in and they drove off, just left me standing there in the road. *Hee hee!*"

None of the rest of us shared his confident glee till we got down to the Galley for lunch, where we found the lynch mob that is McMurdo already dining on its favorite morsel: gossip. The word on the street was that Guster was indeed done for, out of here on the next airplane. Chucked for the chooks.

Unfortunately we didn't have much time to celebrate. Our next job turned out to be, not surprisingly, the monster cleanup. And with the weather continuing to improve, it was relatively easy to find the decaying dead using only our noses. We spent the next month and a half picking poultry parts out of every cranny of every building in town, stuffing the cold, greasy bits back into triwall boxes just like the ones they'd come out of before all this craziness got started.

By the time we were done, whatever "done" was, it was late January, almost time to head back to New Zealand and the relative sanity of the real world. I had already made up my mind that I wanted to come back to McMurdo again next season, for reasons I couldn't quite parse out. And fourteen years of working in this far-flung nuthouse later, I sometimes wonder if I ever will.

The winds in Antarctica are legendary. They rise from the South Pole and pick up speed. If you can no longer see Minna Bluff, a Herbie is on its way. In the entranceway of all of the dorms in McMurdo LCD signs announce the weather: Condition One is when visibility is less than 100 feet, or wind is greater that 55 knots, or wind chill is greater than -100°F. No one should go out in a Condition One. Condition Two is wind between 48-55 knots, visibility is less than a quarter of a mile, and wind chill is greater than −75°. Condition Three is described as better than condition Two. This is what the weather is most of the time and people move about freely. Jim Mastro's adventure in a storm in the dark of an Antarctic winter is a Condition One adventure.

Jim first went to Antarctica in August of 1982 and stayed for fourteen months. Since then, he has returned eleven times and held a variety of positions, including assistant laboratory manager (summer), laboratory manager (winter), research assistant, science diving coordinator, dive team leader, and cruise ship lecturer. Most recently, he returned to McMurdo Station in late 2005 to serve as interim manager of the Crary Science and Engineering Center. In total, he has accumulated seventy months on the Ice, including two winters, and he has been to all three permanent U.S. stations. Jim holds an undergraduate degree in zoology, worked as a marine biologist for many years, and served as a university instructor. He has a Masters degree in English and has published a number of articles, essays, short stories, technical papers, photographs, and books, including Antarctica: A Year at the Bottom of the World *and* Under Antarctic Ice: The Photographs of Norbert Wu. *Originally from San Diego, he currently lives in New England with his wife and son, where he writes full time. His essay is adapted from* Antarctica: A Year at the Bottom of the World.

Lost in the Storm

* * *

JIM MASTRO

EVEN BY ANTARCTIC STANDARDS, THIS BLIZZARD HAD been brutal. It was the winter of 1986, and for nearly two weeks almost non-stop hurricane-force winds had driven blinding snow across Hut Point Peninsula, bringing activity at McMurdo Station to a standstill. Though the continuing storm had kept anyone from taking a full accounting of the damage, I knew that at least one building, a Quonset-shaped, tent-like structure called a Jamesway, had been destroyed. I had passed it this morning while fighting my way from my dorm room to the biology laboratory, where I worked. Half the wooden frame was gone, along with the cloth that had covered it. The rest lay bare, with a few tatters of fabric whipping in the wind. It looked like the rib cage of a large animal whose flesh had been ripped from its bones.

I had shuddered when I walked by, and not just from the cold that bit through my parka. My sense was that the storm was not through with us yet. A few times the wind had diminished and visibility improved for a few hours, enough for people to start moving around again. But no sooner had we tried to resume normal operations than the storm had kicked up again. The helicopter pilots called these false respites "sucker holes." Antarctic storms were famous for them. A patch of clear sky would appear and the storm would appear to be breaking. A pilot anxious to get somewhere would be suckered into flying into the clearing, only to have the storm close in around him.

Now, as I stood in the doorway of the laboratory and looked out, I wondered if that wasn't happening again. The wind had dropped in the last couple of hours to an almost reasonable twenty-five knots and, except for a few wisps scudding along the ground, the air had cleared of blowing snow. Across the dirt road that ran in front of the lab, a mercury-vapor street lamp cast a circle of yellow light on the snow-covered ground. Nearby, the Chalet, a small wooden structure that served as the NSF administration building, sat dark and empty. Like so many other buildings in McMurdo, it had been shuttered for the winter. I glanced up. Telephone and power lines overhead twisted in the wind.

I didn't like the looks of it, but Steve had decided to take advantage of the relative calm to drive down to the aquarium. Steve was a marine biologist studying single-celled organisms called foraminifera. His live cultures of the critters had to be kept in salt water at ambient temperature, and the aquarium was the only place to do it. It was a pre-fabricated wooden structure called a T-5, identical to the buildings used to create the biology lab. To get there, he'd drive his tracked vehicle, called a spryte, down the hill in front of the lab, make a sharp left turn to keep from driving out onto the now-frozen sea, and travel along a narrow road between the sea ice on the right and a steep hillside on the left.

As with most sprytes, Steve's didn't have much of a heater, and the windows tended to fog up quickly. But the trip was short. After telling me he only needed a few minutes, he threw his parka over the t-shirt and sweat pants he always wore in the lab, jumped in the vehicle, and took off. All he had on his feet were tennis shoes.

I shut the lab door and went back to work in my cramped office.

Caught up in organizing the lab's inventory records, I didn't look up again until some time later. A change in sound had caught my attention. The low background hum of the wind snaking around the rickety laboratory had turned once again into a loud, low rumble, punctuated by heavy thumps as gusts slammed into the back door or tore at the roof. The blizzard had kicked up again.

I went to the front door and cracked it open. The wind caught it and shoved me backwards. If the door hadn't opened inward, it would have been ripped from both my hand and its hinges. Outside, a single light bulb over the door illuminated a solid wall of white. Snow was streaking horizontally through the darkness. I shoved the door shut.

The phone rang. It was Steve.

"I'm coming back to the lab," he said.

I tried to talk him out of it. Visibility was zero. He wouldn't be able to see beyond the windshield of the spryte.

But he was adamant. "I can't stay here."

It was true the aquarium was not a comfortable building. The water in the tanks was maintained at 29°F, about the temperature of the sea. If it was allowed to get much warmer, the animals started dying. So the aquarium itself was kept at about 55°, bearable for an hour or two but not much longer. Also, there were no beds, no comfortable chairs, no food, no bathroom, and no potable water. And who knew how long this latest blow would last? Steve could be stuck there for days.

"If you don't see me in a few minutes," Steve continued,

"call Ratchko." Lt. Ratchko was the U.S. Navy's winter-over Officer-in-Charge for McMurdo Station.

I hung up the phone and waited. It was impossible to go back to my work. The wind had increased in intensity and the entire laboratory was creaking and groaning. I heard a muffled thumping and went to investigate. Storm winds in McMurdo come from the south. Since the lab was aligned south-to-north, the south end took the brunt of the wind as it roared off the unobstructed expanse of the Ross Ice Shelf, around Observation Hill, and down over the Station. As if to empha-size that point, the noise level increased as I entered the back room, which contained a small shop and cargo receiving area. The electric wall heaters were buzzing at top capacity, but the room was freezing. The back door strained at its latch, as though some large animal was trying to force its way in. The thumping I had heard was coming from the plywood roof over my head. It was bucking as if it were about to be ripped off. I remembered the Jamesway I'd seen that morning and headed to a safer part of the lab.

Ten minutes passed, then twenty. It was a five-minute drive from the aquarium to the lab in good weather, and only that long because the spryte was not a vehicle meant for dirt roads and had a top speed of about five miles per hour. I knew Steve would have to stop frequently to keep his bearings, perhaps waiting for the snow to clear long enough for him to spot landmarks. I went to the door and cracked it again. Apart from a small patch of blowing snow illuminated by that naked bulb over the door, I couldn't see a thing. The blizzard was so thick it was even masking the light from the street lamp.

I mentally kicked myself, and Steve, for not getting the radio in his spryte fixed. We'd intended to get it done, but as long as he was just using it to go back and forth from the lab to the aquarium it didn't seem that important. But now there was no way to reach him to find out where he was.

When thirty minutes had passed, I picked up the phone and called Lt. Ratchko.

He took in the news, then paused. "Give him another fifteen minutes. If you haven't seen him by then, call me back. I'll start putting together a SAR."

Initiating a Search-and-Rescue was no minor thing. A SAR meant someone was in serious trouble. More than that, it generally meant that whoever was about to go out and attempt a rescue would also be placed in danger.

But another fifteen minutes went by with no sign of Steve. It was clear to me now that he was lost somewhere in the storm, in a poorly insulated vehicle with an inefficient cabin heater and limited fuel. I called Ratchko back. He said it would be an hour before they were ready to go out. He had to gather the SAR members together, collect their gear, and get their vehicle running. I hung up knowing that they'd never be able to find Steve. Visibility in a vehicle is even worse than it is on foot. Sitting higher up off the road makes it harder to know where the road is. In addition, the spryte's headlights reflecting off the blowing snow would blind the driver, making it impossible to see navigational landmarks, like the faint, intermittent light from street lamps. Add to these difficulties the problem of windows fogging up from passengers' breath and I knew it would be a near miracle if they were even able to stay on the road.

The only way to find Steve would be on foot. Of course, it was strictly against the rules to venture out alone in conditions like this. But I knew my way around pretty well, and if I found him, no one would care that I'd gone. If I didn't, no one had to know. I shed my tennis shoes, put on a sweatshirt, and then climbed into my "bunny suit." This is a one-piece, insulated, wind-proof, extreme-cold-weather garment. During the winter, I had found it to be my best protection against the cold. I pulled on my insulated "bunny boots," giant, white rubber boots with an insulating layer of air between two layers of rubber. Then I put on a thick, woolen cap and pulled a woolen gator over the hat and down over my nose and mouth. Next came the ski goggles, after which I flipped the bunny suit's hood over my head and zipped it shut. Finally, I put on glove inserts and slipped my hands into thick, windproof mittens. After grabbing a powerful flashlight from my office, I headed for the door.

The wind nearly knocked me over the moment I stepped outside. I held onto the door handle for support and looked around. I was in the middle of a maelstrom. Beyond the tiny circle of illumination created by the bulb over the door, there was only amorphous darkness. The snow was so thick it was obscuring every other source of artificial light, and the Antarctic was offering none of its own. On a clear day, I could navigate by starlight. But now, with the sky obscured by clouds and snow, not a single photon of natural light was getting through.

I turned on the flashlight, but turned it off immediately. All it did was brighten the snow in the air before my face, but it probably didn't penetrate three feet. I let go of the biolab door and took several steps in what I knew was the right direction. After moving fifteen or twenty feet, I turned and looked back.

There was no sign of the biolab. I was surrounded by impenetrable storm.

My initial confidence was shaken. This is nuts, I told myself. What good will it do Steve for me to get lost, too? I retraced my steps, leaning into the wind, and with great relief found the biolab door. I pushed it open and stumbled inside.

After removing my cold weather gear, I paced the biolab lounge, trying to think of something I could do. What I needed, I decided, was a lifeline I could tie to the lab and use to guide myself, and presumably Steve, back to safety. After an exhaustive search of the storage room, though, all I could come up with was a roll of string wound around a hollow tube. At first I discarded it as being too flimsy. But when I could find no more suitable rope, I picked up the string again. It would have to do.

I bundled into my cold weather gear again but left the goggles off. The tint of the lens had obscured what little light there was and made it even harder to see. I'd have to do without them. After putting a screwdriver into the string's hollow tube so the roll could rotate freely, I stepped outside. Fighting the wind, I tied one end of the string to the lab's doorknob. Then I headed out again, holding the screwdriver and allowing the string to play out behind me. This time I didn't look back.

Immediately across from the lab stood a memorial to Admiral Richard Byrd. A dirt road ran between the lab and the Byrd memorial. About fifty feet from the lab's door this road intersected the transition road, so-called because it led straight down the hill that McMurdo sits on, across the land-ice transition, and onto the sea ice. On the right side of the road, as you headed toward the ice, were several shuttered buildings. On the left, below the Byrd memorial, a road led to the helicopter pad and gymnasium. Further down, the road cut through a gully, with the helicopter hangar at the top of a steep and rocky slope. At the bottom of the hill, the transition road intersected another road that went left, toward the salt-water intake that fed the desalinization plant. This road was bordered on the left by the same steep, rocky slope, and on the right by the ice-covered water of McMurdo Sound. Several hundred yards down this road sat the aquarium. There was one street lamp on the route. It sat on a power pole outside the hangar, at the top of the rocky slope and overlooking the bottom of the transition road.

I had walked this route more times than I could count, and I knew it as well as I knew the layout of my own room. I also knew I'd have to navigate based on this internal map. One thing in my favor was that the roads had been kept relatively clear of drifting snow. As long as I could see dirt and rocks beneath my feet, I would know I was on a road.

The wind at my back nearly pushed me over several times before I even reached the transition road. Small rocks pelted the back of my suit. Even through the insulation, I could feel the cold pressing in. The wind was driving it through every tiny crack in my clothing.

At the corner of the two roads stood a green flag on a bamboo pole, placed there to guide the snow removers. I almost ran into it. I stopped and looked in what I knew was the direction of the transition road. Still nothing but darkness and swirling snow. But I could feel the slope of the earth, so I started working my way down the hill, keeping my eyes on the dirt below my feet. I was facing sideways to the wind now, and wind-driven dust and small pebbles were blasting my face and getting in my eyes. I began to wish I had the goggles again, but I wasn't about to go back. Instead, I worked my way forward by walking sideways, keeping my hooded face away from the wind and stealing glances now and again in the direction I was headed.

The sound of the wind was deafening, a constant, low-frequency roar that seemed to consume the world. It vibrated through my body, even as it pushed at me and kept me off balance.

I kept moving down the hill, hoping I'd run into Steve's spryte. Perhaps he had made it part of the way back and was waiting for a clear moment before continuing. Then I hesitated, struck by a realization. If Steve was on this road and if he was moving, he'd run me over before he could stop. He might not see me at all. I didn't much fancy getting chewed up by the steel tracks of a spryte.

There was no other choice, though. If I left the road, I'd be lost. I started moving again, hoping that he was not. I tried to keep my bearings by glancing up every few minutes. Occasionally, through a break in the snow, I'd get a brief glimpse of a slightly lighter spot in the sky to my left, which I knew must be the street lamp near the helicopter hangar. In addition, as long as I could feel the downward slope of the road, I knew I was on the right path. I tried not to think of the power lines snaking overhead. If the wind broke one free, it would become a vicious whip in the wind, deadly even apart from the live electricity it carried.

Loose objects, in fact, represented the greatest single danger in a blinding snowstorm like this. A sheet of plywood or a sheet of plate metal driven by hurricane-force winds would be like a scythe. Either one could take off my head. There was no shortage of loose construction material lying around McMurdo Station, including rolls of wire, wooden pallets, and innumerable boxes and crates. But I took courage from the fact that this storm had been blowing for two weeks; most of the easily dislodged material must have already blown away. I hoped.

I concentrated on keeping my eyes on the dirt below my feet. At times, even that would disappear in the driving snow and the darkness, and I would have to bend down to make sure it was still there. It seemed to be taking me forever to get to the bottom of the hill. I looked back the way I had come, but it was as dark and uninviting as the direction I was headed. I looked down again and suddenly the ground disappeared.

I was hanging, suspended in space, surrounded by swirling snow. I became dizzy and disoriented, unable to maintain my balance. My stomach lurched and nausea welled up. Realizing I had walked into a snowdrift, I forced myself to stumble backward before I fell. The vertigo disappeared as soon as I could see dark earth below my feet again.

I stood for a moment, unsure what to do. I had heard of vertigo resulting from a total whiteout condition, but had never believed it could actually happen. If this snowdrift was too big, I might not be able to get through it. How absurd, I thought! To go out into this wind and cold and near zero visibility and be stopped by a stupid snowdrift! If nothing else, I thought, maybe I could crawl over it. But before I was forced to do that, I decided to try a faster approach. I took a deep breath and ran toward the drift. In several steps I was over it and onto hard road again.

I had no idea how far I had gone or how far I had left to go before I came to the bottom of the hill. I knew if I wasn't careful, I might end up out on the sea ice where there were no landmarks. I would be lost, except for my string. Moments later, though, I ran into a pair of flags side by side, one orange and one green. I knew from memory that this marked the bottom of the transition road. The aquarium was to my left, directly into the wind. I headed that way, leaning into the gale.

The wind pummeled me like a living thing, trying to keep me from moving forward. Snow, driven at hurricane force, stung my face. Pebbles and sand flew at me and ricocheted off my suit. I kept my face down to keep from being struck in the eye. Still feeding string out behind me, I pushed into the storm.

There were large rocks in this road, and twice I nearly tripped and fell. Time seemed to stand still, with me stumbling forward but not seeming to make any progress. My heart sank with each step I took without running into Steve's spryte.

Finally, I could make out a dim glow ahead. It had to be the light over the aquarium door. If I hadn't encountered Steve on the road, he surely wouldn't be at the aquarium. Moments later I confirmed that fear. The spryte was nowhere to be seen. I stood outside the aquarium for several minutes, buffeted by the wind, trying to come up with another plan. But there was nothing left to do. I turned around and began heading back, spooling the string back onto the roll as I walked. The going was slightly easier, now that I had the wind at my back. It pushed me along, still pelting me with small rocks.

About halfway down the aquarium road, my string angled right, up the steep hill of loose rocks and dirt that led to the helicopter hanger. The wind must have whipped it up the hill and wrapped it around a rock. I pulled to dislodge it and the string broke.

I was gripped by a twinge of panic. Flimsy as it was, the string had been a psychological comfort. Now I was on my own.

Then I mentally kicked myself. I had found my way down to the aquarium without a string, after all! Of course I could find my way back to the lab. Besides, the wind had probably wrapped my string around all nature of obstructions. It was a silly idea to start with. I stuck the remaining roll of string and the screwdriver into a pocket and continued forward. Glancing upward, I caught brief glimpses of light from the street lamp next to the helicopter hangar. I was getting close. A few minutes later I came to the orange and green flags.

Before heading up the transition road and back to the lab, I paused. There were only two places Steve could be: either he had made a wrong turn and ended up out on the ice, or he had missed the transition road and had continued straight along the shore. If he was out on the ice, he wouldn't survive the night, and there was no way to reach him. With visibility at three feet, he could be lost less than a stone's throw away.

There was a better chance, I thought, that he had gone straight and missed the turn. In that case, he was somewhere in the darkness ahead of me. Snow swirled past my head in an endless stream, disappearing into that darkness. I considered working my way in that direction, but I didn't know the terrain on that side of the road, and there were no markers. To keep my bearings I would have to hug the side of the hill, making sure I was always on a slope. Otherwise, I could wander off onto the sea ice and be irrevocably lost myself.

Twice I started to move forward, and twice I stopped. Something told me this would be a mistake. Reluctantly, I turned right and followed the dirt road up toward the biolab. Once again, I had to keep my face averted and walk sideways to keep the bitter wind out of my face and the blowing pebbles out of my eyes. When I reached the snowdrift, I ran across it as before to avoid vertigo. At the top of the hill, I found the green flag and turned right again. A minute later, the door of the biolab loomed out of the roaring darkness.

Inside, I pulled off my bunny suit and found that the wind had driven snow through every tiny hole, even through the zipper. The inside of the suit was packed. I shook the snow off and went to the phone. I knew Ratchko would be upset at what I'd done, but I could at least save him the trouble of retracing my route on the SAR. I was too late. Ratchko and his SAR team had already left. I found out later they had taken over an hour to get their spryte to the bottom of the transition road, where it had stalled. After spending several minutes getting it re-started, they had turned around and headed back. They had decided that trying to search for anyone in that visibility was hopeless, and their undependable vehicle made it too dangerous.

By this time, several hours had passed. Depending on how much fuel he had and whether his own spryte had continued to run, Steve could be getting hypothermic. I was considering pulling on my gear and giving it another try when the phone rang.

It was Steve.

He sounded shaken. He was in the power plant, which was down at the other end of the station. He had missed the transition road turn, as I suspected, and had run up against an obstacle. Unable to go forward and afraid of going back for fear of ending up out on the ice, he had sat there with the engine running, hoping either that the storm would abate or that someone would find him. The spryte's inefficient heater had barely kept him from freezing. When the spryte ran out of fuel, though, he knew he had to find a way to safety or freeze to death where he was. The storm had not diminished, and it was clear no one would be coming to find him.

He had crawled out of the spryte and discovered that the barrier that had stopped him was a set of pipes that ran down to the sea. He followed the pipes up the hill until he could make out the outline of a building. It turned out to be the power plant. The engineers on watch had been stunned to see him stumble through the door, wearing only sweat pants under his parka and sneakers on his feet.

The next day, the storm was gone. After two weeks of nonstop, brutal wind and blowing snow, the air was clear and dead calm. I walked down the hill, retracing my route of the previous night. A yellow light was flashing, illuminating the snow and the sides of the buildings. I couldn't figure out what it was, until I turned the corner at the bottom of the hill and saw Steve's spryte rammed up against the pipes below the power plant. He had turned on the vehicle's emergency light and had forgotten to turn it off when he left. The battery had kept it flashing all night. From the bottom of the transition road, where I had stood, the spryte was about 200 feet away. The strobe was bright enough to be seen for miles, and I had not had even a glimpse of it the night before.

Then I saw something that brought the hairs up on my neck.

A few feet from where I stood, the wind had scoured out a deep hollow in a snowdrift. There was a ten-foot vertical drop from the lip of the hollow to the frozen ground below. Steve was lucky enough to have missed it, but it was directly in the path I would have taken if I had gone forward. I never would have seen it. I would have stepped into air and tumbled head first to the hard ground below.

POSTSCRIPT: The wind had blown my string all over the station, wrapping it around buildings, telephone lines, and power poles. In the months that followed, I overheard several people wondering where it had come from. Three years later, when I returned to McMurdo Station, the string was still there, still wrapped around poles and dangling from power lines. And people were still looking up at it and asking, "Where the hell did all that string come from?"

I never said a word.

[Oates] did not—would not—give up hope to the very end. He was a brave soul. This was the end. He slept through the night before last, hoping not to wake; but he woke in the morning— yesterday. It was blowing a blizzard. He said, "I am just going outside and may be some time." He went out into the blizzard and we have not seen him since.

—ROBERT FALCON SCOTT, LETTER HOME, MARCH 1912

If there is a hierarchy in the Antarctic, it is those people who winter over who garner the most respect. Making it through a winter—the endless dark, the confined working conditions, the extreme cold, and the small population—can be a challenge. By the end of the winter, most are looking forward to the sun rising and to leaving. However, after a winter at South Pole, Katy M. Jensen is not ready to leave the community that has formed through the dark Antarctic winter. In her essay she describes with love and honesty the complexity and beauty of this small world.

Katy has spent more than four years in Antarctica, including three winters at the South Pole and two seasons as the station's first female area manager. She continues to support the U.S. Antarctic Program in various contract positions, and someday she'd like to visit Jensen Rampart, a set of cliffs named after her in the Darwin Mountains. Some of Katy's best friends are Ice people—especially her husband, Rod, with whom she shares a home and a blue heeler in Saint Paul, Minnesota.

Sunrise at 90 South

⋆ ⋆ ⋆

KATY M. JENSEN

IT IS SEPTEMBER 1993 AND I AM STANDING ALONE AT the geographic South Pole, wind stinging my eyes, snow rolling across my boots in waves. This is the first time I have seen the sun in six months. And to tell the truth, it's not that impressive. There is no flaming chariot speeding across the heavens; no angel's face with a mane of golden rays. Just a pale, egg-yolky blob floating above a frozen ocean.

One of the perks of spending a year at 90 South was supposed to be a chance to see two fabulous equinoxes, complete with awesome mirages. But the guest of honor was a no-show for our sunset party in March and again for last week's sunrise gala, in spite of our pagan attempts to lure it into view with sacrifice and song. This year, anyway, ol' Sol seems to prefer slinking across the equator, protected by a curtain of clouds and blowing snow.

I shouldn't complain. The pre-dawn twilight was glorious, beginning in August with a bright violet glow, then progressing smoothly through early September's raspberry-tangerine, and last week's bouquet of spring pastels. But sunrise brings with it a bittersweet realization that winter is over, and I am not ready to let it go.

For the past year, our little tribe of scientists, construction workers, and support staff has called this place home. It seems like forever ago we zipped up our parkas and tumbled out of that LC-130 cargo plane, our lungs slammed by the altitude and the cold. The first four months were a blur of activity as 125 people tried to jam a year's work into the short austral summer. Our mantra was, "Sleep, bad. Coffee, good!"

Suddenly it was February and most everyone headed north, leaving our group of twenty-eight "winter-overs" to mind the shop. When the last plane of the season took off, it zoomed in low across the sky, wings tipping in a final salute. Our lives became increasingly small, and we lost touch with the world revolving around us. Charles and Di split up, Steven Spielberg shocked the masses with a movie called *Schindler's List*, and, after forty-five years of fighting, Arafat and Rabin shook hands on the White House lawn. But with *The New York Times Fax* for news, we only saw the stories that were depressing or sports-related. In fact, most of us skipped the "news" altogether and headed straight for the crossword puzzle on the last page.

All winter, we have enjoyed a comfortable, protected existence. Now it's time to Ramp Up, get the place ready for summer, and allow the cycle to begin again.

I lower my goggles into place and pull my fur-lined hood low across my face before turning toward the wind. At twenty knots, it kicks up the dry snow like a sandstorm, and the wind-chill temperature of -150°F (-101°C) makes frostbite a real concern. It takes almost ten minutes to stumble across 200 meters of hard-ridged sastrugi to the place where I work. The "Clean Air Facility" is a drafty wooden building that sways in the breeze, but it is my Walden, and I wouldn't trade it for the world.

I sweep piles of encroaching snow off the porch and stairs, and climb up to the roof to wipe frost from the lenses of the light-measuring instruments. After a quick weather observation, I duck inside and shed my cold weather gear, trading my heavy "bunny boots" for sheepskin slippers. With Bonnie Raitt on the stereo and a mug of cocoa in hand, I'm ready to begin the daily rounds of checks and calibrations.

I am a "beaker"—a scientist—an NSF grantee sent here by the National Oceanic and Atmospheric Administration (NOAA) to monitor things that might affect the Earth's atmosphere. The idea is to understand what's in the cleanest air on Earth so we can use that as a baseline to help people better manage the rest of the planet. The owners of these instruments live in Boulder, Colorado, and when they're not analyzing data or training observatory crews, they're *out there*: celebrating the outdoors and remembering why all these things are important.

As our group's field team leader, most of my time is spent collecting samples of air and snow, recording data, and writing reports. Ray is the technical guru who keeps the equipment running, and Carl is heading a special ozone-monitoring campaign. Another NOAA scientist named Kathie uses a mysterious array of beeping black boxes to study atmospheric winds and temperatures.

Everything we have heard about climate change seems to be true because we're seeing it here, firsthand. Carbon dioxide and other greenhouse gases are increasing at an alarming rate. Average temperatures seem to be rising in some parts of Antarctica, yet falling in others. And this year's ozone hole

looks like it might be the worst ever, with significant depletion occurring fifteen to twenty kilometers above the Earth's
surface, where ozone is supposed to protect the planet by ab-
sorbing harmful ultraviolet radiation.

I have developed a certain fondness for the instruments in
our little observatory. For its name, I love the nephelometer,
which measures the optical properties of aerosols. For their
magic, nothing compares to the gas chromatographs and their
ability to separate halocarbons from ambient air. Whenever I
need an ego trip, I can make lightning with a Tesla coil or
build tiny clouds in a Pollak Condensation Nucleus Counter.
But my most favorite job of all is measuring ozone with a
Dobson spectrophotometer. This hulking, metal submarine-
on-a-gurney has enticed me out of bed at ungodly hours just
to point its periscope at the sun or the full moon—through
an open window—regardless of the temperature outside. With
frozen fingers spinning a metal dial, I can attenuate the wave-
lengths of light bouncing around inside the Dobson and figure out exactly how much ozone is between me and the light
source. It's simple, it's ingenious, and it's how British scientists
proved the ozone hole existed when other systems had been
programmed to disregard such low values.

Sunrise means job security for ozone researchers. It's the
returning sunlight that breaks up chemicals in the polar
stratosphere and begins the chain reaction of ozone destruction every year. But right now the sun is too low on the horizon for the Dobson, and the *Nimbus*-7 satellite's instruments
haven't worked since May, so Carl's balloon-based research is
more important than ever.

I hear the front door slam shut, and I catch my breath,
thinking, *Please let it be anyone but Ray*. We used to work together really well, but lately Ray and I have been riding a

rollercoaster of misunderstandings, and I never know what to expect from him. I know it's my job to try to work this thing out, and I plan to. Some day. I just don't feel like doing it right now.

I peer around the corner, trying my damnedest to look nonchalant. It's Kathie. I have never been so happy to see her, and she laughs at my obvious relief.

"You should just talk to him."

"I know. You're right. I will."

She smiles. "Uh-huh."

Kathie has been a good friend all year, and she knows me better than I'll admit. Together we have started a science club, an exercise group, and a "Red Rocks at 90 South" concert series where we play music videos on the big screen, drink fruity cocktails, and dance like maniacs until we're sweaty and tired.

She has just come from the dark room, where the photography buffs are developing copies of our winter-over photo. It's a hundred below zero and we're outside, organized in neat rows and holding our breath to keep the fog from obscuring our faces. It's all perfectly professional...except for the brightly colored jester hats that BK sewed for us from scraps of felt and fleece. Hardly a motley crew, however: we are men and women of varying ages, but that's where our diversity ends. In fact, we represent a good cross-section of middle-class, white America. Our token international representative is a (white, male) British astrophysicist named Andy who gets a kick out of our cowboy accents. "Oh BOY," he says with an exaggerated Texas drawl, and "Good JOB." Looking at the photo now, Kathie and I decide half of us look like we'd stay forever if we could. The other half look haunted and ready to get the hell out of here.

Before lunch, I gear up and walk over to visit Carl in the Balloon Inflation Tower, about a quarter mile away. I dance up the spiral staircase to the Inflation Room and then whistle through the hatch before climbing the ladder into the tiny electronics lab where Carl is sitting, listening to the whirr and burp of ozone data returning from the balloon's transmitter. Ray is there, too, tweaking the antenna to help Carl get a stronger signal. He barely acknowledges my hello, and I pretend not to notice.

Since late August, Carl has increased the number of balloons he launches each week, and we have watched anxiously as the ozone layer continues to disappear above our heads. The experts in Boulder think this year's depletion will reveal leftover effects from a volcano that erupted in the Philippines two years ago. They're right: today's flight registers the lowest total ozone ever recorded on Earth. And it's still early in the season, meaning it's likely to get worse before it gets better. Certainly not good news, but *news* nonetheless, so as soon as the flight ends, we hustle down to the radio room to call our boss in Boulder. He's like a proud papa on the phone. He tells us we're the best crew ever, and to keep up the good work. We smile at his little lie, remembering last year when we were on his side of this conversation. He would gush with compliments and then hang up the phone saying, "They sounded really tired. Didn't they sound tired?" Still, we appreciate his soothing voice across the miles. Whenever we are particularly frustrated, he brings us around with something like, "Of course it matters. Everything matters. But none of it *counts*."

At lunch, people seem to have a renewed energy. Or maybe they're in panic mode, sunrise triggering a new awareness that there's only one month left to get everything done before the summer crew arrives. In addition to the increased productivity at work, folks are suddenly discovering new interests and frequenting the gym. Tables in the galley are littered with travel brochures and Harley Davidson catalogs. A note on the message board chides, "How's the working out working out?" The rest of the board is crowded with a Toasty Self-Test: a list of indications that your brain is beginning to get crispy around the edges. Number 18 is, "You break it off with your fantasy lovers due to their predictability and lack of imagination."

I grab a plate and a monster cheeseburger with a homemade bun. The food here is fabulous. We're on our own for breakfast, but our cook, Kari, supplies two huge meals per day, including an endless supply of desserts and fresh breads. Thanks to a NASA grant, we have a greenhouse that produces more lettuce than we can eat, so there's salad every day. And in June, the U.S. Air Force "dropped by" in a C-141 cargo plane, roaring overhead at 1,000 feet and dropping two dozen pallets of goodies onto the snow. The most treasured items were personal mail and "freshies" like eggs, milk, fruit, and some sort of New Zealand tuber that we never identified, but ate anyway. Airdrop also brought 200 pounds of chocolate and 100 pounds of *People* magazine. I fear my subsequent addiction to both will land me a job in a dentist's office when I get home.

I load my cheeseburger with greenhouse lettuce and grab a seat at a crowded table. Across from me is Jerry, who is our connection to the outside world. He is the "Comms Guy," responsible for collecting all of our data and e-mail messages and sending them home over a serial modem. He is also the keeper of the weekly sign-up sheet for our ten-minute phone calls, so he is understandably popular. The guy is a puzzle, though. On one hand, he was the only one brave enough to eat the forty-year-old LOAF, TURKEY we found in the emergency supplies. But he also seems increasingly paranoid about a ghost that he swears is haunting the Comms office. Not wanting to lose our phone calls and messages, we usually just smile and nod politely when he describes his latest encounter.

The rest of the guys at the table are making a list of things they'll miss most about this place. No one is willing to say "each other," so when the question comes to me, I gush about the night sky…how the stars seem close enough to touch, and how it took me so long to realize the moon was upside down, and how I've never seen such amazing auroras, from rose-colored washes to acrobatic white spirals and spiky teal needles that rained down in all directions. Just about every outdoor venture in June and July ended with us lying in on our backs, giggling and enjoying the celestial show.

But as much as I'll miss all that, I'll miss these people, too, whether they like it or not. Every crew is different, and we'll never be "us" again. Except for four days of R&R at McMurdo Station in January, all of us have spent the last year within a few miles of where we sit now. With no way to leave and no place to hide, we have come to know each other better than most of us know our own siblings. We have become a family, complete with the power to soothe or provoke at a moment's notice. So when I casually begin to remark, "Well, when you've lived together this long…" Jerry is quick to correct me, saying, "We do NOT 'live together.'" Man, he's toasty! His irrational fear of inferred intimacy just makes me want to reach out and plant a big, sloppy kiss on his cheek. Instead, I wad up my napkin and bounce it off his chest.

One of the science projects here is an anthropologist's study of group dynamics: how people interact with each other in isolated environments. By monitoring several winter crews, these researchers hope to improve the winter-over selection process. They also want to determine an ideal mix of personalities for prolonged space flight and other extreme situations. They label us like bugs in a glass case: jokester, floater, philosopher, social shepherd. Stan is not only our station manager, but our emotional leader as well, which is good but apparently unusual. He is sarcastic and caring and kind, and his sense of humor is the metronome that sets our pace. BK is another natural guidance counselor who often has a line of people vying for her attention. Her diverse life experiences, from llama training to forest fire fighting, have earned her an unparalleled confidence and authority that's incredibly attractive. As with most families, we have a small group of favorite aunts and uncles who only come around once in a while, and there are more than a few weird cousins. We have shared each other's highs and lows, consoled couples through breakups, and celebrated news of a baby on the way. He has become a sort of mascot for us, and we insist that the parents name him Ichabod, but I doubt they'll come through. They are more likely to choose something admirable, like "Andy." (I can hear his namesake now: "A BOY. Good JOB!")

The anthropologists' study requires us to fill out annoying questionnaires about emotions we have experienced and people we have interacted with during the week. I always circle "blue," but never "sad." And lately I have tried to hide the fact that I'm spending less time with Kathie and more time with...well...there's *this guy.*

His name is Rod, though most everyone calls him Rodman, and this is his third winter at the South Pole. He's an unassuming Minnesotan who works nights as the maintenance mechanic, quietly ensuring that the place stays warm while the rest of us sleep. We had shared some great conversations, but we didn't really notice each other romantically until the rest of the night shift got involved. I had been staying up way too late with them, sneaking out on snowmobiles, or playing Assassin, or thinking of new ways to make ghost sounds in the Comms office. After a while, the hoodlums got bored and decided to start a rumor about the most unlikely couple they could think of. And the rest, they say, is history: I guess Rod and I fell victim to the power of persuasion. It's been a whirlwind. A great ride. And the newness of it all makes me regret sunrise even more.

There's a commotion by the microwave, which can only mean one thing: a new tub of ice cream has been opened. Our dairy products come from New Zealand, so they are full-fat and (usually) delicious. But in addition to the standard varieties, the ice cream comes in weird flavors like Banana Chip and Hokey Pokey, and we're not allowed to open a new tub until the previous one is finished. The new stuff has been stored outside (average temperature: -57.1°F/-49.5°C), so it's too cold to eat without chopping off a chunk and softening it in the oven.

JP approaches me with a two-scoop cone of Rocky Road.

"Does this smell like diesel fuel to you?" And like a dope, I lean forward to sniff the ice cream, which he pushes up against my nose, laughing at my predictable naiveté.

For his birthday, JP ended up duct-taped to a table. Now he's talking about coming back next year as Station Manager of the Ultimate Winter Crew. It's just like fifth grade kickball and I pray he will pick me for his team.

After lunch, I have to hustle back to Clean Air to catch "Zero Z," or midnight in Coordinated Universal Time. That's when I mark the charts and change the tapes and do another set of observations. As I leave the galley, I notice the wind hasn't quit; I can hear the snow sizzling against the Dome's aluminum shell like grease in a frying pan. Every once in a while, the whole place shakes with a rumble and a *boom*: "Dome Thunder." It's harmless but spooky, like a creaky old house. And ever since April Fool's Day, a life-sized mannequin has hung from a noose in the center of the Dome—a morbid pendulum reminding us not to slam doors or take the last cup of coffee without brewing a new pot.

When I get to Clean Air, I notice Ray's coat in the entry-way. It's too late to turn back...he must have heard me come in...and anyway it's almost Zero Z. I am like one of those cartoons, with an angel on one shoulder saying, "Just *talk* to him," and a devil on the other saying, "No way, this is *his* problem, not yours." I am standing there, trying to decide what to do, when Ray walks up.

"Hey, Katy," he says lightly. "I went ahead and marked the charts early. And we got an e-mail message from Boulder about that missing G.C. data."

As if everything is fine. Is he just messing with my head? Is this the same guy who got righteous about me missing Pollak observations and "relegating" his technical section to the back of our turnover report? Am I losing my mind? He's standing here, looking right at me, explaining what he's working on in his oh-so-patient way. And the whole time he is talking, I am staring over his shoulder at the world map on the wall, getting lost in the colors and wondering why India seems so small. Nothing is making sense! After a while, he says, well it's been a long day, and his back is sore, so he's going to head into the Dome for some coffee and then work in his room. And I think, *Hey, that's cool. Bizarre, but cool: I guess I was worried about nothing.*

Until I see him disappear into the Dome and remember this is the afternoon I wanted to start hauling crates over to the Cargo office.

I can't believe my ignorance, and Ray's duplicity. Cursing, I load a couple of empty nitrogen cylinders onto a sled, hoping "empty" will mean "lighter than usual." But these are big steel cylinders, and they sink my banana sled like a rhino in a rowboat. I try walking with the rope over my shoulder. The sled won't budge. I tie a quick bowline and step into it, wiggling the loop up to my waist. Slow progress. I think of Robert Falcon Scott, slogging along, singing sea shanties. So I start hollering, "Oh, what do you do with a drunken sailor…" but the snow is all speed bumps and baby powder, and the atmospheric pressure is low today, resulting in a "physiological altitude" of 11,099 feet (3,383 meters). *Ray, you weasel! I can't believe you suckered me into doing this alone.*

It takes all afternoon to make three trips with the sled. Mostly because I'm feeling sorry for myself, I stop into the galley for cookies and cocoa after each trip.

Evenings are usually reserved for pinochle or trauma team meetings or basketball, but tonight is "date night" and I'm headed for Rod's cabin by the lake. The cabin is a satellite receiver shack that Rod has converted into a condo, and the "lake" is Lake Patterson, a deep hole in the snow where we dump the station's raw sewage. Two months ago, Rod invited me out here for what I thought was a one-night stand…and he has let me stay ever since.

I'm hoping we will watch a movie together, but Rod has other ideas. We have to do water runs. More specifically, *I* have to do water runs, and he'll talk me through it. We climb into the cab of the 953 track loader, and he reminds me which controls are for the tracks, and which are for the bucket.

I'm nervous, so instead of driving, I begin to jabber.

"So, do you think we'll ever...?"

"Don't talk. Just drive."

"Yeah, I know, but what I'm saying is—"

"Stop procrastinating."

"I know. I will..."

Eventually, I work up the confidence to start rolling, and he tells me stories during the long drive out to the snow mine, where I carefully scoop up a bucket full of pristine snow to take back to the melter. When we get to the ramp that leads up to the roof of the Power Plant, Rod hops out with a shovel to lead the way. Alone in the cab, I am freaking out, barely breathing, certain I'm going to slide this thing off the ramp and into a ditch. I feel like a jet pilot landing on an aircraft carrier, and Rod's just smiling, waving me in. His trust in me is overwhelming. So, with agonizing jerks and starts, I inch the loader up to where he's standing, lift the bucket, and tip it, hoping most of the snow lands in the melter.

"Right on," he says casually. "Next week I'll teach you how to drive the D-6 so you can help me drag the skiway." The D-6 is a bulldozer with a manual transmission. I don't tell him that my father, my best college friends, and many a boyfriend before him have been astounded at my inability to manage a stick shift. Instead, I just smile and say, "Cool."

Afterward, while Rod fuels up the 953, I stop by the Dome to grab some supper from the leftover fridge and a bottle of wine from my room. On the way back out to the cabin, I notice the sun looks somehow different. The sky has cleared a bit, and the air is thick with diamond dust—tiny ice crystals that sparkle like rainbow glitter. And there, stretching away from my feet, is the longest shadow I have ever seen. Longer than a school bus...easily the length of a bowling lane.... I can barely see the end of it and suddenly I feel tall, and thin, and invincible.

Funny how one sunrise can elicit such a range of emotions. I am jazzed. Wide awake and ready for whatever's next. I know I'll miss the upside-down moon, the killer sastrugi, and the mixed bag of auroras. I worry that this fledgling relationship with Rod won't survive the harsh light of reality back in the States. But suddenly I am ready to say goodbye to my South Pole family, the same way I left my parents a year ago, with a hug and a promise to carry them in my heart. I'll even miss Ray, though I doubt we'll ever have that talk after all. I imagine my last day here will be like Dorothy leaving Oz: Love ya, Scarecrow. Take care, Tin Man. Later, Cowardly Lion.

I look around slowly, pledging allegiance to this magic world, promising to come back some day, and bursting with big ideas of things to do in the meantime. Soon, Rod and I will wake up in a place surrounded by trees and grass and big puffy clouds, a place where we can walk barefoot near the ocean and eat fruit from a coconut bowl. A place—though it's hard to imagine right now—where the sun rises *every single day*.

On May 17 the sun disappeared, not to be seen again for seventy days.... On July 22 the sun returned. It was not a pleasant sight that it shone upon. The Antarctic winter had set its mark upon all, and green, wasted faces stared at the returning light.

—ROALD AMUNDSEN, *THE SOUTH POLE* (1898)

The Antarctic retains some of the spirit of the Wild West—anything is possible, and land (except for what has been claimed by government bases) is wide open. If you can find a place to pitch a tent or land a plane, it's yours. In his story Jon Bowermaster describes flying onto the continent with Adventure Network International (ANI), and captures the history and spirit of the company and of its legendary founder, Giles Kershaw.

This little adventure is a tame one for writer and filmmaker Jon who, for nearly twenty years, has explored exotic corners of the world for a variety of national and international publications, ranging from National Geographic to The New York Times Magazine, the Atlantic Monthly to Outside. He has written eight books, three with renowned polar explorer Will Steger. His travels have taken him to seven continents and included two-person sledging across Antarctica, sailing a sixty-foot sailboat across the Atlantic, and first descents of rivers from Chile to China. Jon's exciting OCEANS 8 project is a series of expeditions launched to explore the world's oceans from the seat of a sea kayak.

The Ultimate Risky Business

✦ ✦ ✦

JON BOWERMASTER

I LIKE BEING PLACES WHERE YOU ARE FORCED TO LISTEN to your own heartbeat, commanded by nature to pay attention to the in and out of each breath. Antarctica is one of those places.

It was so windy last night that I thought at one point my tent was going to explode. Literally. Thanks to a trio of pinholes along one seam, the sides of the thin nylon membrane were sucked in by the forty-mile-per-hour gusts, and then exploded outward, making a cracking sound, like an M-80 going off. This went on for several hours.

Such Antarctic winds have driven people mad. The Brits are famous for incidents of wind-and-isolation madness: At Rothera base a few years back, an engineer barricaded himself in the bar for a month, threatening anyone who tried to come through the door with a fire ax. His excuse? The sound of the winds.

When morning came this day, the winds dropped. (Note, I don't say "when the sun rose," since it's up twenty-four hours

in January.) By noon, they were back, gusting katabatics whipping snow across the ground at chest level at thirty to forty
miles per hour. As I trudged across the crusty snow, the wind
whistling inside my fur-lined hood was the sound of freedom—and frostbite.

My friend "Borneo" Steve Pinfield and I spent the afternoon kick-stepping up 1,000 feet of an ice- and snow-packed
bowl, with ice axes and crampons, to the peak of the tallest of
the Patriot Hills. We are 400 miles from the sea, 600 miles
from the nearest scientific base at the South Pole, and 1,800
miles from the nearest town at the southern tip of Chile. Atop
the ridge we are met by even bigger winds, gale-force, blowing up the other side of the hills from the flat ice that sepa-
rates the Patriots from the Independence Range. We look
towards Mt. Vinson, Antarctica's tallest peak, down a long line
of granite, snow-covered peaks separated by fields of ice and
snow, suncups, sastrugi, and crevasses.

With our axes dug in for stability we continue up the
knife-edge of the rocky ridge to the snowy summit.
Thankfully this wind is constant, not gusty. Big gusts would
easily pick us off and dump us over the edge. Everywhere we
look, the wilderness is vast, unending. Pausing to catch our
breath we talk about the slim chance of being rescued should
one of us fall this far from "the world." It's very humanizing
to stand so far beyond civilization, far beyond help.

Think of it this way. Imagine a land the size of the U.S. and
Mexico covered by ice and blowing snow, where temperatures
hang well below zero. Now imagine there are just 600 people
scattered across that entire land, and that you've just been
dropped off in the center. That's what it is like this day, atop
these Antarctic Hills, in the middle of the Heritage Range of
the Ellsworth Mountains. In spite of the fact that many of

these mountains have names, Antarctica is less well mapped than the moon.

But that we are here, in the middle of the last continent, suggests that it is not totally beyond reach. As far back as 1938, Australian explorer Douglas Mawson, who accomplished many firsts, wondered, "from an economic aspect, the frozen South may not attract immediate attention, but who can say what a train of entrepreneurs the future may bring?" Me, I have come south with the most audacious of Antarctica's modern entrepreneurs: a flying company, the only private business operating on the continent.

There is only one way to reach the interior of Antarctica—unless you're a scientist or government-contracted plumber or electrician putting in time at one of the continent's nearly sixty bases—and that's to fly with the once seat-of-the-windpants air charter company called Adventure Network International. The wild-ass fantasy of a handful of dreamer/climbers a dozen years ago, the little company that began as jottings on the back of an envelope is now a multimillion dollar a year outfitter delivering climbers, expeditioners, and fat-walleted tourists to the most remote, most potentially dangerous place on earth. Against all odds, it works.

I have known the operators of the company for many years, but it took until January of 1996 for me to hitch a ride to Antarctica with them. On a sunny, windy day in Punta Arenas, Chile, I climbed aboard a Hercules C-130 cargo plane along with twenty other passengers, including four climbing parties and four individuals who'd paid $21,000 each to visit the South Pole for a few hours. A pair of ANI employees were along for the six-hour ride, including managing director Anne Kershaw, whose late husband Giles—perhaps the greatest polar pilot ever—trail blazed the company.

It is a weird assortment of passengers, but not unusual for ANI. It included a hardened team of veteran climbers from Croatia and Slovenia as well as a couple of doddering grandmothers incapable of putting on their own wind pants and boots. A seventy-four-year-old American woman from Michigan, who claimed she was going to the South Pole "because I've been to the North Pole," admits her friends back home can't figure out why she is so intent on "going nowhere." There was also a pair of veteran North American climbing guides, Skip Horner and Tod Burleson, escorting nine clients of differing experience headed for Mt. Vinson, Antarctica's tallest peak at 17,000 feet. Horner, who first guided with ANI in 1988, remembers his initial flight to Antarctica, which was quite different than this one. "When the plane landed, I think it was a DC-3, the other guide Gordy Wiltsie and I were completely covered with aviation fuel that was basically floating loose in the back of plane. Things have changed a lot since then."

Lots has changed since the early days of ANI. It used to be that the "boys"—veteran climbers and pilots—who ran the operation did not need a GPS to find the brothels in Punta Arenas. Today the company is run by a pretty blonde woman with a preference for paisley hairbands, who considers "gee whiz" an expletive. Probably the best word to describe Annie Kershaw is conservative. And that's probably why ANI is succeeding.

The five-man flight crew—and their Hercules—is from South Africa. This is their second season flying round-trips (at $200,000 a crack), from Punta Arenas to ANI's base camp near the Patriot Hills. They are a perfect crew for this mission, since their experience includes flying through bullets and landing on unlit runways in the dead of night across Africa. Landing a twenty-five-ton plane on a sheet of ice is a breeze, comparably speaking. "This is the kind of nonsense we love," says the captain.

A slight apprehension fills me as I wait under sunny skies on the runway, listening to the wind whistle. It's a far way we're going today, to a distant, isolated place. Planes are hardly new to Antarctica; eighty years ago the Australian Mawson brought the first aircraft to the continent—a Vicker R.E.P. monoplane. Neither are plane crashes—the skeletons of more than fifty aircraft dot the ice, all but a few military or government owned. The worst Antarctic air accident was in 1978, when an Air New Zealand jumbo jet crashed into Mt. Erebus, killing all 225 aboard. My mood is not helped by the most salient piece of information passed along during a briefing from the co-pilot as he demonstrates safety measures onboard. "If we ditch at sea please don't inflate your Mae West's until you are *outside* of the safety door. It's a tight fit as it is…"

Ditch at sea?

The flight over the Drake Passage is actually very smooth. The sea is flat and blue, the sky painted by wisps of white clouds. The drum of the twin-engine props is loud, overpowering, hypnotic. Annie, her blue down jacket pulled up around her head, naps in the last row. She barely slept last night, typical of the night before one of the dozen flights the Herc will make each season. This is the first time she's visited Antarctica this season, and she's going to check on the camp and eighteen-person crew, which is based on the continent from November through early February. She wants to gauge firsthand how the season's gone based on conversations with her on-ice team. A couple weeks from now the camp's kitchen, meteorology, and radio tents will be packed and stored in an underground cave—as will its bright orange Cessna 185—until next season.

Any apprehension diminishes, perhaps falsely, after we cross over the first ice sheet near the tip of the Trinity Peninsula. The bright light reflected off the surface of the ice blazes through the tiny portholes in the cargo hold, illuminating the cabin's dark interior with blinding streaks of white. An occasional crack in the ice-sheet exposes blue-black waters.

After six hours we near the three-mile stretch of rippled blue ice that is the landing strip at the base of the Patriot Hills. I sit with the crew for the landing. One of two co-pilots, standing, shouts over the roar of the engines: "See those hills, to our right? How far away do you think they are?" I guess a few miles.

"Try fifty miles. It is so big down there it is impossible to judge perspective from up here." One result is that in order to set the big plane down it must be guided in by a pair of mirrors held by camp crew on the ground—one at the threshold of the runway, a second near its end. "Everything is so white, so bright, that it is virtually impossible to distinguish where the ice begins. So we just line up those mirrors, drop straight down, and pray."

At the trio of small peaks known as the Three Sails we make a hard right-hand turn. As the plane drops, the captain "quacks" hello over the radio to the base camp with a small rubber ducky. He and one co-pilot are strapped in, as is the navigator sitting just behind. A second co-pilot and engineer stand, unbuckled, bracing themselves for what could be a rough landing, holding onto the metal frame with one hand, bucking-bronco style. There's no use for brakes on the ice; stopping requires throwing the big engines immediately into reverse, then skidding for half a mile, desperately trying to keep the nose straight-on.

The landing is smoother than I expected, in part because I can see it coming. For the rest, strapped down in back, unable to see the ice as it approaches, it comes as a bigger shock, jolt, surprise. When the wheels hit for the first time I hear a few squeals from the cargo hold. We skid for nearly a mile.

"That was smooth enough I'd think you did it every day," I say to the captain, who has actually done it fewer than ten times.

"Highest compliment, mate, highest compliment," he replies.

We are steered to a stop carefully by a man in blue fleece and a jester's hat. The back cargo chute is dropped and bright sunlight and cold, cold air rush in. The plane's engines keep a steady beat—to shut them down in this cold risks not being able to start them again. The camp manager, in the faded orange polar gear of the British Antarctic Survey (BAS) strides aboard, wearing Viking's horns with the world MENTAL printed across its brow. The rush is on to unload the green barrels of fuel, bags, snowmobile, and food and a crew of a dozen has come out to help.

It is 0°F; January, mid-summer. By the end of the half-mile walk to the dozen tents that are the base camp some of the overdressed climbers are sweating, pulling off layers of clothing. Eighteen people live here from November to early February, including the camp's manager (who when employed by the BAS spent two-and-a-half years straight on the continent), two mountain guides, four pilots, two engineers, radio and weather operators, two cooks, a trio of Chilean military men on assignment, and a "client relations" person. It is a true melting pot of nationalities—this season's crew hails from the U.K., New Zealand, Canada, the U.S.,

Australia, Chile, and Uruguay. Also in camp are a pair of Poles and a Norwegian, who are handling logistics for expeditions underway.

After a massive dinner for fifty in a double-Jamesway that serves as the kitchen, two Twin Otters are loaded with climbers and gear, to be shuttled to ANI's base camp at Vinson. No wasting time when the skies are bright and winds are down. As the planes are fueled I walk out for a look around. It is 9 P.M. but as bright as noon. Camp sits at 2,500 feet, on the edge of the blue ice runway, facing the Patriot Hills, which climb to 4,000 feet.

Back in the mid-1980s, Adventure Network knew that to accommodate climbers and tourists it needed a semi-permanent base camp near Vinson, a place to store fuel and food and bodies while they waited to climb. No one besides a government had ever considered building a station in the interior. Siple, the American base 150 miles from the South Pole, was closed in 1986 because the National Science Foundation that runs the U.S. bases decided it was too expensive to maintain a base so far from everything. Nearby is where ANI decided to plant its camp.

The first challenge was finding a good spot. Giles Kershaw—who came to Antarctica with the BAS in 1972 and had since flown more hours over both poles than anyone— had done numerous studies with BAS expert Charles Swithinbank on the blue-ice areas around the continent, looking for those that would make for perfect natural runways. Searching satellite photos, they decided a four-mile long stretch of flat ice near the Patriot Hills would be perfect. It sat at 80 degrees south, 1,800 miles from the nearest city or town, on a plain where the wind came off the mountain and cleared the flats of snow. For Giles the challenges were numerous: No one—not even the best government pilots—had ever tried to land the big planes he was considering (C-130s, DC-4s, DC-6s) on such conditions. And he intended to land on wheels, not skis, another first.

Once the site was chosen, and after Giles relayed hundreds of tons of fuel, supplies, and two smaller planes to the foot of the Patriot Hills, they constructed a completely removable weatherproof tented camp, stocked with enough sustenance to feed three dozen people for a month or more. The camp consisted of a half-dozen sturdy WeatherHaven tents with cots and thermopane windows. Two tents were joined together to make a kitchen/dining room, complete with heaters, gas cook range, and sporadic radio contact. Months of meat and vegetables were deep-frozen in pits. Every move was made difficult by the katabatic winds that roared across the flat ice up to 100 miles an hour and wind chills that dropped below -100.

For nearly two decades, outside the official international scientific community, if something happened in Antarctica, Giles was probably involved. In 1989 he became the first person to have flown around the entire circumference of the continent. Over sixteen years he logged more than 5,000 hours in the air over the continent, more than twice any other pilot. Antarctica was his true home. He loved flying there because there was virtually no bureaucracy, no air traffic control, no flight plans to file. His passion for the continent was the main reason he helped set up Adventure Network. The business gave him an excuse to be there every year.

His last flight was in March 1990. He'd spent most of that season in Hong Kong. Late in February he flew to California to visit friends Mike Hoover and Beverly Johnson, who were on their way to Antarctica to film for National Geographic

Explorer. Giles agreed to go back with them. On a blustery March 5, off the coast of Jones Sound on the west coast of the Antarctic Peninsula, he took Hoover's kit-built gyrocopter for a pleasure ride at the end of the day's shoot. He was in the air just minutes before it was caught by a gust of cruel winter wind and thrown into the icecap.

A week later the Chilean Air Force provided a Hercules for Kershaw's young widow, two friends, and a priest from Punta Arenas, who flew to Antarctica for a full Catholic service. Though several Antarctic mountains already bore his name, the British and American governments agreed to rename the range where he was buried the Kershaw Range.

My trip to the Ice included a couple weeks of sled pulling, climbing, and skiing. ANI guide Borneo Steve has proven to be a perfect traveling partner, in both the tough conditions and the many hours spent inside a small tent. After a couple days testing equipment, we skied away from base camp pulling sleds loaded with seventy-five pounds of tents, sleeping bags, food, ice axes, climbing rope, and fuel for an extended camping trip in the middle of the ice.

Now, some of my best friends are polar robots, men and women who have skied, manhauled, dogsledded, and walked across the coldest parts of the globe. Put them in -50°F temperatures and big winds and they just turn on, as if some key inside their minds had been switched. I'm not like that. I've spent a fair amount of days in some truly cold places, but usually with the promise of a shortlived adventure. I keep going back to cold places for one reason, because of the incredible wilderness that opens up if you are willing to put up with a reasonable amount of uncomfortableness.

Here in Antarctica, just beyond the Patriot Hills, is a perfect example of just such underexplored terrain. At this moment, there were fewer than a dozen people doing the same as we. And no wonder. It's fucking cold. On the day we set out temperatures are -10°F, crosswinds blowing at 10 mph, equaling a wind chill of around -30°F. The wind, thankfully, is across us, though it nearly blows us off our feet a few times, gusting to twenty-five mph.

Pulling the sleds is not so difficult...at first. We glide smoothly over the lumpen ice and the scenery changes slowly, but dramatically. After five kilometers, base camp has disappeared and the flat plains prove to be more rolling; we drop over a ten-foot descent and an entirely new panorama of rugged, snow-peaked mountains—dozens in a row—is unveiled. We are heading for a small, snowy plateau above an ice field at the foot of a hill that leads to the Minaret, an unclimbed, 5,000-foot jewel that Steve would love to try and find a route up. If we kept skiing we'd eventually hit the base of Mt. Vinson, an overland trip that's never been attempted due to an abundance of nasty crevasses.

The exercise layers me with a coat of perspiration, which quickly chills when I stop for a breather or just to gawk at the surroundings—which I try and do with regularity. I don't want to have this experience without looking up occasionally to admire and wonder about where I am at, a mistake made by some of the more driven polar explorers. After ten kilometers we stop for lunch, and the cold and exertion begin to take a toll. Sitting on our gloves, drinking hot water and chewing chocolate bars, Steve takes our minds off the cold with a tale about a New York society lady who came to Antarctica with ANI a couple seasons ago and insisted on being flown back immediately after visiting the South Pole "because it was too cold." She was met in Punta Arenas by her hairdresser, who'd flown down from Manhattan.

After lunch we ski more directly into the wind—did we shift direction, or did it?—and the problem of vision surfaces. With my hood up, its fur-ruff flapping across my face, I can see out of only one eye. Then, thanks to the inverted humidity inside the hood, my glacier glasses fog. But I experiment with putting the hood down and my nose begins to frostbite. Neither option is comfortable and for much of the afternoon I see basically just my ski tips.

One mile from where we will make camp the surface compounds the difficulties, becoming a mix of blue ice and a crusty layer of snow. We are on a slight descent and it is tricky to ski across the patches of ice without the sled—connected around my waist by a harness—banging hard into my back, throwing everything off balance. It is late in the day, we've traveled sixteen kilometers, and it ain't getting any warmer. The toes on my left foot—the foot facing the wind—are beginning to tingle.

Camp is on a flat span at the bottom of our descent, in the shadow of the Minaret. We put up a new Kelty tent, stick it down with bamboo stakes, ice axes, and skis. Extra ice axes are thrust through the harnesses to keep the sleds from skittering off during the day/night.

Dinner is pasta; a walk afterwards shows clouds looming around the tops of the mountains, not a particularly good sign. And the wind has kicked up. Back inside the billowing tent Steve puts me at ease with a story of being stuck in a big windstorm on the flight down from Punta Arenas in one of the Twin Otters. He and his tent mate spent twelve hours with their feet up, pressed against the roof of their small tent to keep it from blowing away. Each kept a knife in one hand, ready to slit the tent open if it began to tumble with them inside, since they'd camped surrounded by deep crevasses. Through the night his Chilean tent mate read out loud in Spanish from the Bible. "I don't know what freaked me out most," said Steve, "the winds or the realization that probably the scriptures wouldn't do us much good at the bottom of a crevasse…"

On January 11, 1988, Adventure Network made history when it sent a pair of Twin Otters loaded with fifteen well-heeled passengers to the South Pole. Most of them were Americans, who had paid $25,000 each for the honor of being the first tourists flown to 90 degrees south. The seven aboard the first plane—which landed fifteen minutes before the second—paid an extra $10,000 premium for the privilege.

When the passengers emerged into the bright sunlight a few were woozy and required oxygen. An eighty-year-old man turned a frightening shade of blue and a real estate man with a drinking problem nearly passed out from lack of a bracer. Those still-cogent visitors traded ball caps and t-shirts with the U.S. government crew stationed at the Amundsen-Scott South Pole base and planted local Lions Club flags in the ice.

Several were "competitive" travelers, who had come this far south—nearly two thousand miles from the nearest town—to check several countries off their "Places I've Been" lists. Most headed straight for the barber's pole that marks the South Pole and fast-walked around it. Members or aspiring members of the Century Club—membership requires having visited at least 100 countries—"captured" eight countries by walking twenty paces around the Pole. But arguments erupted among the country collectors. Exactly which countries could they count? Only those with territorial claims reaching the South Pole were official, and Norway's Antarctic claim has an undefined southern border. By walking around the South Pole had they really been to Norway? Or not?

"For some it was a life-changing experience," remembers Gordy Wiltsie, one of ANI's first guides. "They would go back and spread the word about the importance of preserving this pristine place to an important segment of the population. But most of these folks, once they'd seen the Pole, couldn't get out of there fast enough."

My sled-and-ski trip was one of the great, small adventures of a lifetime, and I thought often about the variety of friends who would love to come South for this one-of-a-kind experience—if they could scrape up the bucks. We saw all weather—bright sunshine, calm, big winds, snowstorms and whiteouts, freezing temps. One night it was so warm in our solar-heated tent we slept on top of our sleeping bags; the next, it was so cold we kept our gloves on inside. One afternoon, coming down a knife-edge slope, our sole map blew out of my pack and is probably still blowing across Antarctica. This was just a few minutes after we each fell, briefly, into narrow crevasses. We skied across slick blue ice, climbed magnificently carved wind scoops, hunted for fossils in piles of rocks and came down a steep hill with visibility at zero, sleds threatening to slide ahead and pull us down behind them. On our last day out it was snowing so hard we had to use the GPS to find base camp. It was Antarctica at its best—trying, yet ultimately rewarding.

Back at Patriot Hills, inside my pink-and-yellow tent, faded from hundreds of days under twenty-four-hour sun, the walls heave and snug with the 40 mph gusts of wind that ripple then expand it. Snow pelts the tent and the wind alternately whistles, hums, and roars. A heavy wash of blowing snow breaks over the tent, leaking an occasional fine spray of powder through small holes along the tent's seams. When the wind pauses, it is otherwise deathly quiet.

It's comforting to be in a tent during a winter storm. Inside, it seems like nothing can hurt, or harm you. But if that thin nylon membrane were to disappear, if through a small slit those fierce winds were allowed inside, or if one of the aluminum poles snapped, it would mean big trouble. On this day I thought about what it would be like to be stranded in the middle of Antarctica in my long johns. I also thought back to the recent late afternoon Borneo Steve and I had shared soaking up rays, shirtless beneath a bright Antarctic afternoon sun.

Fifteen days after I arrived—the final three stuck in place because the blue-ice runway was covered with snow—the Hercules returned at two o'clock in the morning. Out of the back chute stumbled a whole new flock of urban penguins, decked out in bright, clean fleece and wind-stop Gore-Tex, shading their eyes and stumbling stiffly in boots made for steep slopes not flat blue ice.

Within minutes after boarding the Hercules for the return flight, I fell fast asleep. My hood pulled tight around my face, I could still smell the smells of Antarctica, feel the winds and the cold. I didn't budge until we touched down, hard, on the cement runway in Punta Arenas, 1,800 miles, six hours, and many, many worlds away.

Both the introduction to this collection and to my own essay contain quotes from the journals of Robert Falcon Scott. Everyone in the Antarctic has their favorite explorer: the Shackleton men believe in lots of luck and the Amundsen men get the job done. Scott fans are moody.

My favorite narrative of Scott's final expedition is Cherry-Garrard's The Worst Journey in the World. During the winter journey while he, Birdie Bowers, and Edmund Wilson are collecting Emperor penguin eggs, they find themselves weeks from their hut at Cape Evans, in the dark, in -70°F temperatures. A blizzard strikes and they lose their tent. "Face to face with real death," Cherry meditates: "I had no wish to review the evils of my past. But the past did seem to have been a bit wasted. The road to Hell may be paved with good intentions: the road to Heaven is paved with lost opportunities. I wanted those years over again. What fun I would have with them: what glorious fun!"

If there's one thing I can say about my six weeks on the Ice: what glorious fun.

The Secret of Silence

SUSAN FOX ROGERS

"If one is standing still and bareheaded, and exhales a deep breath, one can actually hear one's breath freezing a moment or two after it has left the mouth. What one hears I do not precisely know, unless the actual formation of ice crystals produces a sound, as appears to be the case. The sound itself is not easy to describe; it is rather like that produced by the movement of sand on a beach when a wave washes up."

—Captain Robert F. Scott, *Voyage of the Discovery*

AT THE SOUTH POLE STATION A TUNNEL TEN FEET HIGH and just as wide bores 1,200 feet into the ice of the polar plateau. The walls of the tunnel, hard and shear, contain nicks and gouges from the machine that scarred its way through the ice over the course of six seasons. I walked inside those tunnels in the austral summer of 2004 tracing the course of two large metal pipes, one that carried fresh water into the station, the other wastewater out. But five hundred feet in, the distance marked on the white walls in blood red, I stopped, feeling the weight of the ice above me, below me, around me. There I was, in *the bowels of the Earth at the bottom of the world.* Bundled in my enormous red parka, the hood up, I could sense my body freezing from the inside out, my lungs crisping in the −57°F air.

"This is far enough," I said to my guide Paul. My voice had issued as though through a trumpet mute and the words smacked flat against the walls of the tunnel, splaying out the color of gray. I heard an odd fear mixed in with the voice that was not quite mine. "You get the idea?" Paul asked. Antarctica, and the South Pole in particular, seemed genius at repetition: endless cold, endless expanses of white, endless sun followed by endless dark. So while visiting I had to decide, again and again, how much I needed to "get it."

Spooked by the sound of my breath, labored in the thin air and pressure of 9,000 feet, I nodded. "Yeh, I got it."

I like silence. But silence and the absence of sound are not the same thing. Silence, I seek, while this had enveloped me without warning. It was a deprivation, not unlike the limited food or the short showers of Polar life. My body rebelled against the muteness of the ice, so that when I emerged from the tunnel I felt as if a hearing aid had been inserted in my ear, and someone had turned it on loud. I had been strenuously reaching for sound—any sound—trying, perhaps, to hear my way out of that tunnel.

Though I feared the silence of the ice, I always wanted more. Soon it became clear that the silence, so odd and complete, had worked its way into my body, my psyche; at work was a subtle seduction.

My first experience of Antarctic silence occurred during Happy Camper School, my third day in Antarctica. All NSF participants undergo this overnight training if they are to leave McMurdo. A guide loaded a group of fifteen of us into a Pisten Bully, a squat, miniature bulldozer-like machine used to haul cargo and people around, and carted us out to a location on the Ross Ice Shelf. Six weeks later, I would skate ski past that site and recognize that what we had done was as good as camping in the back yard. But at the time it had seemed a wonderful adventure, much like venturing to the pine trees in the front yard that sheltered the cotton sleeping bags of my youth.

For campsites, it would be hard to beat our Happy Camper location. Twenty-five miles away stood Mt. Erebus, rounded and white, a thin plume rising from the top into an endless blue sky, an indication that the volcano is still active; nudging south of Erebus stood the dormant Mt. Terror (both are named for the ships that James Clark Ross sailed when he entered these southern waters in 1841). Castle Rock, which really is rock, emerged from behind a hill, red-brown amidst endless white. South, in the distance, rested White Island, Black Island, and Brown Peninsula, and then Mount Discovery (Scott's 1901 ship).

In this spectacular setting, we were taught the basics of hypothermia and frostbite, how to fire up a stove. We were told—a half dozen times—to have a plan, and then a back-up plan. Expect the unexpected. Learn patience.

We set up a range of tents, my favorite: the Scott's tent, all sixty pounds of yellow canvas stretched over long poles and secured with deadmen. The tent has no floor, so if it blows away—as it did for those early explorers Cherry-Garrard, Wilson, and Bowers one dreadful winter night—the sleepers remain put. Frozen, but not catapulted into the winds. More solid were the ice caves we constructed by digging into a mound of solid snow. Inside, dark, still, and cramped, I felt buried.

While we dug and tied knots the sun blasted down on us through a piercing blue sky. I sweated as I sawed ice blocks to help two mad scientists build their ice forts. I cut into the solid ice, creating perfect right angles. They heaved out magically smooth, creating exact building blocks. Intoxicated by the work, I tossed off my enormous red parka, rolled up my sleeves and slathered on sun block. But the minute I stopped,

I bundled back into Big Red, aware how frail my warmth was with 600 feet of ice stretching beneath my feet.

That evening, I took a walk with John, a slim Mormon boy, and a senior in college in Utah. Our walk took us several miles out a flagged route during which he explained his research on nematodes. Later in the season he and his crew would sport t-shirts that read: worm herders.

After over an hour of walking we stopped, took pictures of our elongated shadows, of an ice cliff that rose near the hill that led to Castle Rock. "Wait," I said. And we both stood still, spun our heads as if searching for something. I was looking for a sound. The silence, impossible to comprehend, didn't just surround me, it entered me. Like the cold, if I stopped moving, the silence could freeze me.

That night I slept with two pads, and a -20°F sleeping bag with a fleece liner between the ground and me. Warm in my cocoon I could still feel the ice seeping in through my back and thighs, through my pores. My transformation had begun.

I have a photo from Happy Camper School, sent to me by Holly, one of my Ice friends, that shows five of us, three pointing in various directions, and two looking puzzled. The guide had asked us which direction was south. Like magnetic compasses that begin to spin when nearing the magnetic pole, our sense of direction had warped. But in that picture, my arm points boldly in the right direction. Still early in my trip, I had not yet lost my orientation.

But this did not last long. Within days, I felt like a balloonist who has thrown out all of her ballast: light and free but unable to control my movement up or down, and utterly unable to land on firm ground.

In Antarctica people compete to claim they have lived through the coldest temperatures. The Polies who have wintered over always win, claiming numbers in the negative triple digits (the lowest temperature is −115°F). As for the continent itself, the Russians, bless them, take the record with their base at Vostok hitting −129°F (-89.4°C). During my austral sojourn I knew I could not compete. But the continent encourages superlatives: highest, driest, windiest; I wanted to add to the list most silent. Silentest.

I gravitate to places of silence: churches and dense forests and the middle of the Hudson River. I've mused and read about life in monasteries and convents, half envying those living with silent orders.

In company I become gregarious, often talk so much that the next morning the sound of my voice is a rattle in my head. To protect against myself, I avoid company. And so most days I speak very little.

Don't suffer in silence. Be silent. Day of silence. Silence is golden. Half the time we exhort to speech; the rest we beg for quiet. Silence is power and it's a sign of weakness. Ambushed by the silence of the Ice, I tried to find ways to think about it. Like Scott trying to locate the sound of his breath, I reached for comparisons: the silence of dawn, the silence of desolation. But they all were false silences and I abandoned them the moment I found them. Next I attempted to establish a moral order of silence: this silence is bad and that is good. But that, too, failed. It became simply: this is more silent; this I can endure; this I can not.

Each experience of overwhelming silence, though, made me feel that I was the chosen one who got to experience this nothing of sound. This made me feel as if the silence and I were in cahoots; it was one of my secrets.

I could never linger with the silence for too long. Still, I wanted it and the strain of reaching to hear something made my nerves taut.

＊

While in the Antarctic all of my senses switched on high. First, sight. I stretched to distinguish the shades of white, then the variations of blue in the sky. The first time I rode in a helicopter across the Ross Sea, the range of greens in the ice there appeared exotic. On land, I strained to make out the dot of a Weddell seal basking near a break in the sea ice. My eyes ached with the effort.

Then came smell. The ice encases smells, so the nostrils, in their innocence, flare, seeking to adapt. For a while, I thought my nose had shut down. There were real advantages to a smell-less world. While walking in the Dry Valleys I'd stumble across the freeze-dried body of a seal that had strayed inland some fifty miles. Why these seals are there remains a mystery to scientists. Unless the windblown sand has buffed the seals to their bones, they are intact, fur in place, eyes looking skyward, flippers making a final faint gesture. I stooped next to these seals, and, without the smell of rotting flesh, the smell of death, could peer in at their toothy, lurid grins.

Layers of government-issue clothing shielded my body from the wind and cold; in every other way I was exposed in that landscape, my senses unzipped. This is a dangerous way to move through the world. With my eyes and ears and nose flapped open, anything—or rather everything—found its way inside. What entered felt unfamiliar and yet the tightness in my chest felt oddly familiar. Reaching for a sound, I craned my neck, a wild anticipation that something great was just about to happen to me. Hope enveloped me; the impossible seemed possible. The early explorers lived with hope—they had to. Cherry-Garrard writes that he was never as happy as he was those two years on the Ice. Happiness. It stands out as an emotion in his story because so few emotions are present. I pushed that a bit further, took that happiness and called it love.

Before I went to Antarctica my friend Emily joked: What lies at the bottom of the Ross Ice Shelf? Then she'd smile in her disarming manner. "Your heart." She was right. I had become cynical, and while I believed in love, I no longer believed that people actually fell in love. That was a silly, modern construct, one that allowed for high drama and lots of gift buying, and a subject for writers and film producers to make money on. I did not have many allies in my beliefs, because evidence abounds to the contrary: people are falling exuberantly, publicly, ridiculously in love every day. I thought it all slightly disgusting. But suddenly here I was with all of the symptoms.

I fell in love in the Antarctic, which means I fell in love with Antarctica.

There are places in the Antarctic where silence is most absent and McMurdo, the center of falling in love, is one. Helicopters take off, their beat a regular part of the day, and there are trucks backing up, the relentless beep like a bad headache. There's the rumble of shuttle buses, a hum in the overheated dorms, the laughter in the galley. This all unfolds twenty-four hours a day, the work season short and so the work a continuous stream.

McMurdo was intoxicating, but whenever I could, I left. One trip was to Cape Royds where I discovered another place where silence is absent: a penguin colony.

I arrived at Cape Royds by helicopter on one of those beautiful Antarctic days—searing sun, a lapis sky, and visibility to the horizon—when all is right in the world. In the helicopter I wore a headset that helped screen out the considerable roar of the machine, but also allowed me to speak to the pilot, Paul. He is a young, tall, thin, chatty British boy, who delighted in his British heroic heritage and so flew me over the exact route Cherry-Garrard, Wilson and Bowers followed from Hut Point to Cape Crozier in the dark of an Antarctic night to collect emperor penguin eggs. We crossed the Ross Ice Shelf, rounded Erebus and dropped down into the camp at Crozier. That this took only twenty-seven minutes and not three weeks baffled me. We only had enough time there to load up David, a penguinologist, and his assistant Jen, and then we were whisked off to Royds.

Cape Royds is where Shackleton settled his 1907 Nimrod expedition and with good reason: a deep harbor in Backdoor Bay, open ground, and a lake with fresh water for his ponies. His hut rests in the shelter of the wind. David led me on a faint path in the crushed basalt toward the colony, my white boots taking two steps to his one large blue boot. Before I could see them I smelled them. "That's something," I joked. "What?" "The smell." The sulfur practically burned the back of my nose. He cocked his head. "I don't smell anything." Since he too smelled a bit like a penguin after weeks in the field with no shower, I understood. "You'll get used to it," he said. Yes, I thought, how quickly we adapt to the unknown, the unimaginable.

We strode past signs that read: Do Not Enter, Area of Special Scientific Interest, and within twenty feet I almost stepped on a penguin lying amidst the rocks. I looked around at a sea of 1,500 nesting Adélie penguins.

Unlike many people, I did not come to Antarctica for the penguins. And yet in the next five hours as I stood among those penguins my fascination grew. Sure, I was taken with their endearing behavior, how they determinedly took small rocks to build their nests, or walked purposefully from one place to another often tripping over small boulders. And, I admired their elegance. Out on the fast ice, which was breaking up, they moved gracefully, tobogganing along, and then diving in the water. In Pony Lake their speed and grace lovely, I imagined them fine breaststrokers popping out of the water then gliding underwater. But there is another side to penguins that I hadn't expected: the violence. And the noise.

Penguins are not all neat and tidy in their black and white tuxedos—many have guano smeared onto their white chests, or blood trickling down their sides from a recent skirmish. The elements are not kind and they must nest high up so that wind-blown snow won't bury them and then later, as the snow melts, flood their nests. If the cold and wind and snow don't get them, they have predators on land and at sea. In the water they fear leopard seals. On land skuas, those large scavenging birds, hover, ready to steal eggs and chicks. Cracked eggshells litter the ground, and carcasses of freeze-dried penguin chicks abound, legs twisted in awkward positions. One day I witnessed a real slaughter. A skua took a fairly good-sized chick by the scruff of the neck and, unable to lift it and cart it off, dragged it away from the nest. Joined by a hungry mate, the skuas slowly tore the chick apart. It was an excruciating slow process during which the chick continued to peep and tried to flee, flesh exposed. When they were done, only blood-splattered snow remained: red against white, vibrant, but mud splattered as well from the chick's valiant struggle. For days after, its desperate peep roared in my head.

Nothing compares, though, with the clanging sound of nesting penguins. There is little open ground in the Antarctic and so areas such as Royds constitute prime penguin real estate. Stones with which they build their nests are also at a premium.

Establishing their nesting space, therefore, becomes a contest, an aggressive affair. They want to be close enough for protection but far enough apart that they can't peck their neighbors. As they set this magical distance, they flare into raucous fights. The noise they emit begins low, like a transmission trying to turn over and as they peck at each other it gains momentum so that it is more like a donkey braying. But this bray is more like a jackhammer, staccato. Below this chaos of sound, the call of hungry chicks.

A storm trapped me for several days at Cape Royds, while winds gusting to forty-five knots brought snow to the icy world. Eventually, the fly on my tent, crushed and battered, lost its integrity. Lying in my tent, the yellow walls lit through the night by the unending glow of sun even amidst a storm, I begged for quiet. The tent walls shuffled, a rattle that takes the nerves and shakes them. It is like someone snapping a towel or sheets, but inside your head, and relentlessly. The wind would momentarily calm, and disarmed, my shoulders would relax until snap, the flapping resumed. For most of the day I shared a Rac Tent—a larger tent with a wooden floor—where David and Jen and I made casual conversation, made meager meals, read books, wrote emails that were miraculously sent through a satellite connection, and listened to chunks of ice scuttling across the roof, a sound like squirrels racing for safety. We shared books we cared about, and they shared information about penguins. We did not share secrets.

But we did not talk that much, really, because someone who lives his life with penguins, as David has, does so for a reason. He spends as much of every season in the field, avoiding trips into McMurdo. Out in the field, stripped of all material ties and needs he embraces the wind and ice, and those birds of his. In David there was a deep freedom from need—food or any of the luxuries of life. He would have been a good member of Amundsen's austere expedition.

"I'm not a good conversationalist," David confessed one night as I tried to pull a story out of him. Something about him, about the place and those funny birds had a strange effect: a different sort of silence descended. This was the silence of no phone and no beeper and no obligations. This was the silence of waiting. This was the silence of peace, or of God. There was nothing to do but practice patience. My mind drifted, dulled a bit, and then became calm, as close as it has ever come to its own silence.

Here is a secret about the Antarctic, about life in McMurdo: it's a sexual playground. In the women's bathroom stands an enormous tin can, one that originally contained ten pounds of beans, and is now filled with condoms. The supply dwindles with the regularity of the tides. This at first surprised me but then my surprise seemed naïve. Stick a thousand intelligent healthy adults into dorm rooms and we will begin to act like eighteen-year-olds again.

It wasn't just the dorm effect, however. I had to figure that what I was experiencing, this stretch of the senses that I called love, others felt as well. Only their love found as its object a warm body. It was like joining a lively carnival, cheerful and without shame. Since all compasses are confused so near the pole, so too is the moral compass.

Couples arrive on the Ice and uncouple, couples form and disintegrate back on solid ground. People leave spouses at home and find their Ice spouse season after season. Wedding vows held no meaning; pledges of faithfulness to those left at home are breached with ease: what happens on the Ice stays on the Ice. These people are as resourceful as penguins—a stone will do for a nest.

Every day the people who work season after season on the Ice risked something; pushing the edge was a way of life. They clearly feared the ordinary. And so they learned a certain fear-lessness in facing the elements, and that became a way of life. Why not in love as well?

What I realized was that the only thing certain about most of these furtive loves is that they would have to say goodbye. Antarctica is the land of goodbyes: no one gets to stay. Every large cargo plane flying back to New Zealand carried some-one in tears, or else left someone behind in McMurdo, watch-ing the sky, waving and hoping the plane would circle back, unable to leave. In McMurdo, broken hearts litter the ground like eggshells.

If I did not believe in falling in love, I even more did not believe in having one's heart broken. Plates or glasses break, but the heart is a muscle, flexible, even elastic. It might tear, it might bruise, it might even stop, but a heart can't break. And yet….

I knew I could not take home the silence that had entered me so surely; it would give over to the roar of life. Too quick, I'd resume my orientation in the world; I'd shift into my wary approach to love; I'd recognize the smell of death.

Cherry never really had a life after the Ice, his heart still there with his comrades that he adored, and the hard life that gave him focus. He wrote a book, *The Worst Journey in the World*, to keep those two happy years alive for him. I write this essay, edit a book. And in this way, I learn, again, how hard it is for any love to survive. To survive *in* Antarctica takes a big red parka and bunny boots, it takes imagination, the willingness to live disoriented, and the determination of those penguins braying into the air. But to survive Antarctica takes something else. Cherry did not find it; he is not alone.

While in McMurdo, people come and go helicoptering or flying off to places with mysterious names, like Dome C or Blood Falls, to do things I could not begin to imagine. McMurdo is a government town, and as such is acronym heaven—we wore our ECW (Extreme Cold Weather) clothes, picked up at the CDC (Clothing Distribution Center). It was when I met ET who worked for MEC in the SSC, and was employed by RPSC that I gave up trying to understand what people actually did when they said they were going to work. In his essay, Jason Anthony takes some of the mystery out of AGO 1 as we join him at this far-flung camp. The details of daily life in such an isolated place are marvelous as Anthony is a keen observer of his sur-roundings. As he works, he's not immune to the beauty of the landscape and to the absurdity of what he is doing at AGO 1.

Jason Anthony has worked in the Antarctic for eight austral summers. His Antarctic essays have been published by the Missouri Review, Seneca Review, Isotope, *worldhum.com,* Alimentum *(forthcoming), and in* In Pieces: An Anthology of Fragmentary Writing. *One essay was selected for the* Best American Travel Writing 2007, *while another was a Notable Essay in the 2006 issue of* Best American Essays. *His web site of Antarctic essays and photographs is www.albedoimages.com. He teaches English at The Deck House School in Edgecomb, Maine.*

AGO 1

⋆ ⋆ ⋆

JASON ANTHONY

NOVEMBER, 2000: AFTER FIVE SEASONS OF FAIRLY civilized Antarctic work, I took on an ominous job offered to me at the end of the polar summer by a drunken friend. Kip reeled across the floor of McMurdo Station's darkened carpenter shop during its massive end-of-season party in February and shouted over Pink Floyd a slurred version of the question we all ask at the end of an Antarctic contract: "Hey man, are you coming back next year?" When I shrugged the shrug of the restless, he yelled an eager if unpromising offer: "You should come back and work for AGO next year. It's crazy!" AGO (pronounced like the end of "Winnebago") is the Automated Geophysical Observatory program, notorious for some of the most difficult work in the United States Antarctic Program (USAP). Kip had graduated to management, and would be doing the hiring.

Eight months later, I was back in McMurdo preparing to journey outward with a few others to a string of isolated motes across the top of the godforsaken East Antarctic ice cap. Bella, the lead groomer, and I will join engineers Joe and Rudy on journeys to AGO 1, AGO 4, and AGO 5. Another team will be flying out to 2, 3, and 6. East Antarctica is the coldest and most inaccessible geography on Earth, a plateau of ice ranging from one to three miles deep, larger than the United States and, except for some windblown bacteria and a handful of people in government-issued parkas, empty of life.

AGO teams visit these sites only once a year. The engineers download the previous year's data and reset, rebuild, or replace the cold electronics and weather-beaten instruments for each AGO unit. Each site has a collection of experiments measuring, among other things, electromagnetic radiation (EMR) from the sun. These experiments are particularly concerned with the massive bursts of energy that storm over the Earth's poles after the eruption of solar flares.

Our four-person team will fly out to AGO 1 by Twin Otter, a small sturdy bush plane used in all the wild corners of the planet. While the engineers do their work, Bella will show me how to smooth out at each AGO site a 10,000-foot landing strip for a huge propane-laden LC-130 Hercules aircraft. Now updated to run on wind and solar energy, AGO sites during my stint were still dependent on a difficult delivery of 3,000 gallons of propane, which would power the automated facility through the upcoming winter. The Hercs land on massive skis (thus we make a "skiway," not a runway), which damage easily on rough landings. The last thing the Guard wants, aside from crashing with several tons of propane, is to do maintenance on a plane out at an AGO site. Such intensive, complex work is nearly impossible in the severe cold of the high plateau.

Nervous about doing what was rumored to be brutal work, I had heard that at AGO sites groomers commonly battle altitude sickness and frostbite, repair snowmobiles endlessly at -30°F below, and find themselves stuck for weeks because of weather.

Working as an AGO skiway groomer was my first pure fieldwork job, after a few seasons taking shorter or milder journeys throughout the USAP as I worked fueling aircraft. I'd lived in tiny permanent outposts just a short helicopter ride from McMurdo, and spent several weeks in temporary tent cities during the mellow West Antarctic summer. Most work in the USAP takes place on McMurdo's stony shoreline, where secretaries and plumbers stroll between dormitories, work centers, and the cafeteria. But AGO sites harken back to the old days, when a few souls were flung by groaning plane to camp in the flat white heart of cold.

Joe, the lead engineer and general AGO mastermind, had already done nearly thirty of these trips over the previous several years. He talked to us with his soft-spoken Alabama voice about how we want things to go, and how badly they might go. "We really need to look after each other out there, guys. Temperatures should be around -30°F. Check each other's faces for white patches, and take it easy snowmobiling and shoveling. Warm up when you need to. Keep track of each other. We'll be a long way from home, and if you're hurt it might take a few days to get you to McMurdo Medical, much less to a real hospital in New Zealand. Things should go fine, but remember that it can get really difficult really quickly out there."

I'll know in a few weeks whether to thank Kip, who now sits warm and safe in his office.

Thank God for Bella, I kept saying to myself, as she led me through the 10,000 details of planning food, overhauling gear, and preparing ourselves for all contingencies. She taught me how to rebuild engines for the thirty-year-old snowmobiles used to groom the skiways. She tested radios while I gathered oatmeal and pesto; she packed up spare snowmobile parts while I searched for bamboo poles. We put together our medical kit and purchased our liquor. We scratched items off lists; she and I both made new lists.

I learned in those days with Bella how to assemble a field camp from McMurdo's logistical maze. I knew town intimately from five summers of work, and Bella knew what life in the field required: between us, with Joe's input, we built a raft of cargo and food for our journey.

Bella fled Cape Cod years ago for Alaska, and has worked many contracts drilling ice cores in Greenland and the Antarctic. She stood out among McMurdo's swarm of red parkas because of her large fur hat, spun from the hair of her best sled dog.

The heart of American Antarctica is McMurdo Station, a nearly graceless town of over a hundred prefab structures, busy with forklifts and trucks moving cargo to and from planes flying to New Zealand, South Pole station, and the field camps. McMurdo squats on the volcanic rock of Ross Island, but offers a heartbreakingly beautiful view of the Transantarctic Mountains across forty miles of frozen ocean. The view is heartbreaking in part because few of the 1,200 people who keep McMurdo humming are given a chance to see it up close. Four-fifths of the residents are contract workers who keep town and transportation running, supporting the famous science done by the other fifth. Most residents never leave McMurdo.

Bella and I were leaving in a few days, crossing the mountain barrier to what seemed to me a very uncertain fate. The work ahead was colder, higher, and more remote than anything I'd known.

✳

> He was lost! Lost in blizzard land! Lost in vast spaces
> that spread about him for thousands of miles! Lost
> without food or fuel! Lost with a crazy man, whom he
> and his companions had to wheedle, cajole, and threat-
> en to keep him moving at all! Lost without a compass
> in the Antarctic!
>
> —F. W. Dixon, *Lost at the South Pole*

November 8: On suspicion of emerging schizophrenia, Rudy,
the electrical engineer who was to fly with Bella, Joe and me
to AGO 1 was told that he would not be allowed into the
field. A bright Ph.D. student, this was Rudy's first trip to the
Antarctic. Now it looked like it was also his last.

Small idiosyncrasies like changing his name en route to the
continent (a sudden mystical interest in Valentino had
prompted Ron—his real name—to ask to be called Rudy), or
obsessive staring at McMurdo's women (he was asked to leave
from at least one workplace) came first; then public statements
on telepathy within dreams and aliens in Antarctica gave us
pause. McMurdo's rumor mill was buzzing about our odd expedition partner and his *X-Files* sensibility. None of his quirks
were dangerous vices, but because Rudy's distance from predictability grew rapidly as the date for deploying to East
Antarctica neared, Joe grew wary and asked Steve, the manager of field science support, to interview him. As a moun-
taineer, Steve had dealt with personality problems in remote
settings before. When his square questions were met with
round answers, he reluctantly banned Rudy from heading out
with us into the great white unknown.

None of us were happy with the situation. Joe needed
Rudy's expertise and the extra pair of hands. Months of

planning had just been lost. Indignant at the possible injustice, Bella kept saying: "We wouldn't think twice about this guy's ideas back home. I know people in Alaska who think they've been talking with aliens for years."

She and I had been annoyed that Rudy would sometimes drift off from our preparations, only to be found later apparently attempting telepathy while gazing far too intently at an annoyed woman, but mostly he did his work and did it well. For his part, Rudy was quite upset, worried about both his image in the McMurdo community and the future of his Ph.D. work. But his protest was quiet and short-lived; the look in his eye told me this wasn't the first time he'd had trouble.

One idea of insanity defines it as the inability to choose among false alternatives. What better landscape to place the object of an invisible fantasy than the tabula rasa of the ice cap? How would we manage Rudy if he fought to prove his delusions? What if he took a snowmobile and headed out to nowhere at full speed?

So the USAP clipped Rudy's wings not so much for the foolishness of his ideas or our confidence that he was unfit, but for the consequences, the what-ifs.

Rudy's compass went awry a short time later. He announced publicly, going table to table in the galley, that the mothership would be arriving at noon next Thursday to pick him up in the parking lot. But come Thursday, our engineer had to settle for delivery by a cadre of upper management, who hustled him off to a quiet room before booking him on the first flight north.

Thursday was a sad day for everyone but a gang of chuckling spectators, some of whom arrived wearing alien masks and toting cameras. As I watched Rudy, bewildered and distraught, being led away to his strange fate, I also noticed, as no one else did, a strange bank of fog surge over the peninsula and swarm into town precisely at noon.

November 13: Arrived at AGO 1. Bella and I flew in the Twin Otter for four slow hours into the strange heart of cold. (Joe came alone with the rest of the gear on the second flight several hours later.) Leaving McMurdo, our plane immediately ramped up from sea level to aim through the mountains, up through local turbulence, the small plane jolting and dropping, kicking forward.

The Twin Otter was unpressurized, unheated, and packed to the roof with 2,000 pounds of cargo. We stared at the jumble of gear bags and food boxes haphazardly strapped down, crammed in within inches of us. In a crash, all of it would spill over us like water from a broken dam.

We kept very quiet within the deep drone of the Otter. As the increasing cold seeped into us, Bella and I began the familiar Antarctic descent into the catacombs of the self. Hood up, chin down, feet braced against the cargo, we spent our time in a zone somewhere between mild hypothermia and simple flight-driven sleep.

Waking mid-flight, everything motionless but for the blurred props, I looked out to see we were still floating above the scattered ice-drowned peaks at the inside edge of the Transantarctic Mountains. Still a long way to go. We were drifting up to 10,000 feet, making our invisible path to a little white spot in the midst of an absurdly powerful emptiness.

November 14: Bella, Joe, and I tucked ourselves into our new home, an orange 8x16-foot insulated box on posts. The AGO box was shipped in by Herc several years ago. A modified shipping container that looks like a hybrid of a small RV and an engineering lab, it contains a pile of electronics, a TEG (a thermoelectric generator, which somehow generates power from the burning of propane), some cupboards and shelves, and four fold-down bunks. As ascetic as it may sound, the luxury of stepping off a plane into a weatherproof cube in East Antarctica changes everything. We were safe and comfy on the far side of the moon.

Outside, a full-on ground blizzard raged, with 30-knot winds at −34°F limiting us to 100-foot visibility. Yesterday, after each flight, the Otter pilots stuck around only long enough to unload and refuel; in twenty minutes, they were back in the air, a few empty hours away from home.

The wind rose quickly after our plane landed, with Bella's hood shaking around her head as she radioed McMurdo.

"MacOps, MacOps, this is AGO 1, AGO 1, on 10.995, over. How copy, over?" For a moment, she and I stood there surrounded by our boxes, bags, and bamboo on the edge of a runway overrun with last year's sastrugi. Beyond the runway and our AGO box there lay a flat white lifeless ice plateau the size of America. Beneath us, two miles of ice pressed the continent into the Earth's mantle.

The ground blizzard hit us an hour after Joe's plane left.

After landing, Bella and I threw the essential gear and do-not-freeze items into the AGO box, and then began the struggle to set up our toilet tent. With the wind already at 20 knots, the heavy canvas Scott tent fought us like a wounded umbrella. We finally managed to get the feet planted and its anchors tied off. I moved inside to dig the outhouse hole while Bella tried to set up her sleep tent. Despite the hassles of camping at −35°F, she wanted her own cold space. Even after I shuffled over to help her, however, with the wind now at twenty-five knots, she decided to give up until a better day.

A "ground blizzard" brings no precipitation; rather, the wind rises to a force strong enough to stir loose snow up into a low maelstrom. The snow flies in a stream only several feet high, so that we can sometimes climb above it into a clear blue sky. When a thin veneer of loose snow covers an upwind area larger than Europe, however, life becomes difficult: a day-long ground blizzard will bury everything we own in a crystal-built cement.

We spent the day listening to Marvin Gaye (Bella) and reading Rilke (me) or science fiction (Joe). Even though the wind swept around and under the insulated box, we kept quite warm with a portable propane heater. Looking out one of our two tiny end-windows at the white froth, I felt like one of three sailors lost in some deep ocean fog. Visibility was less than a hundred feet, the toilet tent a pale yellow blur.

We were supposed to be in and out of AGO 1 in six days, but already our clock's ticking had slowed to a hypothermic pace. With the storm here and Rudy absent, our trip was bound to be extended.

I'd like to think that if Rudy had made it out to AGO with us, the hard beauty and strange reality of what surrounded us would have helped focus him on the work at hand. Or maybe the stress of the otherworldly emptiness might have sent him over the edge. We'll never know.

What I found in myself again was my pleasure in hard weather and extremity. A stormed-in day at AGO 1 was much more agreeable than the anxious packing for AGO 1. A journey begun is always better than a journey in preparation, and now I'd arrived, snuggled into the corner of the future I'd worried about for the last eight months.

Joe, who has done more of these trips than anyone, said that the wind at this site has two characteristics: "It always blows, and it always blows from the same direction. Usually it blows lightly, but not this time, I guess."

*

The outlook was by no means encouraging, as the surface still bristled with huge ice undulations as far as the eye could reach. It was just as though a stormy sea had suddenly been frozen solid...

—Edgeworth David, *The Heart of the Antarctic* (1908)

...the plateau over which we are now travelling resembles a frozen sea...

—Roald Amundsen, 1911, quoted in
Scott and Amundsen

The snow was getting more and more uneven the further south I went. The ridges crossed at right angles to my course and looked like a heavy sea that had suddenly frozen solid.

—Børge Ousland, *Alone Across Antarctica* (1997)

The surface of Antarctica is in motion, relentlessly sculpted by the wind into sastrugi. The universal description of sastrugi is of an ocean frozen in motion: it's the inescapable metaphor brought down from the liquid north. Travelers' imaginations have been strung together in Antarctic literature as a continuum of land-or-sea aesthetics. Present-day descriptions of the plateau, by adventurers, journalists, or USAP workers, still use this stock image.

Any other metaphor would violate scale by comparing the texture of sastrugi to, say, sand dunes or the undulations of fresh whipped cream. Sand dunes grow far too large—sastrugi are usually just knee-high, though may reach six feet—and feel far too soft underfoot. Sastrugi scarcely dent, much less break, under the weight of a passing ski or snowmobile.

The form of a moving wave is beautifully recreated in the slow-sculpted surface of snow. On the water, both wind and wave are fluid; on the ice, only the wind flows, while the snow is pushed along like dust, adhering, degrading.

Whether landing a Herc on a glacier, adventuring by ski to the South Pole, or grooming a skiway out of the squall-carved surface, we still find the frozen sea waiting as it has for eons. And as soon as our species turns away from the ice, the snow will crest and fall across our small history like waves over spindrift.

*

> What are they doing in Heaven today,
> where sin and sorrow are all done away?
> Peace abounds like the river, they say,
> But what are they doing right now?
> —Washington Phillips, "What Are They Doing
>   In Heaven Today"

November 17: Waking with these 1920s gospel blues lyrics in my head after a fever-wracked "night" of restless sleep and difficult dreams, I found myself sweating in an orange box on stilts in the empty heart of Antarctica's bright twilight zone, which might, from a comfortably distant overflight, look like heaven. Life in the clouds and all that…

Washington Phillips was a little-known preacher from Texas who recorded a few songs and sermons with his high beautiful voice about the same time Admiral Byrd was down here on his first expedition, talking loosely of creating a perfect scientific community in this icescape. The two twentieth-century moral universes of church and utopia have informed American Antarctica right up to this point: We're still part of an exploration that glorifies science and pays lip service to the language of faith. Every explorer cited the grace and handiwork of God, and we still maintain a shiny white chapel in the center of McMurdo. But the increasingly comfy USAP has replaced the talk of Providence with the pleasures of easy living in an exotic locale. The chapel sees more yoga classes than services. We support science that cares less about heaven than the turbulent mathematics of the heavens.

What was I doing this day? Dragging my ass around, for one thing, but at least momentarily clean of obvious sin (isolated with Joe and Bella from worldly temptation, too ill to drink wine with them) and too caught up with the wild strangeness of this life to consider sorrow. Grumpy from sleeplessness, I bundled up against what seemed the temperature of outer space to shovel out boxes of food and a snowmobile buried for a long year in the dooryard of our little AGO haven.

The wind had come down some, so Bella set up her orange Scott tent and moved her gear out of the AGO box. We needed to run the snowmobiles a bit, to move gear around and pull buried cargo out of its rock-hard drifts. It was far too cold to start the machines with their keys; even pull-starting them at -35°F is like tugging a horse that strains against its reins. I planted my foot against the snowmobile's 750 pounds and threw my whole body backward to earn a half crank from the engine; on the next few tries the cranking improved, and then it reluctantly started. Soon it would be time to wrestle these beasts during long days of skiway grooming.

The body's only heaven here are the frames built to protect it. Our cubes and tents that keep us warm and wired to other people are our local version of the afterlife. After several hours of messing around in the cold, I ascended the ladder to find heat and friendship above the frozen clouds, and aspired to a songless night with peaceful earthbound dreams.

✳

"MacOps, MacOps, this is AGO 1 on 10.995. How copy?"

"AGO 1, AGO 1, we have you weak but readable. How us, over?"

"We have you loud and clear, MacOps. IS IT BETTER IF WE YELL, OVER?"

"Loud and clear now, AGO 1. How are you doing, Over?

"ALL IS WELL, MACOPS, ALL IS WELL. WE HAVE THREE SOULS ON BOARD AND ALL IS WELL. DO YOU HAVE ANY MESSAGES FOR US, OVER?"

Each morning, we called in (as required of all camps) to MacOps (McMurdo's communications center) to say we're alive, don't worry about us, and to see if there was any news for us from the other AGO team, AGO scientists at home, the flight planners, or friends. HF radio transmissions are an ephemeral thing, and even the loudest holler can sometimes sound like a feeble whisper in the blizzard of static.

Sometimes we've had to call South Pole when McMurdo could not receive us, and ask them to relay our messages. Pole's antennas are not as powerful as McMurdo's, but we're closer to them and don't have to worry about the elevation drop from our ice cap through the mountains to the coast.

Even after several days here, the morning transition from warm breakfast and familiar voices on the radio to our parka-clad existence in the planet's Empty Quarter is still a shock. The waves of hard snow at our feet are more real and yet more strange than the frail invisible waves that throw our voices across the continent.

November 20: Making a skiway is a beautiful and completely absurd task. To make a skiway 10,000 feet long and 150 feet wide out of a wilderness of hard sastrugi, we tow a homemade grooming machine only four feet wide. We might as well mow a swath through an overgrown field with a pair of scissors. And just as grass grows back, so our little pragmatic Nazca line scratched into the field of topographic chaos will soon be wiped away by the next ground blizzard.

The groomer, which consists of 800 pounds of improvised angle iron, does two things: four forearm-sized iron fangs shatter the surface into chunks, which the blade then crushes into fragments small enough to be evenly spread. The groomer doesn't do these things at the same time however; we harrow the 2 million square feet of the skiway, loading area, and turnarounds before removing the teeth and doing all 2 million square feet again with the blade.

The teeth and blade are set as deeply as the snowmobile can handle, usually just a few inches. Set them too shallow, and the groomer bounces along, scratching the surface at random; set them too deep, and you might go through the windshield. Once the surface is bladed, the fragmented snow sinters into a rough pavement.

Bella and I took turns, working at full throttle for several hours at a time. Anything slower is useless. Hunched down behind the windshield, we end up both tense and bored, and always cold. We droned up and down two miles of sinuous white space, swaddled in thick layers of insulation, bucking and jumping over the rough sastrugi. Inside mittens the size of footballs, our right thumbs grew sore as hell from applying constant pressure to the throttle.

Sastrugi form in parallel with the prevailing wind, long waves of accreting snow porpoising out of the plateau. We build skiways into the prevailing wind as well, the groomer riding up and over narrow forms that threaten to tip us over.

I was thrown off the snowmobile only a few times, though each time I raced up and over sastrugi narrower than the machine I made ready to jump. And this is one of the easiest, smoothest AGO sites. At AGO 6, the sastrugi reach over three feet, and persistent storms will carve up a new skiway a couple times before the Herc arrives with the propane.

With any luck, we can do the job in two complete passes of both tooth and blade. This can take several days. Harder to remove, however, are the larger undulations in the skiway, swells beneath the waves, which could cause a Herc at high speed to slam a wingtip into the snow. These require intensive passes to bring them down, a few inches at a time.

In 1971, a Navy Herc crashed on the East Antarctic ice cap: no one was killed, but the Navy abandoned the plane. Seventeen years later, the Navy dug the Herc out of the ice, repaired it, and flew it back to McMurdo, but only after another Herc servicing the summer-long repair operation had crashed, killing two people.

Herc crews will not shut down their plane's engines on the East Antarctic plateau, even at South Pole station. At a primitive AGO site, they want to land and leave as quickly as possible. Parking it for repair at cold altitude means days of work and weeks of logistics. Other Herc flights would fly in people and equipment, which means flights taken away from the South Pole or elsewhere. One bad undulation on our skiway can easily affect the whole Antarctic program, including the lives of those who fly the planes.

Bella spent hour after hour working on these larger swells in the last two days, trying to make them friendly. I was up until 6 A.M. the "night" before, obsessed with blading the last portion of the skiway. Taking our safety rules to heart, Bella didn't sleep either, because she sweetly worried about me, popping out of her tent occasionally to see the little red-and-black dot that was me careening through the whiteness.

Grooming is a wild job in the furthest reaches of Antarctic climate and American logistics, and the absurdity of all this frenzied back-and-forth in the center of nothing did not escape me as I somewhat happily mowed this insane lawn.

*

I used to wonder sometimes whether the people who suffer from hunger in the big cities of civilisation felt as we were feeling, and I arrived at the conclusion that they did not, for no barrier of law and order would have been allowed to stand between us and any food that had been available. The man who starves in a city is weakened, hopeless, spiritless, and we were vigorous and keen.

—Ernest Shackleton, *The Heart of the Antarctic*

No one starves in Antarctica anymore. Ross Island, once the desperate bit of rock that held the only full meals available to Shackleton, now sports Antarctica's big city. McMurdo is a law-and-order (or at least bureaucratic) town that tries clumsily to be civilization, and the living is so easy that tons of food per year are wasted.

Joe, a thin man who grew up on rich Southern cooking, told us one night after dinner that "the South is really bad for a person's figure." But he was talking about the Antarctic, not Alabama. Only new McMurdo employees are surprised that they can gain weight on the cafeteria's fat-rich diet. The same is true at the low-altitude West Antarctic field camps. We run the risk of filling out our ECW (Extreme Cold Weather) gear on the greasy food we crave after moving in and out of the cold all day.

Even in East Antarctica, gaining weight is not uncommon. While Russians at bitter Vostok Station (higher and colder than South Pole station) still grow thin eating from an impoverished potato-based menu, the well-fed Pole fattens up its managers and pencil-pushers. Outside, however, where calorie-sucking temperatures repelled the vigorous Shackleton, the cold still gnaws away at carpenters and mechanics.

The success of technology means, in part, that we can be on the far edge of nowhere but still be neither vigorous nor keen. Joe, Bella and I enjoyed this Antarctic irony, but not as much as we enjoyed the angel hair pasta with pesto and scallops.

*

There are three kinds of people—those dead, those alive, and those at sea.

—Anacharsis, 6th century B.C., quoted in *Antarctica Ahoy* by Juhan Smuul

November 23: Our work at AGO 1 was done, but we were not. Joe updated some science projects and nixed some others. He and I renovated the strange TEG (gluing thin sheets of mica to wired ceramic tiles, among other things), while Bella and I finally brought the bumps and undulations on the skiway to within reason for a deep-field Herc landing.

The loss of our electrical engineer accounted for some of the cancelled science work, but bad planning (incomplete designs, missing parts) by researchers in the States had made some of Joe's other tasks impossible. A scientist with no experience in the Antarctic is never able to foresee the long list of problems caused by extreme weather, rough transport, and lack of spare parts. Joe made patient phone calls to the U.S. via scratchy high-frequency radio in order to explain to a geophysics professor just why their carefully wrought project was unworkable in our cold reality: "There's nothing I can do, over. Sorry, over."

AGO 1 was teaching me something I'd heard in passing as I moved in and out of camps in previous seasons: Nearly everything you plan in Antarctic fieldwork should have an extra 50 percent to 100 percent built in as a safeguard. Going out for a week? Bring at least ten days of food, plus some emergency rations. Think you'll need twenty hours of helicopter time? Beg for thirty before the summer begins, and be ready to explain at summer's end why you ended up using forty. Bringing one of the indestructible nothing-can-go-wrong HF radios? Bring two, just in case.

Day after day, the flight that should have come to pull us out cancelled because of bad weather in McMurdo, or was de-prioritized because of the vast number of flights needed to keep South Pole operational. And finally, we were told by MacOps that our flight did not make the pre-holiday schedule.

So we knew we were stuck with nothing to do for at least the next four days. The long Thanksgiving weekend in McMurdo, with our friends gathering in the galley for the annual feast, would be savored without us. And I felt like whining about it.

I'd learned so much about how to make a field camp come to life, but I still hadn't learned how to bring my life to the field camp. In the midst of a journey few had made and most would love to make, I had a warm box to sleep in, was keeping good company, but was suddenly and hopelessly ready to go. As if anything about AGO 1 had taught me that we were in control of our fate.

So a few days of impatience awaited me in this bland white space: days to fill with occasional work (touching up the skiway, organizing cargo, etc.), reading, cooking the best of our very frozen food, and walking to and from the horizon.

I'd already spent hours photographing sastrugi arching into the cold air. Bella was as happy as a Cape Cod clam at high tide: she searched for finger-wide microcrevasses or napped in her tent. Joe was on his sixth sci-fi novel, and slept like a cat in the warmth of the TEG.

What was scheduled as a six-day trip was stretching toward sixteen days.

As for Anacharsis' people, I felt like part of a very minor subculture: those alive, drifting on a dead sea.

Thoughts while walking the whiteness: *Why is there this nothing rather than something...? The enormous scale of absence in this landscape, the depth of alienness, the invisibility of memory, and the absent facts of consciousness tell us that ice itself is not enough. It wants definition, or we think it wants definition, and for me only a negative definition fits.*

Poor Rudy. Dreaming too hard of complexities outside the pale of everyday human existence, he missed visiting this simplicity outside the pale of everyday human existence. This place, if we can call it a place, is a remnant of the great silence that predates us and the consciousness that gets us into so much trouble.

I owe Kip a beer.

November 26: We lost communications with McMurdo because of high solar flare activity. A burst of intense electromagnetic radiation flattened out all Antarctic radio signals, leaving us (and Pole, McMurdo, and every other camp) listening to pure snowy static. In theory, only a few days would pass before the EMR would fade.

This comms blackout made a mess of our lifeline to McMurdo. When we can't make our daily all-is-well call to MacOps, then they have no idea what's happening with us. We would treat any injury here as best we can, until the airwaves cleared. We broadcast our existence "in the blind" in case radio operators in town or at Pole might hear us. Mainly, we needed to know when the Herc with the AGO propane and our ticket out of AGO 1 would launch.

We were simultaneously preparing for a longer stay and sudden departure.

Meanwhile, I was in the middle of one of Joe's sci-fi books, in which the imminent destruction of the planet is signaled first by massive EMR at the North and South Poles, disrupting communications and isolating polar residents from the news that the Earth is about to boil over and break apart.

I have more leisure than I shall probably ever have again. Thanks to the routine way I do things, my opportunities for intellectual exercise are virtually unlimited. I can, if I choose, spend hours over a single page in a book. I thought tonight what a very full and simple life it is—indeed, all I really lack is temptation.

—ADMIRAL RICHARD E. BYRD, *ALONE*

On Thanksgiving and Christmas workers get two days off—except, of course, for the people laboring in the kitchen and the dish room. So for the holidays people volunteer to help out. On Christmas 2004, I found myself in the dish room at McMurdo with two National Science Foundation representatives. We swapped stories about home and family as people dropped off their clean trays (rarely does anyone waste food) and wished us a Merry Christmas. One fellow poked his head in, saw who was working and asked: How many NSF reps does it take to wash a dish? Truth is, it's pretty mindless work washing dishes. And as I looked around at the churning dish machine and cafeteria trays it all looked just like the dish room I'd worked in in college. It is like dish rooms throughout the world. Who comes to Antarctica to wash dishes? I wondered.

Phil Jacobsen holds the record (National Science Foundation approved) for washing dishes in Antarctica. After spending fourteen months as a dishwasher, Phil nearly went insane. So he returned to McMurdo for two more seasons to learn what went wrong. Phil currently lives in Salt Lake City, Utah and is writing a book about his experiences.

The Big Chill

⋆ ⋆ ⋆

PHIL JACOBSEN

THE ICE RUNWAY AT MCMURDO STATION IS NOT ONLY at sea level, it is the sea—the Ross Sea. The ice has been shaved smooth so that cargo planes can take off and land on the ocean's surface.

I didn't know it at the time, but stepping foot off the ice runway and into an airplane to fly to the South Pole, I was leaving what would soon save my life: sea level and oxygen.

Five months earlier, I had left Salt Lake City to live in Antarctica. I'm not an adventurer, world traveler, or thrill seeker of any sorts. I've been to Canada and Mexico, but have never owned a passport.

I had read some books about Antarctica. One was a story about a guy who took a ship called the *Endurance* and a gaggle of sailors to Antarctica. These sailors and this captain were going to do some cross-continental exploring, but their boat got stuck in the ice and they almost all died. The boat sunk and everyone had to eat penguins until they were rescued. The End.

Just because I've read about Antarctica did not mean I wanted to live in Antarctica. I've also read a lot about Watergate, but I've never wanted to be a Republican.

But I did want to follow a girl. I was in between relationships when a girl friend of mine, Penny, asked if I wanted to go to Denver and attend an "Antarctic Job Fair." I thought, "Hell, I would have simply gone on a date. So, sure, I'll follow you to the bottom of the world."

Come to find out, it wasn't that simple. To work in Antarctica we had to compete with nearly fifty thousand other people applying for less than one thousand available jobs.

So, when the National Science Foundation, through their government contractor Raytheon, offered me a year contract, in a windowless room, to wash dishes for 981 people, it was an opportunity I couldn't pass up. For a place to live, $4.88 an hour and the opportunity to work sixty hours a week washing dishes for scientists at a town called McMurdo Station, 850 miles north of the South Pole, I could experience Antarctica.

Penny got a job as a janitor. I quit my life in Utah and moved to McMurdo. And I washed dishes and I washed pots and I washed pans until my knuckles cracked and my fingers bled.

Until one day there was a dishwashing emergency at the South Pole.

"Jacobsen," Tina my dishwashing boss said. "The dishes are piling up at the South Pole. You may not be the best dishwasher in McMurdo, but you're the one I'd like to get rid of. You're on the next C-130 flight to the South Pole. Pack your bags."

When I arrived at the South Pole, I tried to ignore the preliminary signs of pulmonary edema or high-altitude sickness—shortness of breath, headaches, inability to walk short distances, difficulty breathing.

I knew everyone at the South Pole was breathing the same

air I was; but it seemed their air had more oxygen in it than mine. I talked to a few people about my problem until I was blue in the face. The overall consensus was that I should go see Dr. Silva, get hooked up to oxygen, or face the cold, hard fact from the bottom of the world: you can't hack it, go back to sea level. Instead, I went to work washing my dishes.

A word about Dr. Silva: If you've read the book *Ice Bound* about Jerri Nielsen, the lady who had breast cancer at the South Pole, or if you've read almost anything about current happenings at the pole, the name Will Silva is bound to show up. When I left for the South Pole, he was one of the icons I was looking forward to meeting. It was going to be like reading about Watergate and then meeting G. Gordon Liddy.

As I was working the first week, a bald man with very cold-looking exposed ears came up to the dish window and said, "You're new here. My name is Will." He then reached out and shook my rubber-gloved hand. Besides being unable to breathe and barely knowing my own name, I didn't realize I was shaking hands with my hero.

There's a TV screen in the galley at the South Pole that constantly updates the temperature, wind chill, and barometric pressure of the South Pole. The temperature always seemed to be -47° with a wind chill near -70°. Although the altitude of the pole is 9,301 feet, the barometric altitude read 10,400 to 11,000 feet.

At 11,000 feet it seemed too low for altitude sickness. Besides, I'm from Salt Lake City, certainly not the Mile-High City, but it is 4,000 feet or so above sea level. And, although I'm not an avid mountain climber, I have hiked higher than 11,000 feet at some point or another. Hadn't I?

It didn't matter what I had done in Utah, I was at the South Pole and I could not breathe.

"Go see Dr. Silva," my friend Mark said. "Suck on some oxygen. I think you need it."

I didn't do it.

After spending six days at the South Pole, I lay in my bed on Friday night breathing in gasps that sounded like I was breathing through a water bong. The next day, I decided I'd check the altitude of Mt. Timpanogas and other mountains around Utah I had climbed. As soon as I woke up, I thought, I'd go to the internet and check those elevations.

I never woke up, because I couldn't go to sleep.

The feeling is best described as lying in bed and slowly suffocating. It's not that I didn't want to get up and go see Dr. Silva; it's that I couldn't. I couldn't move. Couldn't breathe. Couldn't will the energy to get help. Couldn't believe it was suddenly this bad.

As I lay in bed, I tried to diagnose my illness, completely ruling out the obvious high-altitude sickness. On Friday I had lugged my gear across the South Pole camp and moved from one shelter to another—from what's known as a Jamesway into a tent-like Hyper Tat. The Jamesway was brown and dark. The Hyper Tat was blue and dark. It was like living in a Louie-Bloo Raspberry Otterpop versus a Hostess Ho-Ho.

After moving, I had gone back to work for three hours, then walked to an area at the South Pole where the air is supposed to be the cleanest in the world. I met some friends and we ran around the geographical South Pole. We ran around the world. We ran around a lot.

It was obvious to me then that in the running around, my lungs had been frostbitten. I reckoned they looked like a freezer-burned piece of high-fat hamburger.

My diagnosis, however, didn't help me move.

At 6 A.M., when I should have been getting up to go to

work, I simply could not get out of bed. The nearest phone was in the bathroom. The nearest bathroom was outside—50 yards and -50° away.

If only I had some food in my room—enough energy to get me from the bedroom, to the medical building housed inside the large silver geodesic dome that protects the main buildings (galley, medical, a few residences, and communications) from the frosty elements. I looked on my floor, hoping the last guy who lived here had left behind something more than his piss jar. A few crumbs from a midnight snack. Anything.

Peering under the bed for the first time, I spotted a stained tin can—the chamber pot of the last resident. In the can was a urinal mint calcified to the bottom and sides of the olive can.

Soccer players en route to a match in Chile once ate their best friends to survive death. In the Donner Party, family members ate other family members to survive. I asked myself if the nutrients I might gain from another man's urine could be enough to save my life? Is it better to die gasping for air or choking on a frozen urine chip? I decided to die trying.

First, though, I'd get dressed then head out the door juiced on the piss. I took a gurgled breath and struggled into my pants. I tied my shoes. I didn't need a shirt, just my warm National Science Foundation jacket. I grabbed the sleeve and yanked the jacket off a hook above my head onto my body. It hit my chest with a thud. Goose down should not thud.

Then I remembered. A month earlier, Kevin Hoefling, the scuba diver who cuts holes through the ice and then dives into the Antarctic Ocean beneath ten feet of ice, gave me a Cadbury chocolate bar. "Put the candy bar in your sleeve," he told me, "because in Antarctica you'll never know when you need emergency energy."

Seven times that very day and six times the next and eleven times on Monday and once on Sunday, I felt like I was having a chocolate emergency. I had opened the Velcro on my sleeve, pulled out the candy bar and then put it back in my sleeve. Even on my flight to the South Pole, I thought I was having a chocolate emergency.

Thank God for will power. Thank God for Kevin. Thank God the candy bar was still there. In one mouthful I ingested all the calories, fat content, and sugar that one Cadbury bar could offer. I got out of bed and staggered the quarter mile to the silver dome of the South Pole.

I have no idea how long it took to get into the medical building, but I can remember every step. On the door to medical a sign said something like, "Please use the door on the other side of the building." I don't recall exactly what the sign said, because I didn't understand the words. I stumbled through the door that said, "Don't go through this door" and said: "Help, I need some oxygen."

But the only person there was a patient. She told me the doctor was the fourth door on the left.

I started to walk away from her and realized I couldn't count to four.

"I can't count the doors," I told the other patient. "Will you tell me when I'm at the right door?"

"O.K.," she said. "One...two...three...four. You're there."

I felt like I was walking down an endless hallway, making no progress. One million one...one ...mill...i-on...t-w-o."

Finally, I knocked.

"Jesus Christ! What the...!? Jesus Christ! I just went to bed a minute ago! This better be important!" shouted the voice on the other side.

Will Silva opened the door.

"Will, I need oxygen."

"Jesus Christ, Phil! It's 6:30 in the morning!" Now his ears seemed like they were burning.

Then, peering at my face, more quietly: "What's wrong, Phil?"

"I think my lungs are frostbitten."

"There's no such thing."

I was still focused on my inability to count. The number four, in one of the quadrants of my brain, seemed so unattainable. "A, B, 3, R...1, 3. Shit."

As I tried to count, Will took my vital signs. My resting heart rate was 125 and my blood oxygen level was 54. During the physical to come to Antarctica, my doctor said I had one of the lowest resting heart rates of a fat guy she had ever seen. My heart plugged away through the cholesterol chambers of my body at a calm forty-two beats a minute. The average man has an oxygen rating of 100. My oxygen physiology of fifty-four rated me an F. I was flunking out of breathing. I was seriously ill.

Will gave me a gas mask full of oxygen and soon I said aloud, "One. Two. Three. Four. Can I go to work now? There are lots of dishes that need to be washed."

"Phil, look at your lungs," Will said pointing to the X-rays. "You were two to four hours away from possible death."

Apparently, being able to count to four didn't necessarily mean I was healthy. There are a lot of numbers after four. After getting the X-rays of my lungs it was obvious to everyone I had full-blown pulmonary edema. My lungs looked like bags of whole milk. I was told I wasn't going to be allowed to wash dishes at the South Pole. Not today. Not any day soon.

Within five hours, a C-130 landed at the South Pole and I was medevaced out with a 314-pound green tank of oxygen.

I spent some time in the hospital and a few days of bed rest in McMurdo. My lungs cleared and I was back behind the dish machine again.

From that day on, I kept two chocolate bars in the pocket of my coat.

I had not anticipated that the work would present
any great difficulties.

—SIR ERNEST SHACKLETON (1915)

In the fall of 2004 in a mock election in McMurdo, George Bush lost and Jules Uberuaga was elected mayor of McMurdo. It's hard to spend any time in McMurdo and not meet Jules. Self-described as five-foot-two/six-foot-four, Jules is an exuberant storyteller with twenty-seven seasons on the Ice to draw on. For the past twenty-five years she has operated bulldozers, grooming the ice runway at Willy Field. When I met her she invited me out to "push snow." That's an invitation no one would pass up.

Jules has met almost every celebrity who has visited the continent from Sir Edmund Hillary to Al Gore and has visited many corners of the continent, from the tip of Mount Erebus to the dark catacombs of underground Byrd Station. When not working on the ice, Jules spends time surfing in New Zealand or whitewater kayaking on the South Fork of the Payette in Idaho.

Uberuaga Island, located in the Ross Sea, is named for Jules.

True Point of Beginning

✦ ✶ ✦

JULES UBERUAGA

WHAT WAS TO BECOME THE BIGGEST ADVENTURE OF MY life started in 1978 not long after my twenty-fourth birthday. I received an excited phone call from my mom asking me if I wanted to work in Antarctica. Never having considered the prospect I told her I would think about it. My mother was working in Boise for Holmes and Narver, the civilian contractor that provided logistical support for the National Science Foundation's Antarctic program. In actual fact it was my mother who was keen to go and since she couldn't fit it in she wanted me to live out her dream. I managed to land the job after a lengthy process of interviews and stringent physical exams. I still believe to this day that the crux move in getting the job had something to do with my unique approach to arriving at the interview. When the company rep walked into the lobby of the hotel in Missoula and called my name he seemed to be surprised that I had hitchhiked 300 miles from Idaho with my Labrador retriever, who was standing guard by my pack.

When I got the call about the job, I was living in a remote logging camp in Idaho. Just before I left the job for the summer, a guy I was working with got crushed on the log deck; I was the one standing next to him. Though I learned many years later that the man survived, this was the first of a series of events that snapped me out of some sort of innocent reverie.

South Pole station was to be my ultimate destination. Located at 90 degrees south; bottom of the world; nearly 10,000 feet in elevation; average temp -56°F...so the dog-eared brochure that I had read and reread claimed. I pored over the few pictures that showed a geodesic dome, bearded men cloaked in heavy parkas running machinery, and a mission statement of the goals of the Antarctic program. I poured over every piece of literature I could find including Sir Ernest Shackleton's gripping tale *Endurance*, to prepare myself for this surreal place.

In October of 1979 our small team flew from a Navy base in California through the Pacific on a military transport plane arriving in Christchurch, New Zealand. This was the home of Operation Deep Freeze. Since the early '50s the U.S. Navy had been administering the operations and logistics of Antarctic bases. I was part of the small civilian crew that was interfacing with the Navy at the various stations and camps around the continent. After receiving our cold-weather gear we boarded a LC-130 bound for McMurdo Station and then on to the South Pole 850 miles inland from the coast. I stood on the flight deck of the cargo plane as we floated over endless miles of white expanse, occasionally punctuated with immense mountain ranges surrounded by sheer untouched emptiness. Then there it was, a tiny dot on the vast horizon, the actual South Pole. We touched down on a groomed snow airstrip and taxied to a halt next to a large geodesic dome with connecting steel tunnels partially buried in snow.

Brimming with excitement and awe, I stepped out of the plane into a mild -50°F and was ushered down into the labyrinth of the station. So began what was to be the most unusual summer of my life.

My job title was general field assistant. I was to be involved with many aspects of station operations including fueling buildings and airplanes, handling cargo, building aircraft pallets for shipment, shoveling snow, fire fighting as part of a secondary team, grooming the snow runway with heavy equipment, washing dishes, assisting scientists with a range of projects, as well as scooping clean snow up with a loader and dumping it into a hopper, which melted it into potable water for the station. All of these tasks were part and parcel of the many requirements to run this remote, high-altitude station.

For the first month or so I was the only woman on station. I was then joined by a twenty-two-year-old female civilian (one of the nicer titles the Navy had for us) physicist who was going to spend the winter there with seventeen men. I was just a summer-over employee who was to depart the station in February leaving the winter-over crew to manage the place until opening flight the next November.

One of the unique tasks I was asked to do was to help organize a celebration of Admiral Richard Byrd's fiftieth anniversary of the first flight to the South Pole. I painted a large portrait of the *Floyd Bennett*, the Ford trimotor plane that he flew, and hung it up above a large stage we had prepared for the event inside the dome where the ceremony was to be held. The station was festooned with decorations and the event was to be held on November 29, 1979, fifty years to the day of the historic flight. The station personnel were awaiting the arrival of a planeload of dignitaries including two surviving members of Byrd's expedition and a congressional committee. During the day preceding the flight I was assigned to my normal task of fueling cargo planes that arrived throughout the day, delivering fuel to the station. During the refueling process the flight crew would chat amiably with us about goings on about the continent. It was at this time that the pilot mentioned that he had heard that one of the tourist flights that regularly flew down to McMurdo Sound had lost radio contact. He added that this was not that unusual, probably just a run of the mill loss of radio communications at that point. These flights were the luxury version of elite tourism. Gourmet meals were served as famous mountaineering guides like Edmund Hillary lectured to the passengers as the planes made low-level passes over Antarctic scenery as the champagne flowed.

The day passed by as more fuel flights came and went and still the pilots mentioned that the plane had not been heard from but not to worry as loss of radio comms was routine. The last refueling flight of the day brought different news. A grim message from the flight crew said that there was a tragedy unfolding: Air New Zealand flight 901, a DC10 carrying nearly 300 people had not returned to New Zealand. The aircraft couldn't fly that long without fuel. It was down. The U.S. Navy launched an air search-and-rescue mission in the surrounding region of McMurdo Station. South Pole station has stellar radio communications due to its location and the air-to-ground comms were relayed through our radio room. I sat quietly amongst the crowded comms center as I listened to the pilot's transmissions as they circled above McMurdo Sound trying to find this aircraft. Then the words I so well remember came over the crackling radio waves. "We have the wreckage in sight." The third largest air crash in history at the time had been spotted. What was to become a subject of intense legal battles and inquiries for ten years was now a national tragedy for New Zealand. The flight crew had lost their way in a whiteout and were desperately trying to find their location whilst the passengers were engaged in a celebratory mood, unaware that the plane was about to slam into the side of the 13,0000-foot volcano Mount Erebus, killing all aboard.

The NSF representative Dr. Richard Cameron called the entire station into the main mustering area. He stood before the stunned crew and told us in a tearful voice that in the entire history of Antarctic exploration more lives had just been lost in the last few hours than in all the continent's history. In the days after the crash we followed the events that took place in McMurdo but life eventually began to fall back into place as our daily work routines swung back into action.

Christmas celebrations, foot races, jumping out of the sauna and running naked around the world, science lectures, and the arrival of real-life explorers at the geographic pole all filled our imaginations and had us brimming with excitement with just how cool we all were to be in this amazing place.

Amidst the high spirits of the holidays our gang of mischief-makers felt a moral obligation to uphold one of the long-standing traditions of station life: the venerable practical joke. One such prank took place during our New Year's Eve celebration. As the party was building in intensity, we singled out the station electrician who was well on his way to joyously ushering in the New Year at the bottom of the world. Wildly encouraging him with toasts to Idaho, and toasts to the Queen, he splashed down whiskey until he dropped to the floor stone cold out. We then descended on the poor fellow. With speed we whisked him off to the medical building where we laid out our hapless victim and set to work. Acting with the deftness of a team of skilled surgeons the doctor instructed his new assistants to begin plying the victim's leg with wet strips of plaster from toe to hip. Had the doctor not intervened with a touch of compassion I'm sure we would have impounded the lad in a complete body cast. After finishing our handiwork we let a stream of well-wishers file in and sign the cast with messages of warm condolences whilst our victim snored away. Feeling pleased with ourselves we then made another assault on the party. Much later in the midst of our reverie the physician approached us with worried news. The patient was wildly thrashing around and in danger of breaking his good leg with the heavy cast. We silently slipped out of the party like a gang of grave robbers and dutifully assisted the doc in restraining our victim while he removed the cast. As in all well-executed practical jokes the true dilemma lies in containing your mirth while you drag out the ruse. In this instance it was certainly the case as we presented the still unaware and desperately hung-over fellow his signed cast at the New Year's dinner whereupon he confessed that he couldn't determine the cause of much bruising on his leg. This admission set the entire station into a gut-busting frenzy of laughter.

I only spent two seasons at pole but the memories from those years are vivid. My second season, the arrival of real-life explorers filled us with excitement. In 1980, the much-esteemed British explorer Sir Ranulph Fiennes, along with Oliver Shepard and Charles Burton were attempting to circumnavigate the globe via the Greenwich meridian. They were crossing Antarctica from the coast via South Pole by snowmobile and proceeding to McMurdo Sound where their ship, the *Benjamin Bowring,* was to pick them up in February. We were expecting them in December. This group had spent the long Antarctic winter holed up on the coast in a small encampment preparing for the team's departure the following spring.

News sped around camp one day that a small plane was nearing South Pole station. Air traffic in the skies at that desolate latitude is not a common sight. We had heard that the small craft buzzing towards us was flown by none other than the much heralded Antarctic pilot Giles Kershaw, who at that time was said to hold the record for being the only person to circumnavigate the entire continent in a small plane. Giles' deep and enduring love for the Antarctic began with his British Antarctic Survey experience and continued on with the elite Adventure Network, the first private flying service that catered to private expeditions. As the small plane touched down and taxied to the front of the station a crowd gathered to greet these fascinating guests. As Giles stepped from the plane I was surprised to see that he had a rather pampered and urbane look: white fedora, tight jeans and million-dollar smile. With him was Lady Virginia Fiennes, who seemed gaunt and reserved by comparison. She stepped out of the plane carrying her perky Jack Russell terrier "Bothy," who was dressed in his own parka and booties. I squealed with delight at the sight of the first dog I had seen in ages. No one seemed particularly interested in the fact that it was a violation of the Antarctic treaty to bring a pet along. We were just happily entertained at the wee fellow raced around and barked with glee.

The mission of Giles and "Jenny" was to provide logistical air support for the ground team. Giles decided to set up a tent to await their arrival. Technically speaking we were not allowed to provide "support" for any private expeditions, but feeling sorry for our guests sleeping out in the sub-zero weather we invited Giles, Jenny, and Bothy into our haven.

Enjoying sumptuous meals, soaking in the hot tub, taking showers, and sharing stories we soon developed a warm bond with these exciting visitors.

As they awaited the arrival of Sir Ranulph Fiennes and the others, time was spent not only making repairs on the plane but recording the antics on film of the much-lauded wonder-dog Bothy who was adored by the British public. Bothy was a film star in his own right, though much time was devoted to keeping the camera away from the little rascal as he prac-ticed his own form of entertainment: vigorously humping everything in sight.

The radio room kept the station posted on the exact loca-tion of the expedition and it was this advance warning that had us lined up near the ceremonial pole at the moment they were due. Looking out from the station one sees a vast unin-terrupted expanse in every direction, framed only by the horizon. Squinting our eyes we could see three tiny figures growing larger by the minute as they approached. Finally our eyes beheld what seemed to be large fur-covered animals astride snow machines pulling sleds. Upon arrival, with all due ceremony, Sir Ranulph Fiennes took off his fur mask, pulled icicles from his beard, announced his team's arrival at the South Pole in a stentorian voice, and then hugged his wife. We all launched hearty cheers. These men were reduced by severe cold, dehydration, and continual windburn into gaunt figures whose faces were marked by patches of dead skin and sunken eyes. Nothing, however, could match their joy when we handed them steaming mugs of hot tea.

We extended hospitality to our new arrivals and we all sat at the dinner table with Sir Ranulph regaling us with stories as we ate. I could see people stealing glances at these hearty explorers, as I believe no one had ever seen men eat so much at one sitting and live to tell the tale. After a few days of rest, the trio bid their farewell to the station and we all waved them off into the vast wilderness. As I watched them depart I entertained my own private curiosity as to whether I had the grit, stamina, and drive that these people had to conquer my own personal adventures.

My first season at Pole, I shared a living space, a large military tent called a Jamesway with four young fellows with whom I worked. We separated our living areas with blankets, affording us some privacy from each other. We were a happy exuberant lot living life to the fullest (as much as you could at the South Pole) and always getting into mischief. Casey Jones was one of our tent mates and our chef; a lean and impish New Englander, he regaled us with gourmet meals for which South Pole station was known for. This was a place that you could eat to your heart's content and let the intense cold burn it off as fast as you could consume it. Casey, like the rest of us, was athletic and physically ambitious. After finishing his rigorous cooking schedule he would go jogging along the runway or a break in routine during the day would allow him to find our work crew and help us with shoveling, chipping ice, or whatever arduous task we were doing so he could burn off some excess energy.

The construction foreman had formed a small crew of us to excavate a large upright air duct that had become filled with ice and snow. The air duct had a small man door at ground level where the debris was to be shoveled out and loaded on sleds and dragged away. Our group merrily worked away laughing and joking as we so often did, finding solidarity in these mindless physical tasks. Clearing the snow from the air duct we soon realized that we would be putting ourselves in danger if we continued on chipping and shoveling, as we were now standing below the column of ice that was entombed in the duct towering above us. A lengthy discussion ensued and we decided to abandon the project for the time being. To this day I do not remember how it came to be that Casey and the station doctor decided to help out on this abandoned project.

A few days had passed and I was back at my normal routine operating heavy machinery outside the station, transporting snow to the melter to make potable water. I had just slid down the ladder that allowed me into the station's archway tunnels when I spied a figure moving briskly at the end of the corridor. At 9,300 feet and -50°F temps you just don't see people running in work clothes. Somehow in that place in my mind where fear resides I just knew that something bad was happening. I took off running, following the moving figure into the small room where we had been working a few days earlier. As I entered the subterranean chamber, dimly lit and casting an icy gloom, the first thing I saw was one of my fellow workers standing with his face inches from a wall, just staring silently at nothing. The few times in my life I have been witness to an accident an odd thing seems to occur. All action slows down, my vision blurs into a single point of focus that unfolds in slow motion as my mind searches for context. *What the hell is happening here and what should I do now?* That moment at South Pole was exactly that.

I focused on a large pile of ice rubble before me with a person's feet sticking out. Other than the frozen figure in the corner the station manager and I were the only people there at that point. Without a word in that cold silence he and I began to dig, wildly clawing at the rubble, throwing blocks of ice, pawing at snow with my mittens, clearing debris from the prone figure. In a polar environment we learn to identify people heavily garbed in winter apparel by specific clothes they wear, and often by a certain gait or signature scarf or hat. I remember going through a mental list of who this might be. People began to arrive, including the doctor. I distinctly remember the sheer silence and people desperately laboring to help this injured comrade rise from the rubble. I whispered to the doctor, asking if there was anything he needed and he told me to get a backboard and a crutch. As we freed the prone figure from the debris it was then that I realized it was my impish friend Casey. We then slid the backboard beneath him and tied the crutch along the length of his spine. All hands lifted him up and it was then that I clearly saw him. His tortured lifeless form, arms hanging limp.

I stood there horrified by the scene before me. I had never seen anyone die before, and was trying to convince myself that this was not the case and that he would be fine. Yet deep down inside I knew that this boy would not be joining us again in our pursuit of life. I was shaken from my trance by the command to race to the radio room and inform the comms tech to have the recently departed aircraft return to pole immediately. As I breathlessly spilled out the details to the radio operator I heard him tell the pilot to return to pole as we had grave injuries; they had to return immediately. As he repeated this plea to the aircraft I could hear his voice departing from the steady calm that is the hallmark of communications techs, pilots, and air controllers. As the plane landed, we all hurried to our positions on the refueling team. Keep moving, keep busy, refuel the plane, these were all the things I knew I had to keep doing to help bring a positive outcome to this surreal event. The plane landed and we began to fuel it. A paratrooper's door under the wing of the plane opened up just as a vehicle slowly moved out of the station towards us. The truth became clear. A green body bag was handed over to the navy loadmaster. As he loaded it into the plane he looked into my eyes and said, *I am so sorry for you all.*

The door slammed shut and the plane was gone. All of this probably took place over a course of twenty minutes. That night as I sat in our big tent staring dumbly at Casey's belongings. I thought, *That's it. Just like that life ends.* His running shoes, goofy t-shirts, camera. All of it was just lifeless stuff without the animation he gave to it. We packed his belongings in a box to send home. I lay in my bed that night thinking about his parents way back in New England, unaware that the National Science Foundation was about to place a call to them that would change their world, that all their dreams of a good life for that boy of theirs would be dashed in one instant.

The season was nearing an end and the days after the accident melded into the arduous task of the station closing for the winter. All our sorrows were slowing being absorbed by physical exhaustion and daydreaming of impending freedom in that beautiful South Pacific country, New Zealand. As I sat in the back of the plane on my day of departure I couldn't help but ponder my future and relive the past events of the summer at the South Pole. Even though I thought at my young age that I had the world by the tail, I also had a new awareness that as young and invincible as I felt I had better try and make the best of each day. As I had learned that summer, something sudden and unforeseen could quickly wrest my grip from this beautiful life.

Had we lived, I should have had a tale to tell of the hardiness, endurance, and courage of my companions which would have stirred the heart of every Englishman.

—ROBERT FALCON SCOTT, FINAL LETTER, MARCH 1912

While in McMurdo, Mount Erebus dominates. Rising to over 12,000 feet, this graceful, snow-covered volcano emits a plume of steam from its summit crater that, on clear days, trails into the sky. Named for Captain John Ross's ship, Erebus, which sailed into McMurdo Sound in 1841, this volcano is the southernmost active volcano in the world.

During the 2002-3 season, GPS specialist Beth Bartel had the opportunity to spend five weeks with a science team studying Erebus. She celebrated Thanksgiving, Christmas, and New Year's on the volcano. She and the science crew lived between two huts and each had a tent for sleeping.

While on the volcano, Beth assisted with the high-precision GPS work, using high-tech instruments to measure the volcano's motion. Since then she has worked full-time for a group called UNAVCO, which supports all sorts of science groups using GPS. She spent the next two years working out of McMurdo Station in the southern summer and working mostly on projects in the Arctic in the northern summer. After getting her fill of the cold, she left the poles to explore Hawaii, the Galapagos, southern Italy, Ethiopia, and even Nevada. Erebus remains the "trip of a life time."

Seeing Mount Erebus

$\star \; {}^{\star} \; \star$

BETH BARTEL

FOR FIVE WEEKS, WE LIVED ON SNOW BETWEEN LAVA flows on the edge of the volcano. Sarah, Bill, Nelia, the Richs, and myself, with others coming and going. We slept in tents and spread our living between two huts; we installed geophysical instruments to monitor the volcano and meteorological instruments to monitor the weather. I was the new one to the mountain. Each of them had been there before, each of them had had experiences there, each of them had stories. For me, those five weeks consisted of constant discovery. Some of the discoveries were good and some were things like discovering the tedium of rocking cables. This is a story about one of the good ones.

It's about two-thirds of the way through our field season, and we've been held inside for the past five days by a storm. The main hut, while comfortable, is tight: It is kitchen, living room, dining room, closet, and workspace all within one small box. We've been mostly quiet the past few days, reading and tinkering and knitting and watching movies, but today there is a different atmosphere in the hut. Maybe we can feel that the storm is breaking.

Still, all morning, the wind pushes against us and blows snow around us and we venture outside only to go to the bathroom, which is located in the second hut out back. Nelia teaches Sarah, Rich E., and me how to play the card game "Oh Hell." I mend my gloves, torn again on the dark, sharp, lava rock on which we work, stitching up the fingertips with bright red tent repair thread for the third time this season. Sarah, who is the camp manager, makes us a hot lunch while we discuss watching another movie.

At around 4 P.M., we notice that we can no longer hear the wind against the hut. "How about a trip to Cones?" Bill suggests. There is no hesitation; the hut turns to motion. We gather our layers from cubbies and the clothesline hung next to the stove and hooks by the door. I don't know how these guys do it, but they can go out some days with their entire faces exposed—just sunglasses covering their eyes—when I have to completely bundle up, and still I get cold. Today, we all put on full field attire: it's still only about -30°C outside. I take no chances—I use balaclava, hat, goggles, and the hood of my issued parka to cover every part of my head except a small triangle of skin at the bridge of my nose. I'd cover that, too, if I could—it's already been frostnipped twice.

Outside on the styrofoam-squeaky snow, the world is milk. We call this fog "skank," and it has plagued us much of the season so far. "Ready?" asks Bill. "Ready," we say. We head to our favorite Ski-Doos, whose mechanical quirks have become their personalities. Mine is called Fang. I have my own mechanical quirk—earlier in the season I caught my ribs on a wooden post, and starting the Ski-Doo is painful. I tighten my chest before I give it a pull. On the third pull it starts and I climb on, the engine rumbling the seat beneath me.

Bill is out first, and then Nelia, and then Rich K., and then me. Rich E. takes up the rear, mostly to make sure that we all stay together. (Sarah is in the hut getting started on dinner, probably relieved to be rid of us.) I have gone from fearing the Ski-Doos to loving the Ski-Doos, but still I have to concentrate to keep up. This is a new route for me, with new and reputedly impressive views. Shortly after leaving camp, however, I see nothing but the white of the skank. There is no Bill, no Nelia—just the black and yellow form of Rich K.'s back and Ski-Doo that I am trying to follow through milky whiteness. The light goes flat and the tracks disappear before me. What is snow, and what is sky? I strain my eyes to tell, and imagine the distinction between the two. What lies beyond, in the skank? Nothing. There is me, my Ski-Doo, motion, the grumble of the motor, a form ahead of me which I approach but never near. The milky void goes on forever.

I am shaken when I can finally make out Bill up ahead, because he has turned off our trajectory to the right. I am afraid he will disappear completely into the abyss; I am afraid that if I follow, *I* will disappear into the abyss—I am going to overturn my Ski-Doo into a rut or fall over a cliff of ice or slam into a white wall at the edge of our white world. I see Nelia turn off, and then Rich K., and I follow. I don't fall off the edge of anything. Instead, we pull up next to a rocky outcrop of gray lava protruding from the snow. Rich E. pulls up behind me. I can taste the salt on my balaclava in the moist mixture of breath and snot; Bill's neck gaiter is crusted with ice, as is Rich E.'s beard.

Amongst the rocks are pieces of equipment—a box containing a seismometer, another containing a GPS receiver, both to measure the motions of the volcano. A wind generator and solar panels are bolted to the rocks in various ways to keep them from blowing down in storms like the one we've just weathered. Rime ice embraces everything—rime ice on the wind generator, hanging heavy on the guy wires, protruding from the snow even. Clinging to the rocks like clams. I pull a handful off a guy wire and it crumbles in my glove.

Bill, Nelia, and Rich K. start in on the site, freeing the equipment of rime ice and rewiring the seismometer. Rich E. and I are tasked with laying cable from the instrument site, where we stand now, to a repeater site on a nearby ridge that relays the data to McMurdo Station. Laying cable has become our specialty. We pull a spool of cable from a Ski-Doo, slip an ice axe through its center, and carefully unwind the spool as we make our way sideways up the ridge. This task feels particularly awkward in my issued boots, which have thick soles and flimsy everything else so that I struggle to not roll my ankles. Up top, a snow-covered mast rises white against the white sky; attached to it are three or four antennas, all covered in rime ice as well. We take a brief rest—there is nothing to see—and make our way back to the instrument site along the same route, placing rocks periodically on the cable to hold it in place. (Rocking cables isn't so bad in good company.)

Shortly after we return to the group, in a moment in which I am doing nothing, the skank clears. In a matter of seconds. Now it is here, now it is gone. It thins as I watch; by the time I get my video camera out of my warm coat, pull off my overmitt, and start panning, only the higher ridges are still shrouded in skank, and by the time I finish they are completely clear. The milk is gone.

I see a world around me. What the skank merged together as one, the sun differentiates into shapes and forms. There is a horizon, with blue above and white below. I can see the repeater tower up on the ridge Rich E. and I have just come back from, its bright white cloak of snow bright against the blue of the sky and closer than I thought. Closer still, I see ice towers. Not just one, but many—a line of them leading uphill, their forms irregular and full, as if someone had dropped globs of gooey marshmallow onto the volcano's slope. The lowest one, which is also the closest, pumps out steam from an opening at its top. I can't see it happening, but this volcanic steam is building the ice tower as I watch, freezing against its walls to make it bigger.

Then, upslope, there is the volcano. We are on the volcano—it is all around and under us—but there upslope is its summit, and I can see it clearly now, snowy slopes steepening up to its rubbly top where the plume lazes upwards into the sky. In its depths, it harbors a lava lake. I cannot see the lava lake, of course, but I try to imagine where it is, if I had X-ray vision and could see through the snow and rock before me.

"You should go to the edge," says Rich E. He is crouched in front of a battery box, checking voltages. "See how far down you can see."

Rich's suggestion turns me away from the summit and towards the sea. He is referring to the edge of the caldera, in which we have been living and working—a long-ago eruption emptied out the volcano and caused it to collapse in on itself, leaving a void, the caldera, which has since been filled in by new eruptions of lava and ash. While a new cone grows in its center and there is no longer a big hole in the mountain, the slope still changes from steep to gentle at the caldera's edge.

The caldera rim looks far away. The terrain looks difficult, especially in my wobbly issued boots. But what am I doing standing here? Getting colder. I have been slowly getting cold since we left the hut—it seeps in inevitably through my layers, not as a sharp pain but as a slow ache that dumbs and dulls me. I am starting to feel dumb, and dull. Get moving. I pick my way through the rock, stepping carefully on the snow in between. My legs warm up as I walk. I'm not sure where to go. Do they have a regular spot? Do they walk out on one of the ridges I can see protruding into the void? Where exactly is the edge?

When I reach it, I know.

The world drops away below me and my eyes grow wide. I am not standing at a sheer cliff; instead, the snow-covered slope plunges almost gracefully away from me, arching white and concave into a sea of clouds. The clouds go on forever. They reach out to the horizon and beyond: east, west, north, south, the world is directionless. There is only the mountain we stand on, and the cloud world below. What dwells in this cloud world? I wonder. I imagine fairytale creatures: Goblins and trolls and ice fairies, maybe Hobbits, or the dragon from *The Neverending Story.* (The people and machines of McMurdo don't even cross my mind, even though I am looking essentially straight towards them.)

Down in the cloud world, there is a great battle. One cloud bank, to my left, crashes into another. I stand directly overlooking the seam between the two. I feel like I am presiding over the clouds. I am an ice princess, in silly-looking blue boots, presiding over the clouds. I am presiding over the clouds and all the creatures that dwell within, everything in my imagination. And not only are the cloud banks crashing together, but the one on the right seems to be diving down at the seam and folding in on itself, recycling itself as if it were a cloud conveyor belt. I film all of this. I start with the ridge at my right, the one that Rich E. and I were just on laying cable back before I was an ice princess, follow its curve down out of my view, and end with the battling clouds.

When I am done filming, I bid the ice princess goodbye and return to the rest of the group.

The forms of ice towers loom close as we speed back to camp on our Ski-Doos. I feel like I have been spied on, like these big odd-shaped piles of snow are trolls that were watching me from the fog on our way out while I had no idea that they were there. As much as I want to look around and take it all in, I find myself concentrating on the bumpy trail in front of me and on keeping up with Nelia. I am braced forward in my Ski-Doo. My fingers are doing well on the heated handle, but my throttle thumb is starting to feel cold. There are things I can do about it but I just keep on, and let my thumb get colder. Soon my thumb stops aching, which disturbs me; numb is bad.

We arrive at camp behind the others. Nelia and I pull up between the two huts and park our Ski-Doos facing the volcano's steaming summit, as if they are ready to take off towards it at a moment's notice. We unload our gear from the Ski-Doo boxes and head into the back hut to organize. As usual, the preway stove is on and the hut is warm. I exhale into the heat and allow my body to relax. I have hardly a minute of repose before I start to feel my thumb. Nelia is feeling hers, too. "Uh-oh," she says, "I think my thumb is warming up." "Me, too," I say. It's starting to hurt. We pull our gloves off and wrap our hands around our warming thumbs and cradle them against our bellies and start to howl. "Ow ow ow ow ow!" we exclaim. My thumb feels as if it's been hit with a sledgehammer. It throbs, it aches, and there's nothing I can do except stand and warm it and howl and wait.

When the howling and the throbbing stops Nelia and I put our mitts back on and head back out into the cold to go next door. Even though I've been out in it all afternoon, the cold takes me by surprise and stings the inside of my nose, freezing my nose hairs. Crimeny. The wind generator is starting to hum again, signaling the onset of more wind.

Inside the main hut, we are greeted by the tantalizing smell of potatoes cooking and then by the sight of a cheese and olive platter, tuna dip, potato chips. I put my gloves in my cubby, hang my balaclava by the stove to dry, and take a seat at the table to relax. Soon, there will be halibut and potato pancakes and broccoli, the much-appreciated fruits of Sarah's labor while we were out getting cold.

After dinner, Nelia points out interesting clouds from inside the hut. One is a vertically balanced feather-looking cloud, which I go out to film. I stay outside to watch a bank of bulkier clouds move steadily and with purpose across the sky, like a herd of elephants. Where are they going? Outside my tent, snow snakes race belly down along the surface. What is their hurry? There is always something to see. Why move so fast?

The night is of special interest to me. There is something about the air, the water, the ice, and the land, which fixes my attention and makes sleep impossible. There is a glitter in the seam, a sparkle on the ice, and a stillness in the atmosphere, which fascinates the soul but overpowers the mind. There is a solitude and restfulness about the whole scene which can only be felt; it cannot be described.

—DR. FREDERICK A. COOK,
THROUGH THE FIRST ANTARCTIC NIGHT, 1898-1899

Food is a big subject on the ice. Because of the cold, the body craves fat, trying to strap on that extra layer of protection. So I found one group of scientists eating Ritz crackers topped with butter and in McMurdo the soft-serve ice cream machine is always available. No one goes to Antarctica for the cuisine but in some remote camps, terrific meals are prepared from frozen foods like salmon or steaks (keeping the food frozen is not much of a problem).

Chronicles of early expeditions focus obsessively on food—there was a terrible monotony to the biscuits and hoosh that was their staple. Beyond the boredom of their diet, the threat of scurvy haunted these early explorers. Mark Lehman, who has cooked at all three U.S. stations—McMurdo, South Pole, and Palmer—sees his work within the tradition of these early cooks who needed to keep everyone healthy in mind and body. Mark's kitchen is heated and to light his stove he flips on a switch. He doesn't need to figure out how to make seal tasty or melt ice to cook, but the challenge of keeping the crew happy remains.

Mark has spent six summers and a winter between each of the three United States research stations in Antarctica. He grew up in Indiana then, after working a summer in Yellowstone National Park, moved to the northern Rockies. Currently, he resides in Bozeman, Montana, where he is working on undergraduate teaching degrees in both History and Spanish.

Food for Thought,
Foods as Fuel

✦ ✦ ✦

MARK LEHMAN

SITTING CROSS-LEGGED ON THE COOL, SHINY TILES OF
our third-grade classroom floor, my school friends and I huddled around a small globe. A favorite game when the weather
was too poor for outdoor recess, we each, one by one, turned
the world into a gentle spin. With closed eyes and eager anticipation we announced, "I'm going to live right HERE!"
And with a sharp touch to the orb's surface, a rested finger
foretold the future. Landings in the middle of the Atlantic
Ocean or the far north of Canada constituted a "do-over" and
we sang, "HA! Nobody lives THERE!" At the time, what I
knew of Antarctica was that I liked it because it was filled
with penguins and, for some reason, was easy to remember
during geography lessons. I do not recall ever pinpointing
Antarctica during our game, but I suspect if we had, it would
unanimously have been voted a do-over.

Outside, darkness lingers in this pre-dawn hour.
Celebrations of mid-summer and solstice, eight weeks ago
now, exist only in memory, and winter beckons. I pass through

the doorway, and with the back of my left hand feel along a wall for a familiar switch. The long and narrow room I have just stepped into floods with light. Across the dining area, a row of tall glass windows act as mirrors, reflecting an image of myself and the plastic tables and chairs that surround me. Dressed simply in tan Carhartt pants and a short sleeve t-shirt, I stare at my image, and the silent, blank expression on my face reveals that I am still half asleep. I locate my favorite kitchen apron from a stack of neatly folded laundry, and tie it snugly around my waist. With drawn-out yawns and unhurried stretches, I repeat the steps of the day before. The simple push of a button provides, in minutes, eight cups of freshly brewed coffee. The quick twist of a few dials gently warms the electric oven, griddle and range. A turn of the tap produces a steady stream of fresh water, carefully measured for hot cereal. I pull butter from a refrigerator to soften and pick through the few remaining fresh fruits, mostly bruised oranges and apples.

In the bakery, I attempt to work quietly, so as not to disturb those sleeping just upstairs. The gentle tap of an egg shell coincides with sounds of an electric mixer creaming butter and sizzling hash browns on the griddle. After nearly six months, I know this kitchen well and a natural muscle memory guides me through many steps. Left leg sweeps the oven door closed, cupped fingers ease back the lid of the deep sugar bin and a long reach is just enough to grab a clean wire whisk from an open drawer. With a flowing rhythm, I work as if I am in my own home. I cherish this time. Moments alone are rare in this place and the simplicity with which my day begins brings peace.

Certainly, thousands of sous chefs around the globe are opening their kitchens in like manner, yet I am different from them. I am working in Antarctica. This small scientific research station, known as Palmer, is one of the more isolated dwellings on the planet. The small peninsular island we call home is surrounded by frigid ocean water and a dangerously crevassed glacier. Visitors must travel four days by sea from South America, crossing the rough waters of the infamous Drake Passage. Depending on one's perspective, this place can act as either an oasis or an entrapment. Teamed up with our head chef, Marge Bolton, the two of us take responsibility as the morale committee for the forty-two souls who live here. But this is no simple task. Our re-supply vessel last delivered Chilean "freshies" nearly two months ago and although fresh eggs, potatoes, onions, and cabbage, are still available, the produce walk-in now seems an empty chasm.

By 5:30 A.M., I am moving more quickly. Freshly baked cookies cooling, activated yeast working inside a rising batch of dough and the smells of crisp bacon fill the kitchen and creep upstairs in search of stirring scientists and workers. Soon, the early risers will be coming through and I know them as well by the sound of their footsteps as I do their habits. Indeed, I could nearly set my wristwatch to the minute they step through the door. Coffee black, coffee with milk, cup of herbal tea, and a hand-peeled grapefruit. One by one they visit me. With each, words are exchanged. Weather today, weather yesterday, weather tomorrow, weather last week. I am comforted by this repetitive conversation.

With breakfast prepared, I need to begin planning for the lunch meal, but opt first for a mug of coffee and a bit of fresh air. From the far end of the dining room, I step outside onto a second story wooden deck. A breeze blows gently south-southwest and I am pleased the often overwhelming stench of molting elephant seal is not so potent today. Removing my ball cap, I turn my face into the wind. Chilly yes, but it pushes against exposed cheeks without bite. The ambient temperature hovers around freezing and the soft flap of the American flag above me indicates I can comfortably remain here a while longer. The rising sun is not yet visible but a lightly colored pastel sky indicates a new day has arrived. A dramatic, snow-covered range of distant mountains dominates the horizon to the south. At their base, massive icebergs, like strategic battle-ships, move position in water as if readying for war. Much closer, a talented pair of terns dances acrobatically in flight as they scour the water's surface for a meal. Calls from nesting penguins, gulls, and other sea birds are audible from small is-lands not far from where I stand. Just shy of them, a few seals share an ice floe which bobs in the patterned swell of the ocean. Across an inlet of still water, I observe clusters of col-orful vegetation, mostly moss and lichen clinging to boulders, rocks, and patches of gravel. I listen and watch for whales. This perch, mere steps from my workplace, offers a 180-degree panorama of Antarctica in its most classic form.

In the past seven years, I have spent more than thirty months of my life working as a sous chef between each of Antarctica's three United States research stations. One might guess that I take inspiration from some famous culinary genius like the French chef, Auguste Escoffier, or Emeril, the more modern and better-known television personality. But my pas-sion in cooking does not lie in mastering the culinary classics; it rests in the connection I feel with the people and environ-ment that are a part of the history of this place. Perhaps it is presumptuous, but I feel a kinship with those who have worked the Antarctic galleys of the past. The stories of expe-dition cooks who began baking bread and brewing coffee in these southern latitudes a century ago are remarkable to me.

Recently, I have been reading of Adolf Lindstrom, who cooked in Roald Amundsen's galley. Spending the long austral winter of 1911 crammed into a tiny hut with eight other Norwegian men, they were keen to become the first to reach the south geographic pole. In studying Amundsen's book, *The South Pole*, I find common ground in a small section in which he paints a detailed picture of Lindstrom's morning routine. As my post requires now, Lindstrom was also the first to rise each morning. But while modern tools and technology help me to warm the range, make coffee and find water, Lindstrom's duties were much more complicated.

> *Br-r-r-r-r!* There's the alarm clock…nine men were sleeping in a room 19 by 13 feet.… A frightful crash! That's Lindstrom slipping out of his bunk.… One! two! three! and there he stood in the doorway, with a little lamp in his hand. It was now six o'clock.… The first thing he does is to lay the fire… he pours paraffin over the wood.… A match.… The water-pot had been filled [with snow] the evening before, and he had only to push it to one side to make room for the kettle.… He grinds the coffee till his cheeks shake to and fro—incessantly. After a quarter of an hour's hard work, he has only ground just enough. Now it is half past six. On with the coffee! Ah, what a perfume!

Any reader who delves into the heroic age of Antarctic exploration can discover the wisdom in the expression "Food is Love." It seems almost that a rare page is turned without some sort of reference to food. Many historical experts celebrate Roald Amundsen and Ernest Shackleton as premier expedition leaders of their day. A central ingredient to the successes of each man can be found by looking deep into the core of the ships. In their galleys, Amundsen and Shackleton respectfully laid down the foundation for survival and hearts were won through close attention to the bellies of the crew members. In both Amundsen's 1910-1912 *Fram* Expedition and Shackleton's 1914-1916 journey of *Endurance*, many untold thanks are owed to their chosen chefs. While under very different circumstances, both Adolf Lindstrom and Charles Green affected their respective crews with contagious doses of optimism. In each story, morale among the men was high and the contributions of Lindstrom and Green cannot be underestimated. To these adventurous men, food was love, but more importantly it was the critical connection to life.

The Norwegian-born Amundsen knew well the value in making food a priority, for it was not his first journey to the Antarctic. Indeed, thirteen years before his *Fram* Expedition, in 1898, he traveled to this southern continent as a young officer under the leadership of the Belgian Commandant, Adrien de Gerlache. In early March, unexpected pack ice trapped their ship, *Belgica*, forcing them to winter-over. In the ship's cramped and limited space, the crew of nineteen men struggled to survive until the sea ice finally freed them again thirteen months later. Provisions onboard the *Belgica* were ample but the tinned foods were bland in flavor, not adequate in vitamin content, and failed to prevent disease. Still, many of the men refused to eat the nutrient-rich fresh meats available and sickness set in. In *Helpless in a Hopeless Sea of Ice*, T.H. Baughman wrote, "Early on, seal and penguin had been tried but rejected." The expedition surgeon, Dr. Frederick Cook eventually intervened and, against the wishes of de Gerlache, forced a change in diet. Dr. Cook recognized that food lent a lethal hand to the negativity which consumed the group. In his book, *Through the First Antarctic Night*, Cook took from his

own May 20, 1898 journal entry, "Everybody having any connection with the selection or preparation of the food, past or
present, is heaped with some criticism…. The truth is, that we
are at this moment as tired of each other's company as we are
of the cold monotony of the black night and of the unpalat-
able sameness of our food." Amundsen reflected on their plight
aboard the *Belgica*. "On July 22 the sun returned. It was not a
pleasant sight that it shone upon. The Antarctic winter had set
its mark upon all, and green, wasted faces stared at the returning light." Baughman reported that, "Several men showed signs
of insanity and most were incapacitated in one way or another.
Most recovered, although Amundsen had to accompany one
insane sailor back to Norway after the expedition." Wisely,
Amundsen took note of these experiences, selecting Lindstrom
as expedition chef for future polar exploration.

Like Amundsen, Shackleton also learned hard lessons during an early visit to the Antarctic. In 1901, he traveled to
McMurdo Sound as a young officer with Robert Scott's
British Antarctic Expedition. Nearly dying from scurvy himself, Shackleton made the health of his crew a priority during
future trips to the southern continent. Thus, while docked
years later in Buenos Aires in October 1914, he prepared his
ship, *Endurance*, for what would become his most famous expedition. One of Shackleton's most important decisions, he
smartly fired his cook before departure for being "indifferent"
and "drunk." English chef Charles Green was hired as the replacement cook and over the course of the next twenty-two
months, performed well under unthinkably harsh conditions.
In Frank Worsley's book, *Shackleton's Boat Journey*, he stated
that, "Sir Ernest always set great store on the best food and
cooking possible for his men. Owing to this constant care,
none of the men under him ever suffered from scurvy."

Swiftly, Green cleaned up the galley and began to demonstrate a jovial manner and team-oriented spirit. In February of 1915, with the ship attempting to break from heavy pack-ice, the crew worked many strenuous hours, trying to cut out a channel of open water. Lansing wrote, "Even frail Charlie Green, the cook, hurried through his bread-making to join his shipmates trying to saw the ship clear."

Today, this tradition of careful planning continues and all potential galley hands are rigorously interviewed for job openings. Months before I deployed to the South Pole for my first season on the ice, I shared a telephone conversation with executive chef, Sally Ayotte. Stating her expectation with straightforward conviction, she said simply, "The South Pole proudly serves the best food on the entire continent and this season will not be an exception." I giggled. Best food on the continent? Any marketing genius would surely love to lay claim to such a statement. However, it was not until I actually arrived at the South Pole and started meeting men with nick-names like "Stretch" and "Big John," that I realized just how immense the pressures would be. With average summer temperatures hovering around -30°F, hard-working "Polies" eat incessantly, as both men and women bring voracious appetites to the galley. Every day at 11:15 A.M. the crew forms a long line near the serving area, sweating in fuel-stained, insulated Carhartts. The warmth of the room thaws ice-covered faces and beads of moisture drip to the floor. Eagerly watching for a signal from the kitchen, they are ready for a feed. Certainly, the Antarctic cooks of today will never comprehend the pressures faced many decades ago, but our post remains the same. The morale and vitality of the community is a direct reflection of the food and atmosphere we create.

With pride, we task ourselves to serve flavorful foods for the staff's varying needs and interests. Pleasing everyone all the time though, is near to impossible. At a minimum, three meals are inspected daily by our peers. Every entree, every starch, every vegetable, every sauce, every side salad, every soup, every dessert, and every loaf of bread we produce gets judged. In the South Pole galley today, a copper-colored bell hangs high above the serving line. This seemingly insignificant emblem of brass is hardly noticeable, being medium in size and simple in design. Over the years though, it has become a tool cherished by galley hands. A handmade sign next to the bell states clearly, "WHINER ALARM!" Chef "Cookie Jon" Emanuel, who introduced the idea, laid the ground rules, insisting, "It's always the cook's discretion. Only ring it if necessary but when you must, just make sure everyone in the galley hears it clearly." Once, the alarm rang in response to a construction foreman who complained loudly about his freshly baked hamburger bun, which was topped with sesame seeds. "What am I?" he demanded, "A freaking bird?" DING! Later in the same season, someone shouted, "Can't you people ever serve chicken without bones?" DING! And on another occasion, a young woman showed us her angry face and hardly touched bowl of soup, saying "Hey, what *is* this? It doesn't taste like Campbell's at all!" DING! Fortunately, these rare but deserving "alarms" were always accompanied by the supportive communities' mocking round of taunts, boos, laughs, and jeers from the entire South Pole crew, aimed at none other than the whiner himself.

Historical research reveals similar scenarios occurring in Antarctica's first galleys as well. Amundsen wrote of his crew, "No one says anything so long as the food is good; but let the cook be unlucky and burn the soup one day, and he will hear something." Indeed, much was at stake and the pressures were very real. Worsley included in his book a passage about Green: "The seamen, recognizing a good man, did not exercise their time-honoured right of growling at the cook." And Amundsen pointed to the "fabulous rapidity" with which the Norwegian crew ate hotcakes for breakfast, mentioning "Lindstrom knows how to prepare them in a way that could not be surpassed in the best of American houses." He respectfully logged, "If it is a cook's best reward to see his food appreciated, then, indeed, Lindstrom had good wages." Without question, the tasty food and healthy atmosphere provided by each of these men contributed greatly to the optimistic attitudes among their teams.

In a similar way, the dynamics of today's Antarctic galleys are reflected in station morale and from season to season, I have witnessed how our work critically moves humans in a positive or negative direction. At both Palmer and the South Pole, the galley acts as a magnet, with food drawing people together in friendship and camaraderie. Populations are small enough for residents to participate in the menu planning and for special occasions, even volunteer to be the cook. I have rolled sushi with a painter of Japanese heritage and fried handmade egg rolls with scientists from China. I have turned a spit of lamb with a heavy equipment operator raised in Greece and prepared a traditional Mexican breakfast with a Hispanic cargo handler. I have assisted a team of electricians with a steak-and-lobster dinner and borrowed a family jambalaya recipe from a Cajun construction worker. With each of these, meal time always became a welcome celebration of community spirit and cultural diversity.

In experiences at McMurdo Station however, the obtrusive wall that divides the kitchen from the dining area, also divides the crew. In peak summer, more than one thousand souls rely on a staff of sixty galley hands for their sustenance. In a flurry of preparation for a single meal, I have produced instant mashed potatoes by the tens of gallons while simultaneously creating the soup du jour in a steam-jacketed kettle large enough for two adults to bathe in. Maintaining a flavorful and creative touch is a great challenge and with the exceptional yields required, seasonings are measured not with dainty tea-spoons or by the quarter cupful but rather by pouring and dumping directly out of the containers. Efforts to accommo-date every individual appetite on station are futile and even though the menu options offer more variety to these residents than either South Pole or Palmer stations, the McMurdo din-ing area is a breeding ground for negativity.

Indeed, people living in the Antarctic today no doubt suf-fer from bouts of "want." Some might justify a hamburger lacking fresh lettuce and tomato with the overused phrase, "It's a harsh continent." A sharp historical perspective though reveals that today's quality of life in Antarctica is far from harsh. While many of the early explorers endured weeks and months without bathing or a simple change of clothing, mod-ern plumbing offers us laundry, showers, flush toilets, and even an automatic dish machine. Although Palmer and South Pole are without television reception, the soft, cozy couches in our lounges provide a welcome retreat with choices from an end-less collection of movies. Internet and satellite telephones allow correspondence with friends and family on a conve-nient and regular basis. In the dining area, a news report and crossword puzzle are printed daily for reading material and a live NPR feed can be streamed into nearby speakers. By comparison, when Shackleton hired him in 1914, Green sent letters and money home from South America to England. Sadly, the correspondence never reached its destination as a German cruiser torpedoed the ship carrying them. Thus, Green's family had no idea of his whereabouts until nearly two years later, when they read of the parties' newsworthy rescue from Elephant Island. As the events of World War I transpired, Shackleton's men spent multiple months without any outside contact. Today we are overwhelmed with updates of our own war.

I am humbled when considering the hardships men like Lindstrom and Green faced. In the early Antarctic kitchens, the cooks were responsible for everyday tasks we would never consider today. Most stayed busy butchering seal and penguin, so fresh meats could be served. Quarrying snow and ice for water was an endless job and stoves needed constant stoking with wood or blubber. Because all resources were vital to success and survival, dogs and ponies brought down as work animals were often shot and used as sustenance. Some groups even took advantage of the plentiful supply of penguin eggs, harvesting them when in season for use in breakfast omelets. Amundsen called Lindstrom's post as chef, "the hardest and most thankless work on an expedition like this." And Lansing reported of Green's remarkable commitment during winter aboard the *Endurance*, "While the others worked only three hours each day, Green was busy in the galley from early morning until long after supper at night." Still, the efforts of both men led eventually to the success of their companions.

As grave as the situation became for Shackleton and his men, lives were no doubt saved when they chose hope over despondency. A week after they had abandoned ship and set up temporary camp on the sea ice, an *Endurance* crew member logged in his journal on November 4, 1915, "...all we seem to live for and think of now is food. I have never in my life taken half such a keen interest in food as I do now—and we are all alike.... We are ready to eat anything, especially cooked blubber which none of us would tackle before." Less than three weeks later, on November 21, the men helplessly watched their crushed ship disappear into the icy depths of the Weddell Sea. Their situation was bleak at best and recognizing the need to keep spirits high, Shackleton wisely called to Green for a special meal. Indicating their healthy state of mind, all hands were delighted with the menu selection of fish paste and biscuits. Lansing reported that one of the expedition surgeons wrote in his journal, "Really, this sort of life has its attraction. I read somewhere that all a man needs to be happy is a full stomach and warmth, and I begin to think it is nearly true." But facing still another nine months of brutal conditions, their quest for survival lasted until August 30, when Shackleton heard the call from his men, "All safe, all well," as he landed a rescue boat on the shores of Elephant Island. Remarkably, every man lived to tell their extraordinary tale of endurance.

Although in a much less threatening situation than Green faced, Lindstrom, too, set up his fellow Norwegians to reach their goal. Describing a typical menu prepared by Lindstrom for the winter crew, Amundsen reported their unique but sufficient diet. "For supper, seal steak, with whortleberry jam, cheese, bread, butter, and coffee. Every Saturday evening a glass of toddy and a cigar. I must frankly confess that I have never lived so well. And the consequence is that we are all in the best of health, and I feel certain that the whole enterprise will be crowned with success." Indeed, they realized their objective on

December 14, 1911, as Amundsen and his party became the
first men in history to stand at the bottom of the world.

With both arms submerged to my elbows in a deep sink of
warm soapy water, my fingers feel for yet another stainless
steel utensil to scrub clean. I am near enough to the serving
line to greet each staff member as they arrive for lunch and I
watch carefully for unintentional expressions that indicate the
meal's approval rating. Fortunately, today's requested menu of
grilled cheese with tomato soup is happily received. Scanning
the dining area throughout service, I note each clean plate as
a quiet compliment and proudly welcome those returning for
second helpings. It is not complicated cuisine, as yesterday's
seafood Newburg was, and certainly not created from one of
our many specialized recipe books. But I am more than content, both with the meal and in continuing the tradition established in the southern galleys of long ago. Then as now, our
priority lies in creating an atmosphere for a team rich in
spirit. I observe this at the close of the lunch period as my re-
sponsibilities for the day conclude. A waste technician takes
over my post scouring pans, an entomologist puts away a clean
rack of glassware, a marine biologist begins sanitizing tables,
and a carpenter starts to sweep the kitchen floor. I reflect back
on the spinning globe from my youth long ago. Like other
children, I was fascinated by day-dreams of thrilling adventure
to places beyond my own experience. Only now though, do
I understand that with determination, commitment and the
choice for optimism, a youngster's pretend world truly can
become a reality beyond his wildest imagination.

Feb. 22, 1909: It is neck or nothing with us now. Our food lies ahead, and death stalks us from behind.

—ERNEST SHACKLETON, *THE HEART OF THE ANTARCTIC*

Everyone who travels to Antarctica through the United States Antarctic Program goes through a physical examination. The reasons are obvious—medical care is minimal and if anything much more than a band-aid is needed, help is far away. The dramatic story of Dr. Jerri Nielsen, who self-diagnosed breast cancer at the South Pole, brought the dangers of illness on the Ice to the public. Even if necessary, the physical exam is a nerve-wracking experience for those of us who don't like tests of any sort: What if I failed and couldn't go to Antarctica? When I got the email that I had PQ'd (physically qualified) I thought I should throw a party.

Then there's another level of exam—the psychological exam. This is only for those spending the winter or venturing for long periods to remote camps. Glenn Grant, who has spent ten seasons in Antarctica, including six winters, knows this exam well. And he understands the irony of it: How sane could someone be who wants to winter over?

Glenn works as a station Science Technician, which allows him to be involved in all things geophysical. He is the caretaker for a dozen long-term experiments, collecting the data and maintaining the instruments, which places him somewhere between scientist and support worker. He has also worked as a commercial diver and software engineer for global climate models. He is remodeling a creaky 100-year-old house in Port Townsend, Washington.

Shrink Rap

⋆ ⋆ ⋆

GLENN GRANT

IN THE HISTORY OF ANTARCTIC EXPLORATION, POSSIBLY the most celebrated and controversial topic is that of winter-induced insanity. From the beginning, wintering expeditions have sought to avoid the dreaded mental instability supposedly caused by the cold, harsh months without daylight. (Laplanders and Eskimos must have somehow evolved past the hazard.)

The possibility of winter psychosis is taken seriously by the U.S. Antarctic Program. All the stations have strait-jackets in the medical supplies, usually located somewhere near the body bags. Applicants, whether for summer or winter positions, are grilled by interviewers about how they expect to cope with the lack of movie theaters, McDonald's, and *Simpsons* reruns. The final, most dramatic test occurs for the winter-over candidates: The Psychological Exam.

I approached *the psych* with a feeling of certain doom. I just knew that I would be exposed as the mentally-unbalanced, obsessive-compulsive, angst-ridden manic-depressive that I was. All of my mental closets would be opened and the neurotic skeletons would come tumbling out. I would be rejected, and that would be the end of it; no chance at

Antarctica. With great shame, I would return to my lowly job as a software engineer for a defense contractor, and remain sullenly silent when my cubical buddies asked why I didn't go to the frozen continent after bragging about it so much.

This fear was compounded for an unusual set of reasons: The psych exam used to be conducted by the Navy in either Bethesda or San Diego. This was almost considered to be a paid vacation by many applicants. At least it was by those who were relaxed about the whole matter. The Navy had a reputation for being much more stringent with Antarctic service applicants, sometimes rejecting them for relatively minor reasons, psychological or not. The Navy was also responsible for performing background security checks on some defense contractors, and I had been subjected to many grueling Personal Security Questionnaires in which I was compelled to "tell all." The telling consisted of chronicling virtually every misdeed and mental lapse of my entire life, followed by an interview with an investigator, extensive reference checks, and a polygraph test to make sure I had told the truth. Never mind the fact that I had passed all of these tests, been given the necessary clearances and rubber-stamped as having the right amount of okie-dokieness. I was convinced that somewhere along the way an investigator had tagged my inches-thick dossier with a red label saying, *"Watch this guy—he's trouble."* Although the Antarctic psychological examinations were now being conducted by a private evaluation firm, I had a nagging suspicion that this company was communicating with the Navy psychological examiners. They would casually peruse my old records, raising eyebrows at the atrocities contained within until finally rejecting me, astonished that I would even have the gall to apply. My winter-over employment would be denied before it ever started.

To make matters worse, shortly after college I had applied to the CIA—the Central Intelligence Agency, not the infamous Culinary Institute of America. (How does one apply to the CIA, you ask? You call them up and ask for an application. They also advertise in your local newspaper.) I had no idea what I could do for them. Computer stuff, maybe. Whatever. It had the potential for some adventure, at least from a nerdy, computer-geek standpoint. I was flown to Reston for physical exams, technical skills testing, interviews with different branches of the agency, and a polygraph. The CIA does what's called a *lifestyles* polygraph, where, beyond the normal questions about whether you plan on committing espionage and being a traitorous bastard, they also ask you things like *"Have you ever smoked dope while having sex with chickens?"* Or something like that. I had to have the examiner explain several of the questions. The final part of the interview process included a day-long battery of psychological examinations. I left with the distinct feeling that I had blown it somewhere along the way, and when I wasn't hired it only confirmed my suspicions.

For a couple of years I told myself that maybe their budget had been cut, and that they really wanted to hire me but just couldn't. And then I finally got up the nerve to apply again. According to the CIA, applicant records aren't kept beyond two years. That meant I was free to start fresh, and this time I knew what was coming. Once more they were interested in me, and the interview process started all over again. At the initial interview I mentioned that I had applied before but hadn't been hired. Heck, either they would find out anyway or they had no record of my previous application. The interviewer said she'd look into it and tell me what was up.

Two days later I received a call from her. "This is very strange," she said. "They don't want you, but they won't tell me why." And that was that. Branded by the government as a Bad Person for life.

And now it was starting all over again.

The psychological exam for the U.S. Antarctic Program starts with two multiple-choice tests, both several hundred questions long. To compile a statistical perspective on the test taker's mental outlook, the same questions are asked repeatedly but phrased slightly differently each time. For instance, one test concentrates on fairly fluffy true/false questions such as, "I'd rather be a florist than a truck driver." A few questions later, something like "I prefer flowers to machines" may appear. The other test gets right to the point, with questions like: "Sometimes I just feel like killing myself." Presumably a test taker will reveal his or her latent wackoness after answering variations on the same questions so many times they start telling the truth just to break the monotony. The final result for each test is a graph showing where you fit (or don't) within several categories of mental neuroses. Statistically "normal" people are represented by the center line on each graph, and your mental state is identified by Xs plotted in relation to that mean value. An X too far from the middle will cause little alarm bells to go off in the heads of the examiners who review the plots.

There was one other examinee in the room, Chris, and we hit it off immediately. He was applying to do a second year at the South Pole. A *second* year? By my own definition of insanity this was clearly a bad case of it, and he should have been rejected from the get-go. You'd think he would have learned his lesson the first time. Of course, by some standards just wanting to go to Antarctica for a year should be reason enough to declare you unfit for going. Yet here we were, being tested to see if we were mentally stable enough to do something only a mentally unstable person would want to do.

You're not supposed to discuss the tests while you are taking them, but some of the questions were so silly that one of us would spontaneously burst into laughter. We'd have conversations about situations where we had felt like going postal or walking off the edge of the world, as suggested by the questions. At one point Chris laughed at the question, "Voices tell me to hurt people." Yes, he said, yes they do. And they are the voices of his friends, saying he "shouldn't have to put up with the bullshit" perpetrated by another co-worker. With friends like that, who needs psychoses?

The second part of the examination consists of interviews with two psychologists. The conversations are casual, congenial, but probing. They ask how you feel about this and that, and how you think you'll do during the winter. If you show signs of doubt or deception the questions become deeper. It is not a psychoanalysis session, at least not in the traditional sense (Chris was disappointed that he didn't get "shrunk"). It is mostly just an opportunity for the examiners to evaluate your attitude and discuss any outstanding issues. They will also be looking at the results of the written tests, and may show you the computer print-outs. They are trying to judge whether you are mentally secure enough to winter-over in Antarctica, even though they have never wintered themselves.

Employees and scientists returning for another winter-over are still required to go through the psychological examination, although the interviewers acknowledge that the applicants usually have a good idea of what they are getting themselves into. Because returnees generally consider the psych exam to be a paid play day, unless there is something important to discuss the conversation often becomes more of a friendly chat session rather than a rigorous evaluation. During the Navy days, a new examinee was once asked, without any preliminary questions, "What makes you think you can survive a winter confined with a couple dozen other people?" His answer was that he used to work on submarines. Antarctic service is sometimes equated with being on a submarine, and this was exactly the kind of positive experience the examiners were looking for. The entire interview lasted only thirty seconds.

In Freudian psychological circles there is an emphasis on sex. If you've ever had a Rorschach test, your responses to the abstract ink blots are carefully scrutinized for either too much emphasis on sexuality (*"Oh that one also looks like two naked people!"*) or too little, indicating sexual repression. So the ideal answers are generally non-sexual, but when shown a blot that has obvious sexual imagery you should be sure to mention it. I never thought I would ever see one of these tests, but at the first interview POP! there it was. Since I had studied the purpose and methods of Rorschach testing some years before, I already had pre-canned responses to the standard set of ink blots. *That one looks like a fox. Two women dancing. A mask.* I think the examiner sensed my nonchalance because he rapidly gave up on the test.

Years later, during another winter-over psych, the examiners were two women who questioned me in tandem, inquisition style. It was all very rote, no Rorschach tests here. Everything was going fine until I noticed that one of the psychologists was wearing a striking slit skirt, and had crossed her legs in an attractive and rather revealing way. *Was this part of the test?* It was very distracting, and tremendously more compelling than any ink blot. It took a moment, but I decided that it might be best if I concentrated on the matter at hand and not stare at her legs for the remainder of the interview.

My test results were normal. *So much for the accuracy of psychological exams,* I thought. The interviews were brief, to the point, and relatively painless, aside from any indecision about where to focus my attention. Just before they started I had decided that I trusted myself more than anyone else to know whether or not I was mentally prepared for the experience. I didn't volunteer my own opinions of my mental state. At the same time, I knew that I would survive the winter just fine. Their approval was simply a formality. If forced to choose between the harsh rigors of an Antarctic winter or returning to the same dead-end job I had been working at for the past ten years, the greatest mental trauma would be *not* going to the Ice.

The examination processes is, generally speaking, a good thing. It has eliminated many of the alcoholics and obviously unstable participants from the program. A few still leak in through the cracks—the process is not perfect, and never will be. But, in the opinion of some old-timers, many of the worst trouble-makers have been weeded out.

There will always be people who, although normal enough to qualify, still fall off the mental rocking-horse somewhere in the middle of the winter or even in mid-summer. In one instance, a South Pole researcher decided to follow in Sir Robert Falcon Scott's footsteps and ski the 850 miles back to McMurdo with nothing more than the 200 pounds of chocolate that he had secretly stashed. The search-and-rescue team found him a short distance from South Pole Station, towing his chocolate on a sled. They persuaded him to wait for the next flight back to Mactown, which was probably better than letting him die of acne somewhere out on the ice plateau. The chocolate was salvaged by one of the crew and quietly distributed to an unsupported, hungry-looking Belgian expedition that arrived on skis later that summer.

Occasionally there are personnel who spend their winters heavily doped on anti-depressants, although the station doctors are naturally reluctant to discuss the subject. But based on the stories circulated plus my own observations, the worst psychological problems develop over broken love affairs (but that is a subject for another time).

The long winter months of cold, dark, miserable weather and crowded conditions may cause some depression and make tempers short, but it's no worse than, say, enduring a winter in Seattle. And Antarctic winter-overs have the advantage of knowing that when the winter is over, *they* will see the sun again.

Polar exploration is at once the cleanest and most isolated way of having a bad time which has been devised. It is the only form of adventure in which you put on your clothes at Michaelmas and keep them on until Christmas, and, save for a layer of the natural grease of the body, find them as clean as though they were new. It is more lonely than London, more secluded than any monastery, and the post comes but once a year.

—APSLEY CHERRY-GARRARD,
THE WORST JOURNEY IN THE WORLD (1922)

Lucy Jane Bledsoe's story plays out that mantra all hear when they travel to Antarctica: weather controls the continent. Which means that weather controls your plans. In McMurdo high winds keep helicopters from flying and planes from New Zealand boomerang. Weather for Lucy at Palmer involves ice and ships that cannot sail. This leads to unexpected adventure, the sort that involves physical trials that make you feel tough, and beautiful scenery; this is a classic Antarctic tale.

Lucy—whose writing and adventures appear in six of my past anthologies—is the author of three books on Antarctica: The Ice Cave: A Woman's Adventures from the Mojave to the Antarctic is a collection of narrative nonfiction; How to Survive in Antarctica is a cross between a survival guide and a travel guide for kids; and The Antarctic Scoop is a novel for kids. She has traveled twice to the Antarctic on a National Science Foundation Artist and Writers grant, once to McMurdo, and once to Palmer. Her descriptions of crossing the Drake Passage en route to Palmer from Punta Arenas still make me seasick.

Lucy's two most recent novels are This Wild Silence and Biting the Apple. Visit her website at www.lucyjanebledsoe.com for more information on her books.

How to Find a Dinosaur

✦ ✦ ✦

LUCY JANE BLEDSOE

I WAS LOOKING FOR KRILL, THOSE TINY PINK CRUSTACEANS with the beady black eye dots, a primary food source on earth. From the beginning, I was interested in prey, not predation.

When the call came, I'd been at Palmer Station for nearly three weeks and had settled in quite happily. I'd set up a tent at the foot of the glacier where at night I fell asleep to the whoosh and flap of giant petrel wings, as well as the groan and splash of ice calving into the sea. Sometimes a Gentou penguin would be standing by the door to my tent when I emerged in the morning. During the day, when I wasn't out in the field with science teams, my cohorts at Palmer enthusiastically helped me develop characters and a plot for the novel I had been given the fellowship to write, a novel about krill. My goal: making something as plentiful and personality-less as those itty-bitty shrimp interesting to my book's characters and readers.

Cancel krill.

The first thing anyone tells you about traveling to Antarctica is to expect change, and lots of it. The weather rules all, and this season the National Science Foundation research vessel, the *Laurence M. Gould*, had been unable to drop off a group of paleontologists on Vega Island where a few years earlier they'd found a couple of plesiosaurs that they now intended to dig up and bring back to their universities. The sea ice ringing the island was impenetrable. So to buy a few days, hoping the wind would pick up and change direction, do whatever it needed to do to blow the ice out of there, the *Gould* would make its port call at Palmer Station a few weeks ahead of schedule. The National Science Foundation called ahead and gave me three choices: stay on station a few months longer than I'd planned, float around in the southern sea as the ship made its rounds for the other scientists on board, or get dropped off on Vega Island with the paleontologists.

I chose the plesiosaur dig.

Just a few hours later, I boarded the ship with the rest of the research team, four other women and ten men. The seventy-meter *Gould* is a work ship and does not enjoy a reputation for comfort. Still, the cabin I shared with the team doctor had two decent bunks and our own bathroom. The galley was cozy enough with long Formica-topped tables, and the cook served wholesome, tasty meals. The lounge was well-stocked with books and movies. Disappointed as I was to be leaving my friends and project at Palmer Station, I did my best to adapt to the new adventure.

According to satellite images, our chances of getting into Vega Island hadn't improved since they'd tried a week earlier. The alternative, though, was for the paleontologists to abandon years of research, and so the *Gould* chugged north. Vega Island, as well as Seymour Island where we were to drop off some other paleontologists studying clam fossils, are on the other side of the peninsula from Palmer Station, a couple of days' journey, and a much longer one if the ice forced us to go all the way around the tip. The hope was to get through the big opening called the Antarctic Sound. The going was slow through the ice-clogged channel, but we made progress until we arrived at its mouth and got stopped in our tracks by packed bergs.

The only option, other than turning back, was to try squeezing through a much narrower channel, called Fridtjof Sound. The air and water were perfectly still, and total silence gripped the small group of us watching from the bridge as we inched through this passage. We slid by massive ice bergs, much taller and longer than our ship, so close I could almost reach out and touch them. Looking into the water at their glowing blue bodies, knowing that they were many times bigger than the icy crowns looming above sea level, I couldn't help but wonder what would happen if one of those bergs happened to roll.

After long heavy minutes of silence, the first mate, who was at the wheel, said, "You all can talk, you know. Everyone breathe."

A scattering of tense laughter.

But the silence grew even more taut as the captain paced back and forth on the bridge, and up and down from the crow's nest. The walls of ice seem to press ever closer to the ship.

"May I have the attention of everyone on board," the captain radioed down from the crow's nest. We all perked up, expecting to be told to start getting into our immersion suits and the lifeboat. His voice continued, filling the cavities of the ship, "If you look at the cliffs to the starboard side of the vessel, you can see a petroglyph of a huge clam chasing a T-Rex."

Everyone on board cracked up. With the tension broken, I was finally able to notice that it was an extraordinary day. Every ice floe carried a flock of penguins or a pod of fat seals, and as the *Gould* nudged their floating ice decks to the side, or sometimes sliced right through them, the penguins and seals would waddle and wiggle into the safety of the sea. Occasionally, but not often enough, my thoughts wandered to krill, the critters that had brought me to this continent and its islands, and I'd pull out my notebook, try to take notes, or peer into the sea over the railings of the *Gould*, as if some of the crustaceans would offer me insight into how to write a novel about them.

When at last we cleared the channel and nosed our way into the Weddell Sea, a cheer went up. We'd made it. Vega Island came into view and all binoculars were trained on its shores, searching for the put-in. The scientists began fine-tuning their plans for offloading.

However, as we approached, the sea ice grew thicker. In fact, the island was surrounded by an apron of fast sea ice. Soon the first mate was backing and ramming, trying to break through the solid, three-foot-thick slab. The *Gould* is not technically an icebreaker, and with each forward thrust, the bow rode up on top of the ice, sat for a moment until gravity pulled it down to break the slab with a loud *thump*. Each time the ship paused with its snout resting on the ice, it felt to me like the whole ship might topple to one side. The tension from our earlier passage through Fridtjof Sound seemed like a mere tickle compared to the vise grip of anxiety now squeezing the *Gould*.

From the crow's nest, the captain ordered the first mate, "As you get in here, if you think you cannot turn the boat around, DO NOT continue in. Roger that?"

The first mate rogered that, and we continued backing and ramming, making a few feet an hour, straining our eyes toward the Vega Island put-in. As evening drew near, the captain finally decided that we couldn't make it, and we turned around.

Or tried to. The temperature was dropping, quickly freezing the sea ice against the hull of the ship, making movement in any direction impossible.

We were stuck. Our position, I noted, was about 7 degrees north of, and less than five hundred miles from, the place where Shackleton's *Endurance* became stuck in the ice and eventually sunk.

The captain ordered spectators off the bridge. I couldn't very well argue that my krill research required I remain, and anyway, I had a date to take a Spanish lesson from one of the ship's Chilean hands, so I went below to practice verb conjugations. As my enthusiastic teacher made use of the announcement chalkboard in the galley to speed through a couple dozen Spanish verbs, I could only think about the absolute stillness of the ship. He grew visibly frustrated with my poor rate of learning, but I couldn't help thinking about the futility of learning another language when I might not see land ever again. We were not moving. And I knew that it was entirely possible that we would not move for days, even weeks. We needed wind to blow the sea ice out, or sun to melt it away, and there was nothing in the human toolkit to hasten either of those events. My teacher, however, clearly saw the situation as an opportunity: ample time for me to become fluent in Spanish.

Finally I had to plead utter distraction and end my lesson. I packed up and wandered around the ship. Most of the paleontologists had crowded into the lounge to sedate themselves with movies. While the ship's crew tensely went about their duties, the rest of us whispered when we spoke, as if a loud voice would somehow shatter a necessary mental calm. The sea ice continued to hug the ship, cementing itself against the steel. I went to bed.

I awoke some time in the night to the sound of the ship's engine grinding away. I sat up and looked out my porthole to see icebergs moving slowly by. I dressed quickly and ran up to the bridge, where I learned that the crew had gotten out all the fire hoses and squirted the fast ice clamped onto the hull. The strategy seemed like a long shot, and yet it worked, melting away enough ice to dislodge the ship. A new plan, to try to gain access to Vega Island from the north, had also been foiled in the night, and so finally, the paleontologists agreed to be dropped off on James Ross Island, which is adjacent to Vega, where there was open water to the shore. They were hugely disappointed, and yet there was hope: A peninsula on James Ross Island that reached toward Vega Island was composed of the same kind of sedimentary rock, the Cape Lamb Formation, and while they'd be starting over from scratch, it was possible they'd find fossils of interest. As for me, I wanted to sleep with land against my back, and frankly, I didn't care if they put me on the moon; I wanted off the ship.

A few hours later, I stood on deck while a reconnaissance Zodiac buzzed to James Ross Island to see if they could find a suitable campsite. I watched through binoculars as they explored the gravelly bench that would become my home for the next few weeks.

The National Science Foundation never let me forget that change was the only thing I should count on in Antarctica. Still, disappointment was hard to avoid. The paleontologists had to abandon the plesiosaurs they'd found on Vega Island and I had to abandon the krill I'd been getting to know at Palmer Station. Now we were plopped down together for a stay on an island that none of us had ever planned to visit. They intended to hunt fossils, and since there were no krill biologists in our expedition, I planned to join the hunt.

We spent a long day setting up shelters and unpacking crates of food and tools, and then, the next morning, I stood on the shore of the Antarctic island and watched the *Gould* drift away, its orange-and-tan hull a bright bit of fire on the horizon. Two long mournful blasts on its horn, and then it was gone. I looked around at the five bright yellow Scott tents and two mountain tents for sleeping, two more Scott tents for the camp toilets, and one polar shelter kitchen tent just barely big enough for all fifteen of us to fit in for meals. Home for the next five weeks. A delegation of fifteen Gentou penguins waddled into camp, their demeanors at once purposeful and curious, like a welcoming party.

That night the lead paleontologists, Judd and Jim, explained our fossil-hunting mission. We had two primary pursuits: one, mammals (probably marsupial) to show the link between Australia and South America; and two, mosasaurs and plesiosaurs, both of which were big marine reptiles. James Ross Island was vast, with miles of shoreline and thick glaciers capping its interior. I couldn't help thinking, yeah, right, you're going to find a few bone fragments on this frozen haystack. As I walked to my tent, which faced Vega Island with its gorgeously striated cliffs and the sea, I remembered that this beauty would be mine, no matter what else we discovered.

Each day we hiked four and a half miles to our worksite, a big peninsula that reached toward Vega Island, called The Naze. We stayed as close to the shoreline as possible, and at low tides, could make use of beaches, but just when our accumulated footsteps would begin to form a trail that made the going just a bit easier, the tide would come in extra high and drown our emerging trail, or a storm would blow drifts of snow across our path. Most of the time we walked across snow fields humped with dirt and knee-high ice formations, meaning every step required raising one's leg a couple of feet off the ground. The Naze was connected to the rest of the island by an elegantly low, curved isthmus, which was a joy to walk across in its openness. But just before reaching this easier stretch of the hike, we crossed a long bed of mud that sucked in my boots with each step. The changing difficulty of the route required frequent stops to add or remove a layer. The hikes back to camp were all the more difficult due to backpacks full of rock and fossil samples. By the end of our weeks on James Ross Island, the soles of my boots had literally worn all the way through to my socks.

And yet those hikes were my favorite part of the entire expedition, with the extraordinary landscape, the changing tides and weather, making each arduous step a miracle. Usually the team spread out along the trail, each walking at his or her own pace, conserving energy and keeping warm, most of us too tired for conversation anyway. There were times when the route crossed crusts of ice, overhanging the sloshing sea water, when I wondered if hiking alone was all that smart. If the crust broke off, and I fell into the sea, getting out would be next to impossible. I made sure there were always hikers somewhere behind me.

When we reached the worksite in the mornings, we fanned out on hillsides, and dropped to our hands and knees. We crawled, inch by inch, examining every stone in our path, looking for the particular crystal patterns that indicated living matter. We gathered abundant fossils of clams, crabs, ammonites, barnacles, snails, and nautilodes. The most fun were the concretions, spherical stones that we smashed open with hammers to find perfect fossils of crab claws or snail shell spirals embedded in the centers. Over thousands of years, the rock formed around these fossils a bit like pearls form around grains of sand. Each fossil we discovered helped to tell the story of this island during the time period of the Cape Lamb Formation. But what we really wanted were bones and teeth. Some days, when the wind blew and snow fell, this crawling on hillsides was very cold work.

While I tried hard to find fossils, my primary job on this expedition was to look for stories. So I stopped from time to time to take notes about the bigger picture: the weather, the terrain, the moods of my teammates. I watched the body language of the paleontologists, asked lots of questions, tried to discover what made their blood race. This was a particularly reticent bunch, so I had to be all the more observant.

The discovery was quiet. No one screamed, "Eureka!" No one called for help. I just noticed a slight increase in intensity as the two principal investigators, and their star graduate student, began working together in one place, which was unusual.

Judd had found the remains of a dinosaur. I stood for a moment and watched the team work, yellow bluffs behind them, the sea ice not far in the distance, and tried to imagine this giant reptile moseying around on this peninsula, hunting for food or maybe playing with its young.

That night Judd told me everything he knew so far. Surpassing their hopes for a mosasaur or plesiosaur, this set of fossils, including a jaw with teeth, represented a therapod, a meat-eating dinosaur. Dated to the very end of the Cretaceous Period, about 68 to 71 million years ago, this was a time when the connection to South America still existed, so there was a "gulf-stream-like" warm water flow that kept the climate warm. The dinosaur fossils were remarkable, and I loved holding them, imagining their owner, that carnivorous creature from earth millions of years ago.

Travel is always that way: you go in search of one thing and find something altogether different. I wanted krill, the prey crucial to life on Earth today, but instead found an ancient predator, from a time when Antarctica was warm.

Our kitchen tent was outfitted with a laptop, connected to an iridium phone, on which we were each allowed a few minutes of e-mail a night. That night we were instructed to keep quiet about the find until the National Science Foundation could be notified. Jim said, "We're all in this together now," as if we'd committed a serious crime.

For days after the find, we picked over the site of the discovery, making sure we got every last bit of the fossils. Once we'd combed the hillside a few times, we cleared it of all big boulders, heaving them aside. Then we shoveled the remaining rocks into a double sieve. As one person shoveled, another shook this big contraption, so that the dust and dirt fell through, leaving a bed of small stone in the upper basket. These stones were dumped in a pile for the paleontologists to examine, one at a time, to make sure they got every single piece of dinosaur, every possible bone fragment, from the site.

Having found their dinosaur, the paleontologists gave us all a day off, and then the weather gave us a few more days off. I enjoyed having the time to explore other parts of the island. I walked the beach as far as I could in the opposite direction of The Naze, climbed Terrapin Peak which towered above our camp, and hiked out to Hideaway Lake twice. In the evenings we took turns making dinner and sometimes sang to Foster's guitar. Most nights I collapsed in my tent earlier than the others.

Bad news came the day before the *Gould* was scheduled to pick us up. We learned that twenty miles of pack ice separated us from our ride. The crew reported that they'd made two "very aggressive attempts" to get in to us, but weren't able to make it. A couple of science teams were already on board the *Gould* and they needed to get home. So the ship planned to take them to Frei Station, a Chilean base on King Eduardo George Island, where a chartered plane would pick them up and take them back to South America. After that, if possible, the *Gould* would make another attempt to get us. It remained, for several days, entirely unclear what our fate would be.

Not to worry, the camp manager assured us all, we had enough supplies to get through the winter. And while there was no place for a plane to land on James Ross Island, they could certainly airdrop us more food. Then, too, there were icebreakers belonging to other countries in the vicinity. What was at question was whether the United States would be willing to ask for their help in getting us out of there.

As badly as I had wanted off the ship a few weeks ago, I now wanted *on* it. Those evenings, we sang a lot of Dylan: "The answer my friend, is blowing in the wind." A good long blow from the right direction, and we'd be home free, but that wasn't happening.

Meanwhile, backing and ramming the entire way, the crew of the *Gould* forced the ship through ice it was not made to travel. When I spotted the big orange-and-yellow ship on the horizon, I escaped to my tent to have a hard cry of relief. A few hours later, the rescue zodiac landed on our shore. The crew was eager to tell us about their adventure, but there was no time for chatting. The weather was worsening and the tide was rising, and so the orders were given to simply leave our tents and gear, and report to the beach.

We boarded the zodiac and zipped out to the waiting *Gould*, where I climbed up the ladder onto the lower deck and headed for a hot shower. Warm and dry, with a mug of hot tea, I went up to thank the crew on the bridge. There I learned that it might well be another few weeks before we arrived back in Punta Arenas, Chile, due to miles of pack ice we had to plow through.

In the end, they did break down camp that day, bringing all the gear aboard, and then we set off for the north, once again backing and ramming, moving a mile or two each eight-hour watch. As the ship sliced through the pack ice, the penguins ran and slid on their bellies, getting out of the way. One time, though, they all stopped on the edge of the ice and didn't jump in. A leopard seal slithered up from the water, sending them squawking in the opposite direction.

I sat on the bridge, where the first, second, and third mates all played music on a good sound system as they drove, chatted, and watched the bergs and wildlife. For hours I strained my eyes toward the horizon and saw nothing but more ice. The future days were entirely unknown; even the satellite images presented guesswork. I couldn't quite accept being on this ship for weeks to come, and yet knew that my acceptance or non-acceptance was irrelevant. I tried, from time to time, to think of the swarming krill, which feed on the algae living on the underside of sea ice, just below us. Stories are as unpredictable as journeys, and this one, too, would have to change.

Then, much sooner than expected, a thin blue line appeared on the horizon. Open water. A couple of hours later, we slipped out of the pack ice and into the sloshing blue sea.

Oct. 27, 1915: The ship was hove stern up by the pressure, and the driving floe, moving laterally across the stern, split the rudder and tore out the rudder-post and stern-post. Then, while we watched, the ice loosened and the Endurance *sank a little.... The twisting, grinding floes were working their will at last on the ship. It was a sickening sensation to feel the decks breaking up under one's feet, the great beams bending and then snapping with a noise like heavy gunfire.*

—ERNEST SHACKLETON, *SOUTH*

Holidays on the Ice can be marvelously liberating (forget about food and gifts!) and can also take on a layer of intense loneliness as all traditions and family are far away. Or, as it was for Traci J. MacNamara, it's another day, but this one spent at Happy Camper School, an Antarctic tradition.

For those who travel to the Ice, McMurdo is your likely destination (1,200 people live there in the austral summer, which is about one-sixth of the population of the continent) or at least a stop-over. Traci's essay takes you on a tour of McMurdo, and into Building 155, the hub of Mactown.

As a geographically restless adult, Traci has spent almost twenty months at McMurdo Station; she has also lived in England and France. Before her first nine-month stint in Antarctica in 2003, Traci taught first-year writing at the University of Colorado in Colorado Springs. A freelance writer since 2002, MacNamara's most recent writing has focused on life at McMurdo Station and has appeared in Vegetarian Times, Backpacker, LEO Weekly, Isotope: A Journal of Literary Nature and Science Writing, *and in* A Leaky Tent Is a Piece of Paradise: 20 Young Writers on Finding a Place in the Natural World.

We Ate No Turkey:
A Holiday on Ice

* * *

TRACI J. MACNAMARA

INSTEAD OF SPENDING THANKSGIVING DAY AS I USUALLY
did in Colorado Springs—watching the Macy's parade on
TV in my pajamas—I was shivering in my work clothes on
the McMurdo Ice Shelf, learning how to make a storm-wor-
thy shelter by cutting dense snow into blocks with a paper-
thin saw. Snowcraft, as our mountain-savvy instructor called
it, was only one portion of McMurdo Station, Antarctica's
two-day survival skills course optimistically called Happy
Camper School.

The course, required of all workers and scientists at
McMurdo, started on a Thursday morning in the Field Safety
Training Program conference room, where our instructor
Brian led twelve first-timers to Antarctica through the lecture
portion of the course. Novices, we were. But it was Brian's job
to get us into Extreme Cold Combat Shape in less than forty-
eight hours, and by the end of our tenure on the ice shelf, we
would be firing up stoves and lashing down mountain tents,
all—of course—with great rapidity in order to outsmart the
gale-force winds and popsicle-death scenarios he concocted
in order to keep us moving quickly. When he wasn't in

Antarctica, Brian—tight-bodied and exuding a spirit of adventure—worked as a guide in Alaska, but at McMurdo, he was a member of the highly respected Field Safety Training Program team (F-STOP for short), a group of sexy men and women who spent their lives in rugged environments and then migrated south for the austral summer to teach McMurdo's scientists and support staff how to survive them.

After Brian introduced us to our Happy Camper objectives, he briefed us on cold-weather health hazards, their symptoms, and their remedies. Before lunch, I felt confident knowing the basics of hypothermia and its telltale signs—the fumbles, mumbles, and grumbles.

"Talk to your partners to determine their LOC," Brian said while pointing to a white board scribbled with notes about how cold weather affects a person's level of consciousness, "and help them out before they get into that irreversible phase. If you notice that anything's off, start with some food and water and get them moving around." Besides those suggestions, Brian offered a few other ideas about how to prevent and treat hypothermia while he gestured with his hands and we watched, motionless and mostly bored, from our chairs.

Of hypothermia's remedies, one above the others captured my imagination. F-STOP Brian told us that it is possible to warm up a hypothermic body by stripping it naked and putting it in close proximity to another naked body. "In extreme cases," he clarified, "you can use direct body heat to rewarm a hypothermic individual." Ideally, the second naked body would be warm, and these two naked bodies together would be skin-to-skin within a sleeping bag so that an ailing individual could reap the thermodynamic benefits. A few giggles followed and a few glanced around the room.

In the early afternoon, we piled into the back of a Delta, a bright orange vehicle shaped like an ant but sized like a dinosaur. A few passengers sat up front with Brian in a bench seat in the vehicle's cabin, and in its passenger compartment, we strapped ourselves into rows of seats that lined its boxy sides. Moving forward on the Delta's five-foot-diameter inflatable snow tires, we left McMurdo behind. From the windows in the passenger hold, I could see Observation Hill sliding by as we began our ascent of the dirt road that led out of town. The road cut into the side of Ross Island, and dark mounds of rock rose above us on the left. On our right side, the terrain dropped off sharply and then smoothed out until it touched a frozen inlet of McMurdo Sound. No guardrails lined the road—so as not to impede a plow in the winter—and even though it was wide enough to allow the passage of two vans, I doubted two Deltas could have passed each other safely. In a vehicle that doesn't exceed ten miles per hour on flat, groomed surfaces, we heaved slowly up the incline, where sections of snow and ice interspersed themselves along the road's patchy surface.

I felt nervously excited about going on my first Antarctic road trip, but I hoped that the journey would give me a glimpse of the landscape I hadn't yet experienced from the rocky confines of McMurdo Station. I had arrived at McMurdo less than a week earlier at the tail end of November in order to work a late-summer labor contract as a station General Assistant, and what I had seen in those first few days contrasted with the images I had come to expect. Nearly a year before, Antarctica would have hardly registered in my mind as a place worth going, but when I ran into a friend in Colorado who had worked at McMurdo as a mechanic, he scrolled through photograph after photograph of a place so strikingly beautiful and unlike anything that I had ever seen.

At that time, I was going through a divorce at the age of twenty-seven and living in the dark room of a friend's mom's basement, but during moments of clarity, the images I'd seen of Antarctica continued to replay themselves in my mind. As I imagined the place, a dark mound of land jutted out into a frozen sea, and a soft blanket of snow and ice floated up against it—white and fluffy in the way that clouds appear through the window of a plane. The snow spread itself across an ice shelf in smooth dimples and folds, and I thought that I could find some use for that kind of open space in my life. Frustrations yelled into it would probably echo back beautifully. When I thought about Antarctica, my mind saw an impressive mountain chain stretching across the coast on the opposite side of an ice shelf, an indigo sky framing their jagged peaks. This landscape had drawn me there, but during that first week, I had found McMurdo Station to be surprisingly more crowded and more familiar than the otherworldly place I was hoping for.

My introduction to life at McMurdo began with a town tour, guided by Jim Scott, who was the summer station manager. Friendly and warm-spirited, Jim looked casual in his blue jeans and slate-gray down jacket, and if he hadn't told us that he was the station manager, I would have taken him for just another of McMurdo's contract workers. Another new arrival and I met Jim at one end of a long hallway in Building 155, one of McMurdo's central buildings that housed the dining facility on its lower level and dormitory-style berthing upstairs. We started our tour by walking down the wide corridor that cut through the building from one side to the other. Highway 1, Jim called it, because this hallway in McMurdo's central building was a major thoroughfare. A fine layer of black grit that had been tracked indoors dusted the dun-colored linoleum floors, and the fluorescent lights overhead gave the walkway an artificial white glow. Like a strip mall, Highway 1 was also the location of many conveniences that you would expect to find in any American small town.

The first of these was the barbershop, which offered free haircuts to anyone on station. A clipboard with an appointment sign-up sheet hung on the door, and just past it—a few more paces down Highway 1—we strolled by four large walk-in closets on our left where hundreds of identical red parkas hung in rows during mealtimes, distinguished only by the name printed on a white Velcro tag and slapped on the breast pocket for the season. The McMurdo Station store came next, its door open and four large windows creatively displaying the items that we could purchase inside. Orange and yellow tissue paper created an autumnal scene with travel books and McMurdo Station logo t-shirts propped up in a come-buy-me kind of way.

The station store sold junk food. This, I noted carefully, because I believed that there would come a time when I'd tire of cafeteria food, most of which stayed frozen for up to a year in McMurdo's deep freeze lockers before it showed up on the line. Regular flights in the summer season did sometimes bring in fresh fruit and vegetables, I had been told, but science cargo would take precedence. In the station store, though, other luxury items were waiting. Cadbury's chocolate from New Zealand and Frito's corn chips lined the shelves near the entrance, and farther back against the wall were stacks of canned sodas—including bottles of cream soda and ginger beer. Behind the counter stood a generous supply of liquor, beer, and wine, and a sign that announced: ONE bottle of spirits per day *or* TWO bottles of wine *or* TWO six-packs of beer.

In the other sections of the store, toothpaste and soap—items that I would run out of before returning to the U.S.—stood next to sewing kits and batteries, two things that I had not even considered I might need. Beyond the shelves, a large portion of the store was devoted to souvenir gifts and clothing: Bumper stickers that said "I BREAK FOR PENGUINS!!" and t-shirts with graphics depicting the Antarctic landscape. Wine glasses etched with snowflakes, and martini glasses bearing McMurdo's name. Magnets. Calendars. Pencils and pens. The store's back corner was full of new-release and classic movies available for rental, divided into sections by genre. When we walked out of the store, Jim led us past the station's cluster of twenty-five computers, which offered free internet access and twenty-four hour availability. Before arriving at McMurdo, I signed an agreement saying that I understood my rights as the user of a National Science Foundation federal government computer system. I should have no expectation of privacy while using the Internet, and I could get fired for illegally downloading mp3s—or porn. Then I was given a username and a .gov email address so that I could keep in contact with my family and friends. The McMurdo communications system also enabled us to use calling cards from the telephones in our dorm rooms, and we could phone any location in the world, charged long-distance rates from Brewster, Washington, which was where our calls entered the U.S. Because the number of phone lines was limited, however, incoming calls were not allowed, and during busy times, it could take hours to get a line out. McMurdo is eighteen hours ahead of U.S. Eastern Standard Time and on the other side of the International Date Line, so some math and a bit of good luck were necessary components of those conversations that materialized.

Towards the end of Highway 1—only one hundred paces from its beginning—we came across several administrative offices: human resources, housing, and finance. In between them rested the recreation department. We peered inside and noticed that several young and fit-looking individuals worked there in tightly packed cubicles. A disco ball dangled over their heads in the center of the room while Jim introduced us as new arrivals.

"Well, welcome!" said one of the workers as he jumped from his desk to greet us. "We've got a rec board to help you find things to do in your spare time, and we're always looking for volunteers." He seemed jittery and out of place in an office environment, but another one of the workers sat behind her computer, smiling and tapping away. Before leaving the office, we were directed to the multicolored bulletin board on the wall outside that detailed the week's happenings—sports league events (soccer, volleyball, and basketball), science lectures, and foreign language groups. Lingering for a few minutes in front of the rec board, I noticed that McMurdo also had a band room, a two-lane bowling alley, three bars, and a climbing cave. Jim pointed out the recreation department's gear issue office around the corner. Gear issue was a closet of a room, he said, and that was where we could borrow costumes for station parties and rent skis. When we walked towards a door that opened into the white morning light, I was still imagining what it would be like to wear a tight Elvis jumpsuit while skiing on the ice shelf.

During that first overwhelming week in McMurdo proper, I had started my job as a General Assistant, which required me to show up each day at a labor allocation meeting, where I would be assigned daily tasks such as shoveling snow drifts, or painting shipping containers, or planting bamboo poles in the ice shelf to mark vehicle routes. Some of the lowest paid workers on station, McMurdo's nine GAs seemed to be a scrappy crew of young and healthy workers coming to McMurdo from varied backgrounds, and even though I didn't know quite how I would fit into the team, I felt proud to be a part of it. Other members of the crew were climbers and river guides, musicians, and expert skiers. One had self-published a book. A former university writing instructor, I had experience teaching first-year college students but had never done any type of paid physical labor in my life. Even though I was in good shape, my body ached from the tips of my fingers to the soles of my feet at the end of the first week. I was struggling to remember the names of my coworkers and roommates, and I was still startled with the reality of such a vibrant life at the bottom of the world. For those reasons, the excursion to our Happy Camper School site provided a welcomed release. From the windows of our beefy Delta, I was beginning to see the Antarctica that I had hoped for.

Two miles along a dirt road heading away from McMurdo, we crested the road's highest point and saw Scott Base, the New Zealand Antarctic station, below us at the rocky edge of Ross Island. On the side of the road, a blue sign announcing that we were in Kiwi territory read: "Welcome to SCOTT BASE, Capital of the Ross Dependency. Population: LOTS." The lime-green paint covering Scott Base's largest structure looked out of place on a continent that has no native vegetation, but its design was neat—almost sleek—in a way that McMurdo would probably never be. Although Scott Base was first built around the same time as McMurdo's construction in 1956, only one of its original buildings remained, and a rebuilding project that started in 1976 linked up most of the station's new buildings through a tidy system of corridors. Accommodating around fifty-five scientists and support staff during the summer season and only ten during the winter, Scott Base looked as if it had benefited from forethought in both strategy and design. The station could have fit within a space less than half a football field in length; by comparison, McMurdo's hasty beginnings and its heedlessness to aesthetic principles had made it an unsightly case of suburban sprawl. The Delta slowed considerably, creeping forward in order to descend the road that came within yards of our Kiwi neighbors.

Even though the Scott Base sign that we could see from the Delta's window said in its white letters that Scott Base was the "Capital of the Ross Dependency," the Antarctic Treaty suspended all territorial claims when it became effective, so no country owns Antarctica. But New Zealand, like other countries who made claims before the Treaty became effective, was responsible for the administration of its sector, and if the treaty does not get renewed—or if for some reason it gets revoked—the Kiwis would still hold the claim, which the British government brought into New Zealand's jurisdiction in 1923. The sign, I thought, was indicative of our neighbors' good humor. A black possum with glowing red eyes was perched threateningly on the top left portion of the sign; these annoying non-native creatures now proliferate in New Zealand. Americans outnumber Kiwis in their original territory on Ross Island, twenty to one.

Shortly after passing Scott Base, the Delta jolted through a rocky seam in the road and made its way onto one of the groomed snow roads leading to the late-summer airstrips established on the McMurdo Ice Shelf. Blue flags flapped on bamboo poles that lined the lanes, which had been designated by a sign directing tracked vehicles to stay to the right and wheeled vehicles to merge to the left. By consolidating traffic into lanes based on vehicle type, grooming equipment would have an easier time leveling out the surface when it became too choppy. The bamboo poles had been speared into the snow and were bending with the wind but not breaking.

Just off the edge of Ross Island, we traversed closely along the border of land and ice, the view from the Delta window affording us the best that both scapes had to offer. Of the Ross Island landscape, we could see a wall of rock towering above us on the ice shelf, its top a mushroom of whiteness. Moving further out, we could see that crevasses cut into the surface of the snow, deep wedges looking as if giant-sized hatchets had been tossed into the surface and then removed. An icefall tumbled from Ross Island's side, joining land to frozen sea. In the opposite direction, an icescape stretched out before us, smooth and immense. The bamboo flags marking our lane served as a reference to reality, but when my eyes ran along the road, imagination followed. Black Island and Mount Discovery emerged on the horizon like undiscovered worlds. We could have been in a covered wagon, for all I cared, galloping into the unknown. But we were in a Delta and fast approaching our destination: Snow Mound City.

We tumbled from the Delta and pulled gear from a lone storage container sitting out on the snow, its presence the only marker of Snow Mound City. Our gear included survival bags stuffed with sleeping bags, fleece liners, stoves, fuel, dehydrated dinners, double-thick thermal pads, and tents. F-STOP Brian instructed us to stack all of the survival bags in a huge pile, and then he handed us shovels. Our task was to shovel snow on top of the gear, creating an enormous snow mound and then burrow to its center. Once we pulled out all of the gear, and dug some more, we ended up with a hollowed-out snow shelter called a Quincy. We sweated underneath our layers while piling on the snow and packing it down.

F-STOP Brian managed to do his job with the enthusiasm of a kindergartener who'd had too much sugar for lunch.

When he got out the snow saws for our next lesson, he smiled, corralling us into groups and offering individual instruction on block-building technique. He cut down into the ground's packed surface alongside us and extracted the perfectly chiseled blocks as if they were gold. Surveying the area and then stacking the dense blocks to create a wind barrier around our tents and the Quincy, we established our living quarters for the night. Even though we were all wearing layer upon layer of extreme-cold-weather gear, we became uncomfortably cold as soon as we stopped moving due to sweat chills that followed our overexertion. We were jumping up and down or swaying from side to side trying to warm back up, but Brian only wore a thin yellow wind jacket and an Elmer Fudd-style aviator's hat with flaps that covered his ears. He was casual about the cold, as if his genetic history had at some point crossed lines with a family of seals. I envied him—but then got over it when he retired for the evening to sleep in a heated instructor's hut nearby, leaving us to fend for ourselves with a few mountains of gear and the dehydrated dinners.

We ate no turkey on the evening of the Thanksgiving holiday, but we huddled inside the warm cook tent and slurped down boiling mugs of pasta, whose flavor simulated chicken, broccoli, and cheese. Some ate Black Bart Chili, and their tent mates expressed worry about what that could do to a person in the middle of the night. As I tried to sleep with the evening sun shining through the bright yellow walls of our Scott tent, I nestled in my dry sleeping bag and counted the many things that I had to be thankful for.

Named after polar explorer Robert Falcon Scott, the pyramid-shaped tent I slept in kept me and two others warm inside, even though it lacked a floor. Designed that way so that blizzard conditions would only take the tent and leave its inhabitants behind, the shelter protected us from the elements although its namesake and his companions froze to death on his return from the South Pole in 1912. I was thankful that there wasn't any wind snapping against its sides, and I was thankful that I was at McMurdo and not 850 miles away at the South Pole, where the temperature was probably still at least thirty below instead of the nearly thirty above that it was just outside our tents. With those simple thoughts, I sunk deep into my cocoon and woke in the morning to the high-pitched whistling sounds of a stove that could melt the snow so abundant in our surroundings, even if doing so involved a great effort requiring equal amounts of fuel and patience—all for a measly mug of hot water.

When F-STOP Brian joined us back at Snow Mound City for our second day of training, he rallied us to action. While I had slept comfortably in my Scott tent, those who had cho-sen mountain tents grumbled about the cold, and the others who slept in the Quincy looked as if they had emerged from a sleepover. They were pals, and the experience had made them so. While Brian reviewed the previous day's lessons, we stood exposed in the wind, huddling together in a tight circle until he requested that we re-establish a camp as a team within a fifteen-minute limit—a test of our newly acquired skills. Scurrying about at our stations, we hoisted gear from the bags and tossed down a tent. I volunteered to get the stove going and to bring the water to a full boil (one proviso of the pop quiz), knowing that I could warm my hands on it in the process and then direct the steam across my dry-cracked face.

After a lunch break, we strung out the antenna of a high frequency radio and practiced our radio etiquette, hailing, "South Pole… South Pole… South Pole. This is McMurdo's Happy Campers on frequency 7995. How copy?" And when South Pole replied "Loud and clear, McMurdo Happy Campers," I felt a little giddy over the success of our M.A.S.H.-

style radio. It didn't take too much technology to send off our voices as radio waves beaming through the ionosphere.

Before driving us back to McMurdo, F-STOP Brian had one more survival skill to cover: whiteout navigation. Whiteouts occur frequently in Antarctica because storms bring in blowing snow that can make the white horizon indiscernible from its surroundings. Even though there is little snowfall in the McMurdo area and little snowfall, overall, in Antarctica due to its desert dryness, windstorms scour the ice shelves and toss blizzard quantities of snow and ice into the sky. When it descends, dropping like a ceiling, the resulting swirly mass of whiteness can be so thick that a person could hold out an arm and not be able to see his or her own hand. In a whiteout, a person could get lost on the snow road back to McMurdo. Or fall down and freeze to death in town.

Once Brian had convinced us of the condition's seriousness, he lined us up outside on the ice shelf and roped us together. He handed each of us a white plastic bucket and instructed us to put it over our heads. Then, he led us through a drill that required us to locate a yelping—lost—team member while we had to move as a group with the nasty whiteout-simulating buckets in place. F-STOP Brian had to have been amused watching us knot ourselves into a human pretzel and bump into each other as we stretched out our line and then let it go slack, with the rhythm and ability of a child learning to play the accordion. The activity was not complete without at least a little complaining, and the really annoying thing about complaining with a plastic bucket on your head is that you can only hear the echo of your whiny self. But when we were finished, we had been more thoroughly initiated into our lives in the Antarctic. McMurdo Station—along with its warm showers and cooked dinners and flush toilets—waited just over the hill.

Before leaving for the Antarctic, everyone said that if I wanted to know what life on the Ice was like, to visit the web site bigdeadplace.com. There, I encountered the zany humor ("A Winter-over Appreciates Jello") and intelligent, sharp observations common to Ice people, but with Nicholas Johnson's own unique spin. Nicholas is the editor of the web site as well as the author of a book of the same title, Big Dead Place: Inside the Strange and Menacing World of Antarctica, *which provides a rare glimpse into the world of Antarctic employment.*

The people I met in Antarctica were often restless souls with elaborate, often remarkable "career" paths. Nicholas's biography is one sample. He has worked as a warehouseman in Iraq, a fish-cannery cleaner in the Aleutian Islands, an office manager at a software company, a salesclerk at Banana Republic, a taxi driver in Seattle, an English teacher in South Korea, and as a valet at International House of Pancakes. He has spent five summers and two winters in Antarctica and so should know something about the subject of his essay: going toast.

Toast on Ice:
Wintering in Antarctica

* * *

NICHOLAS JOHNSON

THE SCIENTIST GRABBED SOME PIZZA, SCREAMED AT THE cook that he would fight him, then flipped him off. The scientist had cut in the food line, the cook had told him to get in the back of the line, and the scientist refused. The Galley was crowded with people watching in amusement. It was only a month into winter at South Pole Station.

By the end of the winter, the scientist would be despised, the cook would be fired, the station manager would write someone up for swearing, someone would attempt to sabotage an expensive science experiment, the ice cream machine would become an object of political controversy, there would be scandalous hook-ups, a few shoving matches, some projectiles thrown, and a great deal of graffiti. One of the station's worst drunks would fall asleep outside and be rescued by his crewmates from certain death. A female scientist would stalk her plumber boyfriend after they broke up. Someone would creep into a woman's room, pull her bras from her drawer, and spread them out on her bed. Men became excited at the prospect of pushing this culprit down the stairs, eager for a bit of justified violence in deepest winter.

In Antarctica, everyone goes toast eventually. It's not a matter of *if*, it's a matter of *when* and *how*.

It happens like this: you've followed your personal familiar tendencies from Step A to Step B to Step C, maintaining your familiar psychology all the while, comfortable in your own skin, until that moment when you arrive at a Step Z, that is not quite unfamiliar, but which seems a bit strange. "How did I get here?" you ask. "How is it that Step Y was so usual, but Step Z so unusual?"

That is how you go toast.

At the beginning of winter, the façades tighten, people tend to buckle down and swab their personal decks. A helping hand is easy to find. Everyone is friendly and hopeful marching into the darkness, showing their best. But fast-forward to black August, and the story has changed. Things are starting to slip. The smiles are breaking down. Some are tired and try to get others to do their work for them, others beef up their resistance to these ploys. Lines have been drawn. Helping hands are not always plentiful, and the skirmishes multiply.

Those who crack the hardest are those who believe that they will never crack and thus construct rigid dams to contain their oozing neuroses. These are often people who haven't traveled, or have never taken drugs. They're not accustomed to having their identity shatter to pieces in a moment, having to rebuild from scratch. For them, going toast is a solemn affair. As their inner world slips, they react by trying to control the outer world. They become the hall monitor. They ratchet down on niggling policies and ordinances, holding aloft the rulebook that serves as a powerful exoskeleton to cover up the eroding facade beneath that is visible to everyone in such close quarters. Like Salemites at a witch burning, they are also the first to accuse others of going toast, thus transferring attention from their increasingly rigid and hostile metamorphosis.

Those who fare the best are those who treat their own winter psychology like a foreign culture. It may be familiar in many respects, but at some point it will surprise you, and you demand absolute control over it at your peril.

Antarcticans recognize two places: Antarctica, and everywhere else. In daily conversation, Antarctica is where you are now, and everywhere else is called "the real world." The real world is where you can shop at whichever strip mall you want, vote for either Democrats or Republicans, eat at McDonald's or shop at the local co-op, and choose from an infinite number of bumper stickers for your Chevy or your Volvo to broadcast your real self. Antarctica, with government housing and a crew of temporary contractors, is merely a temporary detour for its inhabitants. Antarctica is a dream state, and our actions there commonly regarded as not quite real.

Life in Antarctica is backwards and perverse. To live there for any length of time is to live in a fairyland. Rather than commuting three hours a day in thick traffic, you've been walking to work in three minutes. Rather than following the latest news of a political campaign that is supposedly vital to your interest, you live and breathe with the local managers. Rather than eating whatever you want, you eat whatever's available. Rather than being entertained, you entertain yourself. Rather than writing off strangers, you must come to grips with each other. Rather than abandoning a job at the first sign of adversity, you have a duty because there are simply no unemployed workers to cover your slack.

When those in the real world consider an Antarctic winter, their wonder is usually focused on how one works outside in -100°F temps, or how one copes with six months of darkness. The answer is that dealing with the cold essentially involves learning how to dress well and to suck it up. Those who complain are weak, those who don't are strong. You may permanently lose some sensation in your ears, nose, or fingers, but unlike the explorers of old, or the skiers who cross the continent for sport, winter-overs always have a warm building nearby to circumvent death.

But, unlike the certainty of the cold and the darkness, dealing with a bunch of people locked up together is a shifting game with no hard rules. There is an infinite variety of unique pathologies. If you then adapt to the common madness, how did you do so? Did you remove yourself from contact with the rest of the crew? Did you cease participating? Did you act crazy to keep others away from you? Did you wear sunglasses every day so no one could see your eyes? Did you put on the polite face? Did you accept others' behavior because it was the path of least resistance? Did you look to the rulebook for easy answers? In short, what madness did you use to combat madness?

By the end of my first winter I was so distrustful of local managers that I was tape recording every interaction with them. These recordings later proved useful in showcasing some ridiculous lies and hilarious doublespeak, but at what cost? A friend of mine, arriving on the August Winfly flight to McMurdo, described this: "You ran up to me in the hall. I hadn't seen you in a year. You had translucent skin and weird-looking eyes and you shoved a tape recorder in my hand and told me to record our orientation meeting." In mirroring the obsessive documentation tactics of the company, I'd become as obsessive as the company. In other words, I'd gone toast.

My next winter, at South Pole, I had learned from this, and barely went toast at all. I simply reported the local shenanigans on the internet, then detached myself and put such events behind me, then listened to Sade's "Lover's Rock" five or six times consecutively. I had always hated Sade until that winter. Odd.

By far the most common method for dealing with an Antarctic winter is a retreat into solitude. A month into my first winter, one of my good friends disappeared from all social activity for about six weeks, then reemerged as a model of stability for the rest of the winter. At the end of that winter, I was shocked to suddenly see someone I had never seen before. Imagine living on a couple dozen acres for six months with no possibility of traffic in or out, and at the end of that time seeing someone you'd never seen before. He was very serious about his solitude, and the effect was like seeing a Martian.

Sometimes the push toward solitude is undesirable. The station manager that winter once received a birthday card from a community member explaining that he was hated by half the station and to please have a really bad birthday. Thereafter the station manager arrived at lunch the minute the food was ready, then took his food away before the galley filled with people.

Often the toastiness is merely amusing, like the time the Pole station manager came into the galley, saw a large chunk of meat thawing in the kitchen, and put it back in the freezer. The cook, who had intentionally left the meat out to thaw, and had experienced other difficulties with the station manager, couldn't handle this small but symbolic attack on his professional territory. For that evening's dinner, he served three flavors of Ramen.

After your winter, you feel slightly out of place, as if you've returned to real society after living in the bush with a tribe of cannibals. Outwardly you may have pasty skin, too much hair, and may be wearing clothes from the skua pile. Inwardly you've gone on a long journey and have discovered new capabilities and deficiencies in yourself. Being back in the real world feels a little strange.

After my first winter, I had returned to New Zealand and was at the Christchurch Antarctic Centre, a tourist exhibit, to take some photos. I was sitting on a bench with my backpack, waiting for the availability and attention of a clerk. I sensed my wait would be longer than anticipated, so took the opportunity to use the bathroom. When I returned there were two agitated clerks by the bench, one of them speaking into a walkie-talkie.

"Is this your backpack?" one of them said.

"Yes, I was using the toilet."

"You cannot leave this here," he barked at me. "No one knows what's in it, it could be a bomb."

"Uh…"

"After what happened in New York, you simply can't do that."

"Yes, sir."

He marched off.

I knew then I was back in the "real" world which, by definition, never goes toast.

We dwelt on the fringe of an unspanned continent, where the chill breath of a vast, polar wilderness, quickening to the rushing might of eternal blizzard, surged to the northern seas. We had discovered an accursed country.

—DOUGLAS MAWSON, *HOME OF THE BLIZZARD*

David Ainley's essay seems to diverge from the personal accounts in this collection as he meditates on the fate of his penguins and in that meditation comes to conclusions about a subject that concerns us all: global warming. It is in the Antarctic that the effects of global warming are most evident, and most devastating. For David, sitting on the stoop of a RacTent at Cape Royds, thinking about penguins is personal, it's what he does, and what he has done since 1968 when he first traveled to Antarctica as a Johns Hopkins University graduate student fresh out of Dickinson College. He has since returned to the ice twenty-six times working primarily in the Ross Sea area, including Cape Royds, Cape Bird, and Cape Crozier, where the Adélie penguins nest year after year. He has authored or co-authored five books, including Adélie Penguin: Bellwether of Climate Change, which I read while waiting out a storm in a RacTent with David and his assistant Jen Blum at Cape Royds.

When not in Antarctica David works as an Ecological Associate at H. T. Harvey & Associates, an ecological consulting firm in San Jose, California. His research focuses on the effects of climate change and fishery depletion on marine food webs. He is increasing efforts to launch some multimedia campaigns to increase public awareness of the growing take of long-lived fish and minke whales from the Ross Sea, heretofore the last still-intact major marine ecosystem remaining on the planet.

Ainley Peak, rising to 1,240 meters on Ross Island, is named for David.

A Letter from Cape Royds: Of Penguins and Men

* * *

DAVID AINLEY

I'M SITTING ON MY DOORSTEP—A CARGO PALLET SECURED by a cargo strap to a RacTent erected on a bed of volcanic cinders at Cape Royds, Ross Island, Antarctica, the farthest south a ship can travel on Earth—and I'm gazing at a U.S. Coast Guard icebreaker, fifteen kilometers out in McMurdo Sound, the backdrop of which is the Royal Society Range, the eastern margin of the Antarctic continent itself. It is the first of January 2003 and, what has become not so unusual in recent years, the air temperature has risen to 40°F. Thus, I'm sitting in my shirtsleeves in the still air. The ship slowly makes its way through two- to five-meter thick ice to open a forty-five kilometer-long channel. Normally, a channel of twenty kilometers or less has been required, but this year there is more ice. Without the channel, ships would not be able to re-supply McMurdo Station, located at the eventual southern end of the channel; without those supplies much of the U.S. Antarctic Program (USAP), which is dependent upon the McMurdo logistics hub, in a year or two's time, would wither and die.

I hold a two-panel photo of the Adélie penguin colony at Cape Royds, one panel taken in early January 1909 by men of Ernest Shackleton's 1907-09 British Antarctic Expedition and the other taken in early December fifty years later by Rowland Taylor of the New Zealand Antarctic Program (NZAP). Comparing these photos I'm trying to resolve what may be going on with this penguin colony. In his 1959 photo, Taylor framed the same plot of land captured on film in 1909. The earlier photo shows several hundred Adélie penguins, all on their breeding territories, but in the 1959 photo I count only sixty-three occupied territories, no doubt including the same depressions in the guano used by penguins in 1909. On the same date as Taylor, but forty-three years later still (a few weeks ago), I had taken the same photo and they look eerily similar. That is to say, not many penguins were present. In fact, in December 2002 there were fewer than thirty occupied territories. Why is this so?

The question relates to the conditions that led to the larger number of penguins in 1909 compared to either 1959 or 2002. Part of the problem in my mind is that by two summers ago, after twenty years of more or less continual annual growth, the Cape Royds colony had increased by 160 percent from its 1959 level. In other words, the population likely had surpassed the size attained in 1909. I was ready to implicate global warming—and in turn the penguins' increased access to the sea (their food source) as a result of dissipating sea ice. I had labored months on a proposal to the National Science Foundation (NSF) to fund a project to resolve that issue, and after having it approved here I now sat with just the opposite scenario before me: the potential disappearance of the Cape Royds colony in contrast to other colonies we are studying (capes Bird and Crozier). All summer long, a related, more practical question had been before me: How might my colleagues and I salvage this project?

To be honest, since hordes of prospective penguins have failed to show and others that had valiantly made the thirty-kilometer trek were disappearing to locations closer to open water, I've worked to stave off boredom by reading more than a few books. One of them was the delightful collection of essays by Richard Feynman, *The Pleasure of Finding Things Out*. In this book, Feynman, one of the greatest physicists of our time but also a person having the storytelling knack, had marveled at the incredible amount of information that is stored in a single living cell and had predicted that someday humans, too, would duplicate the feat, i.e. store a huge amount of information in an infinitesimally small space. All that was needed was to understand better how cell nuclei organized their DNA atoms and that would lead to advances in microtechnology. This would be accomplished, he said, through the creative, careful experiments that mark the physical sciences. However, at this moment, my thought was that understanding all the physical laws that govern the behavior of cells was not going to resolve the problem lying before those collections of cells coalesced into the forms of Adélie penguins who were struggling before me. I could see that physical forces were at play, but whether or not the colony survived, other than the possibility that the icebreaker might cause the sea ice to go away, depended on whether all those Adélie penguin cells would cope with the chaos that had been injected into their lives.

Actually, the problem is a bit more complex than what a comparison of these three photos of breeding penguins may imply. As I contemplate all this, the icebreaker is backing-and-ramming, trying to punch its way through the fast ice, the term for sea ice held in place within Antarctica's bays and sounds by the land's contours and grounded icebergs. Such a movement by the ship is what is needed to advance through sea ice so thick that it forces the ship's massive, powerful bulk (40,000 horsepower!) to a stop every few ship-lengths of travel. I sympathized with the sailors on board who were experiencing nothing of the supposed romance involved in sailing restless seas, as even at this distance I could hear a dull grinding roar emanating from their ice-pulverizing effort. Somewhat ironically at least as far as this story goes, and likely unbeknownst to those sailors, the ship was passing along a stretch of the Victoria Land coast once occupied in several places by Adélie penguin colonies over 3,000 years ago. Since that time, the annual presence of the very same fast ice through which the ship was now cutting had led to the demise of those colonies, much as the ice now seems to be accomplishing at Cape Royds. Just a few kilometers south of Cape Royds, at Cape Barne, as noted by persons of Robert Scott's 1901-04 Antarctic Expedition, another site had similarly once been occupied. Now just the bowls of stones, from which the penguins constructed their nests, are all that remain.

A few thousand years ago temperatures were generally about as warm as they have become now. We know this from cores of ice extracted from the polar ice cap. With the warmer temperatures, the fast ice no doubt had become considerably loosened, as it had until recently. In other words, during the period when the Pharaohs were constructing the great pyramids in Egypt, Adélie penguins were constructing their own rock edifices along the southern Victoria Land and Ross Island coasts, something which they had not done before and, like the Pharaohs, have not done since. During that period,

3,000 to 5,000 years ago, rather than as now having to trek laboriously at one to two km/hr over multiple kilometers of upheaved ice—this sea ice is not like what one finds in a skating rink—and on legs only a few centimeters long, the penguins were able to swim easily (8-9 km/hr) to and from their colonies in search of their food. In the short polar summer, that saving of time and energy means the difference between breeding or not, and whether or not a colony might be founded or, once founded, whether or not it survives. With the easier travel in those ancient times, the colonies were possible.

Recently, scientists have been dating the bones of penguins found at current as well as extinct colony sites on Ross Island and along the Victoria Land coast, among other things, to track the retreat of the West Antarctic Ice Sheet. The ice sheet reached maximum extent (the Last Glacial Maximum or LGM) about 19,000 years ago, but somewhat before and after, 24,000 to 12,000 years ago, few places on the continent were free of glacial ice. Once the retreat was underway, however, more and more of the coast became accessible. During a short period, temperatures were even warmer (as now). Geologists have termed that very warm, great age of the Pharaohs, 3,000 to 5,000 years ago and well after the ice sheet had begun to retreat, as The Penguin Optimum. Their reasoning has been, and rightly so, that if the ice sheet had retreated to leave gravel capes, which were also lapped upon by ocean waves, then the penguins would soon find them and form colonies. Until last year, given the recent retreat of sea ice along the southern Victoria Land coast (McMurdo Sound), the growth of the Royds and other colonies, and the founding of additional colonies nearby, including re-use of the Cape Barne site, I was thinking we once again were in a Penguin Optimum. In fact, during the past twenty-five years it has been getting very warm here at Cape Royds, especially during winter and early spring. Hence, wearing just a shirt has become not all that unusual in this neighborhood during the summer.

Cape Royds, at 77° 34'S, is presently the southernmost of all Adélie penguin colonies, of which there are about 160 distributed around Antarctica. The penguins breed here, as elsewhere, because, until recently, open water appears by midspring adjacent to its gently sloping land. At most, less than 5 percent of the Antarctic coast is ice free and, further, even less of it is also gently sloping. Having requirements similar to the needs of the penguin—southern location, open water, and gently sloping land—humans have visited and lived in this place, Cape Royds and vicinity, over a longer period than anywhere in Antarctica. Ships could be off loaded, huts could be built, and the golden grail of Antarctic exploration, the South Pole, was as close as it possibly could be to such a logistics base. Thus, in the early twentieth century, several expeditions launched forth from this area. McMurdo Station, continuously under construction since the International Geophysical Year in the late 1950s and twenty kilometers farther south than Cape Royds, had continued that tradition. McMurdo is built where Scott constructed his quarters for his 1901–04 expedition, but as he discovered upon returning in 1911, and what Adélie penguins had already "known," sea ice often blocks water access to the site. Therefore, penguins avoid that spot. On his second trip, Scott was forced to build a hut at Cape Evans, near capes Barne and Royds, where the presence of open water is far more reliable, a fact also known by the penguins. To overcome such vagaries of sea ice, as we have noted, the USAP and NZAP now depend on a powerful icebreaker to chop through the ice.

In 1907-09, Shackleton, dissuaded from use of Scott's facilities at Winter Quarters Bay (McMurdo site), built his base at Cape Royds, within a stone's throw of the penguin colony. In fact, with only slight telephoto magnification, the photo I spoke of earlier could have been made from the hut's doorstep. Cape Royds, however, was not the perfect location for polar exploration owing to the very reason why the penguins find it, or found it, such a great place to nest. The one disadvantage of Cape Royds for human explorers, who sought the easiest routes to the continent's interior, was that one had to patiently wait for the sea to freeze sufficiently each autumn before heavy sledges could then be safely man-hauled from Ross Island across the ice to reach continental shores. Winter Quarters Bay, on the other hand, was immediately adjacent to the Ross Ice Shelf (a portion of the West Antarctic Ice Sheet), across which the continent lay beckoning without need for any sea-ice excursions.

Regardless, an indirect result of the logistics hub built by Shackleton at Cape Royds was the first formal study on the biology of the Adélie penguin. Until then, the penguin had been known to science only as inanimate carcasses (museum specimens). This first description of its biology, "The Love Habits of the Adélie Penguin," was accomplished by James Murray, and was appended to Shackleton's book, *The Heart of the Antarctic, the Farthest South Expedition*. Mostly it is a purely anthropomorphic interpretation of how this bird occupies its time when at the breeding colony. Other accounts of this penguin's natural history written in the same vane were published in the few decades that followed, leading L. Harrison Matthews, a prominent polar ecologist of recent times, to describe this literature as a "mass of anthropogenic nonsense" in his book *Penguins, Whalers and Sealers: A Voyage of Discovery.*

Nevertheless, at a time when Albert Einstein was formulating his theory of relativity and the secrets of atomic structure were being investigated at scientific laboratories in the civilized world, this was a small start toward understanding the ecology of one of the quintessential south polar creatures. Until this point, all that had been written about Adélie penguins concerned how they could help humans to survive polar mishaps, nourish their sled dogs or otherwise make way in a hostile environment. In his diary, kept while de Gerlache's ship *Belgica* was entrapped by sea ice from March 1898 to March 1899, Roald Amundsen, that polar explorer extraordinaire, recorded the capture and eating of 63 emperor and 134 Adélie penguins. To him these birds were victual delights. Amundsen preferred the meat of the smaller Adélie over that of the emperor and when he felt the approach of some sort of illness, it was not vitamin C pills that he popped, but rather raw penguin flesh. In fact, he remained in better health than anyone else on the expedition. During one skiing trip that took several days, he and his two companions threw out the canned soup and instead dined on a concoction of cocoa, apricots, and penguin meat chunks. Later, ever keen to learn how to survive, he extolled the value of using rolled and layered penguin skins to soften the scraping of the vessel's planks by sea ice when it loosened just before the ship was released. Nowadays, inflated rubber "fenders" are used for this purpose.

Further examples of this sort of growing, "practical" knowledge about polar penguins are evident among the journals of various other south polar explorers usually, but not always, upon finding themselves in dire straits. The ultimate use, all in the name of science, was described by Wilhelm Filchner, leader of the Second German South Polar Expedition to the Weddell Sea in 1911-12. In order to save coal, 120 kilos of which was needed to drive the winch for a single deep hydrographic cast, the ship's boilers had been adapted to burn seal blubber and penguins, the latter of which were thrown whole into the flames just after killing. It was not until the time that physicists and engineers had split the atom and had launched by rocket a tiny sphere to orbit the Earth that the first detailed, factual knowledge of the natural history of the Adélie penguin was published. In 1958, William Sladen, a medical officer of the Falkland Islands Dependencies Survey (now known as the British Antarctic Survey), published his observations of Adélie penguins garnered while over-wintering on Signy Island in the South Orkneys. As members of his party fed penguins to their sled dogs, a necessity brought on by a fire that destroyed much of their stores soon after the ship had left, Sladen was tuned in enough that he took notes about the sex, physical condition, and maturity of the victims. He was actually more aware than that; for the first time he marked penguins (using numbered metal bands around their ankles and, later, their wings), so that he could tell individuals apart, even one summer to the next. Accordingly, he dispelled many of the myths about penguin colony life that had grown since Murray's time. Shortly thereafter, in 1962, Rowland Taylor, on the basis of his stay (in Shackleton's hut) at Cape Royds, October 1959 to February 1960, published his now classic, and still the most detailed description yet, of this species' basic nesting ecology, building on Sladen's ground-breaking work and use of marked birds and nests. It was photos taken by Taylor that were now in my hands.

Yes, that was the beginning of a new age in south polar biological and marine science: methodical observation finally had become the standard. A decade after Taylor's study, a decline in the penguin breeding population at Cape Royds, thought then to be the result of disturbance by too many visitors from McMurdo Station and nearby Scott Base (hub of NZAP), led to the Cape Royds colony being declared a "Site of Special Scientific Investigation" under the Antarctic Treaty. People can still come to see the penguins as well as Shackleton's hut but they can only view the penguins from an appropriate distance as identified by a series of small, orange signs. Penguins are now protected entirely from human interference.

While the declining Cape Royds penguin colony led to one of the first specially protected areas in the Antarctic, increased visits by people did not completely explain the colony's declining population trajectory. We've since learned that other colonies around Ross Island, including ones not visited much by people, were also declining then. Before the age when orbiting satellites were used to sense the extent and thickness of sea ice, it appeared that the sea ice during the 1950s and 1960s, if not earlier, did not loosen as early as it has subsequently, and it took longer for icebreakers to chop their way through to McMurdo Station. Beginning in the mid- to late 1970s, with warming temperatures as recorded at Scott Base, the sea ice began to loosen sooner in the spring and McMurdo Sound colonies began to grow. Here and elsewhere on the coasts of the Ross Sea, where 40 percent of the world's Adélie penguin population breeds, all the smaller colonies have been growing—or have been at least until recently. Thus, the phenomenon was not a local one. In fact, except for the west coast of the Antarctic Peninsula, Adélie penguin colonies all around Antarctica have been growing as well.

Along the west coast of the Antarctic Peninsula, which juts far to the north and is bathed by South Pacific waters (14 latitude degrees farther north than Ross Island), Adélie penguin colonies have been disappearing over the past twenty-five years. This pattern, which has received much press, is a response to the recent warming that in turn has led to the complete disappearance of sea ice along those shores. The warming there is far more dramatic than anywhere else in the south polar region. Assuming I may have confused you a bit here: yes, for an Adélie penguin there can be too little as well as too much sea ice to suit its interests. In general, sea ice to Adélie penguins is what forests are to song birds: you remove the habitat and the birds disappear, you grow the trees too thickly and the birds occur at the forest edges. Actually, the Adélie had colonized the northern stretch of the Peninsula coast only with the arrival, with colder temperatures, of what climatologists call "The Little Ice Age." Such a pattern has been revealed by Steve Emslie, an ecologist who has been dating penguin bones found in both living and extinct penguin colonies. The Little Ice Age is the cold period that began around the year 1200 A.D. and that led the Norsemen to abandon their settlements in Greenland, the Mayans to abandon the northern Yucatán, and the Anasazi from abandoning their cliffside pueblos in now arid North America. Apparently, the colder temperatures of the Little Ice Age also brought more persistent sea ice along the Antarctic Peninsula coast and the Adélie penguin followed, its colonies spreading northward. Today, as the region warms, the ice-loving Adélie is being replaced along the Antarctic Peninsula coast by other penguin species that cannot cope with sea ice. Evidence from ice cores extracted recently from the Greenland and the Antarctic ice caps, investigations also funded by NSF, indicate that in most ways, we should be still living in the Little Ice Age. The only difference is the warming air and ocean temperatures now underway and for which we seem to be responsible.

So, here we have the Adélie penguin, increasing everywhere in Antarctica, except along the northwest coast of the Antarctic Peninsula and more recently except at Cape Royds. In other words, global warming has been (at least temporarily) a boon to this species. I have to give great credit to NSF and the New Zealand Foundation for Research, Science, and Technology, which funds my Kiwi colleagues in this endeavor, for supporting research on a member of the charismatic megafauna that has been increasing spectacularly. Usually it requires catastrophe to catch the interest of the agencies that fund ecological research. Thus, with funds and logistical support, we had set out to determine what was allowing Adélie penguins to increase and found new colonies or recolonize sites long abandoned, such as Cape Barne. To do this, among other things, we have been banding cohorts of chicks for the past eight years at each of four colonies somewhat isolated from the others to the north in the Ross Sea. The colony at Cape Royds had been growing much faster, at about 7 percent per year, than the huge colony at Cape Crozier, which recently had hardly been growing at all. Cape Crozier is one of only six Adélie penguin colonies that exceed 100,000 breeding pairs and seemingly, therefore, one would think that penguindom should be faring well there. We had found from our banding that the growth at Cape Royds was in part due to the emigration of the offspring from parents at capes Bird and Crozier and nearby Beaufort Island. This pattern indicated a relaxation of what is known as natal philopatry, or the tendency of offspring to return to their place of birth. A banding study carried out by Sladen's group at Cape Crozier during the 1960s and early 1970s, during that time when the Ross Island colonies were declining, had identified a highly developed sense of philopatry in this species. That was then, however, and this is now. Little Cape Royds and environs, until very recently, had become the place to be, and recruits apparently can be attracted to new terrain more easily than we had been led to believe. Perhaps Cape Crozier and other colonies had become overcrowded and the loosening sea ice had made life at Royds more possible. These were subjects we had set out to investigate.

All this brings us back to the present, to me sitting in my shirt sleeves at Cape Royds, watching the ice breaker go slowly by, thinking about the slow disappearance of the Cape Royds colony, and wondering what to do with this project that had been designed to investigate the whys and wherefores of population expansion. What, indeed, has been going on? Well, the one item in this scenario that I have yet to reveal has been the arrival in this neighborhood, two years ago January, of a huge iceberg that is about ninety-seven nautical miles long and thirty nm wide or roughly the size of Delaware. An iceberg this size had never before been seen by humans. It had broken from the Ross Ice Shelf, as has happened repeatedly from the West Antarctic Ice Sheet while retreating since the end of the last Ice Age. Icebergs this size, I am told by glaciologist Doug MacAyael, may have been produced about twenty times per each 1,000 years since the retreat got underway in earnest (about 12,000 years ago). This particular berg came to rest with one end against Ross Island and the other against Franklin Island some ninety miles away to the north. The iceberg, called B15A by glaciologists (the A-half of the fifteenth sizeable iceberg to be formed within the B quadrant of the continent during 2001), has positioned itself directly across the route taken by Adélie penguins when they migrate between wintering areas and Ross Island breeding colonies in spring and autumn. That is, the iceberg now lies across the route for all these penguins except those from the Cape Crozier colony. Cape Crozier and the wintering area lay to its east; the other colonies are to its west. These penguins first begin to respond to their philopatric tendencies at about two to three years of age; before then they remain at sea among the ice floes. During its spring migration, traveling southwest from the northeastern Ross Sea to Cape Royds, when a pre-breeding two- or three-year-old encounters this wall of ice, it would have to choose between turning left (south) or right (north). A choice to the left would take it to Cape Crozier, while a choice to the right, counter intuitive to whatever is in the bird's mind, would take it on a journey away from its in-tended route before it could round the berg to continue the southwesterly journey to McMurdo Sound (and Cape Royds). Besides this obstruction of migration, the presence of the iceberg also has prevented the sea ice from blowing clear of McMurdo Sound. Therefore, once the penguin got around the berg, it would then have to stop swimming and walk thirty kilometers or more to find Cape Royds. As I've noted earlier, penguins don't like to walk long distances.

My colleagues at these other colonies, like myself at Royds, are reading the numbers imprinted on every band at-tached to a penguin. What we have found is that while Cape Crozier and other colonies have continued to grow in size, Cape Royds has become an undesirable location for young Adélie penguins in search not just of their colony of birth but also a colony where the production of young is possible. In the last two years, we've found very few penguins younger than six years at Royds (age of first breeding is three to five years), but many individuals of those age classes are showing up at the other colonies, including many that were born (and banded) at Cape Royds!

What we have here, friends, is what is known as a "natural experiment." In no way could we ever have orchestrated such a scenario, and by good fortune we have been tagging cohorts of young penguins at our four study colonies hereabouts for the past eight years. In order to understand what we see happening now, in the heroic days of Antarctic exploration, ecologists would have walled off a colony to note the response of its occupants, or even to harvest all the occupants to see how much time and by whom the locality would be recolonized. In this day, when the wink of a penguin eye can send a tourist to cover, we would not even think of doing such an experiment even though experimentation is what has driven the progress exhibited in other fields of science, as so well described by Richard Feynman. Experiments in much of ecology, however, owing to the costs and logistics involved are rarely done, except at very small scales. Experiments are especially unforgiven when they involve what is called the charismatic megafauna—penguins, seals, and whales, etc. For sure, such data could have been collected on other species in the real world, but wasn't (owing to expense), each time a dam was built to block the migration of salmon, a clear-cut destroyed the habitat of forest birds, or a fishery depleted the top predators from a marine system.

What this natural experiment is showing is that the Adélie penguin's behavior is far more pliable than we had believed. Only the birds older than five years, and who have bred before, are bothering to return to Royds to attempt breeding. For them, what worked before should work now, although the fact that it isn't does not dissuade them from at least trying. So, not only is the current Royds population not producing additional offspring (the long treks are just too much), but the young adults produced in pre-berg years are going elsewhere. Cape Royds is disappearing, while the other colonies are not. A high degree of philopatry is seen only in the best of times. Even though icebergs have been calving, circling and running aground along the Antarctic coastline for at least as long as Adélie penguins have existed as a species, we are only now seeing what is an important part of this species' "ecological strategy." In other words, with this experiment, only now can we appreciate that this species can adapt to dramatic, natural changes in its environment.

Without the B15A iceberg, the waxing and waning of penguin colonies, as a response to conditions brought by the retreat of the West Antarctic Ice Sheet, or by the Little Ice Age or Medieval Warm Period, would have remained forever mere abstractions. The patterns would be there, told in the bones lying for thousands of years in the permafrost, but the context would have remained unknown. Now it has all come alive, however excruciatingly slowly it seems to be evolving, i.e. just a few failed nests at a time, as viewed from this particular doorstep at Cape Royds. I'm content, at least, knowing that my colleagues are almost frenzied in their attempts to keep up with all the penguin activity at the open-water colonies.

Of course, now to think of it, unintentionally we may have been running an experiment underway since the days when Rowly Taylor began the first modern investigations of Adélie penguins here at Cape Royds. During all that time, icebreakers every summer have been loosening the McMurdo Sound fast ice at about the time that Royds penguins need to feed their chicks. After the ship makes its cut through the fast ice, thus releasing the ice pressure, huge floes usually break away leaving Cape Royds ice free if it had not been freed already. Perhaps, in response to the colder temperatures of the Little Ice Age and the more persistent fast ice that followed, this colony for a long time had been slowly marching to oblivion, thus explaining its decline during the 1950s and 1960s. A recent analysis by Steve Emslie showed that the now-extinct colony at nearby Cape Barne was much larger in the days of the pharoahs than even Royds is now. I can see the cartoon in *The New Yorker*, a magazine famous for its penguin depictions: penguins standing on the icebound shores of Cape Royds, with their suitcases, waving to the approaching icebreaker, much as the human residents of McMurdo Station will soon be doing. One penguin says to the other, "What do you suppose we do, should they run out of gas?"

Christopher Cokinos takes us on a journey into the interior of Antarctica looking for meteorites, describing both the science of meteorites and the mystery of his inner landscape.

Chris is the author of Hope Is the Thing with Feathers: A Personal Chronicle of Vanished Birds, which won the Sigurd Olson Nature Writing Award. He's also a winner of a Whiting Award and the Glasgow Prize for an Emerging Writer in Nonfiction. His forthcoming book is titled The Fallen Sky: A Private History of Shooting Stars for which he has traveled not only to Antarctica but also 600 miles north of the Arctic Circle in Greenland in an open boat, the Outback in Australia, as well as towns, meteorite craters, and strewnfields in Europe and the U.S. His poems, essays and reviews have appeared in such venues as Ecotone, Orion, turnrow, Science and Birder's World. The founding editor of Isotope: A Journal of Literary Nature and Science Writing at Utah State University, Chris holds appointments in both English and Natural Resources.

He says that despite the experience at the center of this essay, he is keen on returning to Antarctica someday and confesses that of all the places he's traveled, Antarctica is the one that appears most often in his dreams, including the long-lost site of Shackleton's Italian villa somewhere on the coast...

Massif:
Notes from an Unmaking

* * *

CHRISTOPHER COKINOS

I AM SITTING IN A TENT THE COLOR OF PISS.

I am sitting in a tent the shape of a pyramid, no, of a rocket nose-cone.

I might as well be drowning. Encased in rock. On another planet.

I am at the Otway Massif, in the middle of Antarctica, with three other human beings.

The Otway Massif: an island of mountains riven with glaciers, two of which, nameless, flow down to the far end of the pale blue ice on whose near-firn we camp. We are a mile-and-a-half from the massif. Our two tents face one end of the Otway, where dark mountains and ridge line curve like a wind-snapped cape, like a bird's wing, or, I would later think, like an arm about to embrace or strike.

The day we arrived shredded cumulus crossed a blue sky, throwing black on the brown dolorite, animating the otherwise lifeless edifice. Sequences of sandstone and volcanic lahars stain the massif—giant tan patches that I wistfully thought could be some heretofore unknown, prodigious Antarctic lichen. Rising some 3,000 feet from the ice to more than 10,000 feet, with its eroded sides and wrinkled peaks and occasional columns (one stands alone like a finger pointing to escape), the Otway is the most sublime place I have ever seen.

But I am in the tent now, again, uncertain in the yellow light.

My tentmate Johnny Schutt asks, "Flu?"

I've just told him I'm not doing well.

"No," I say. "Depression."

Nearly five weeks before, I sat in another tent, at the LaPaz Icefields, with Ralph Harvey, the chief scientist of ANSMET, the Antarctic Search for Meteorites. We were laughing so hard, my eyes teared up.

Ralph, in an excellent imitation of Smithers: "Sir, my legs are on fire."

Me, doing my best Mr. Burns: "Well, Smithers, can't you pull yourself about by the arms?"

How did an English professor from Utah end up sitting in a tent in Antarctica, recounting the day's meteorite finds and doing impersonations from the television show *The Simpsons*? The easy answer is: I'm writing a book about meteorites—more precisely, about meteorite hunters in history, about their quests—so I asked to go along to what Antarctic veterans call, simply, "the Ice." And I like *The Simpsons.*

Frankly, I was relieved that a person I knew I'd be proving myself to during our camp at LaPaz was someone who could appreciate some manic silliness. It was a good sign that Ralph liked the show enough to indulge in such exchanges, further confirmation of the good feeling I got when I first talked with Ralph about going to Antarctica. After all, he very easily could have turned down a writer he'd never heard of when

I explained my project and my desire to see the most productive meteorite-hunting grounds on the planet—a place where, since 1976, the United States has annually sent scientists in search of rocks from space, a place where, since then, some 25,000 meteorites have been found, comprising 85 percent of the world's total number of specimens.

Meteorites do not fall preferentially anywhere on the planet. It just happens that ice makes Antarctica such fine hunting grounds: It creeps out from high points on the polar plateau—think of giant glaciers—but the ice sometimes encounters mountains, above ground and below. The blocked flow piles up, only to have its surface slowly stripped by strong katabatic winds and by the odd summer day when it's warm enough to sublimate the ice. Eventually, the rocks that were encased in the ice, including meteorites or sometimes *only* meteorites, are revealed at these "stranding surfaces."

Meteorites are, quite simply, rocks. But they are very old. Some of them, the chondrites, are more or less "unprocessed" fragments from the solar system's birth 4.5 billion years ago, including carbonaceous chondrites, which are treasure troves of organic materials. Iron meteorites are the melted and shattered metal cores, the broken hearts, of asteroids. Other meteorites include samples of volcanic asteroid crusts. Some meteorites have been blown off the moon or Mars. These rocks tell us of origins—"a ground truth to the formation of our solar system," as Ralph puts it—and these rocks tell of endings—the long history of cosmic bombardments on other worlds and our own. Meteorites are the alpha and omega of geology and perhaps of our very existence.

This is a recent revelation to Western science, which has paid close attention to meteorites for only about two hundred years. Before scientists accepted rocks falling from the sky (apart from volcanos of course), many indigenous cultures understood that they do. They worshiped these rocks and took heed of shooting stars, seeing in them portents of good fortune or omens of ill.

For years I, too, had looked skyward in the dark, finding the stars—those seemingly fixed, those sometimes streaking—an escape from many inarticulate griefs in my life. Only after falling in love with a woman other than my wife did I understand the night sky not as refuge but as connective solace, another place—like the bedroom—where I could be as whole as possible. I look to meteors and to the rocks they sometimes deposit on the Earth and I understand viscerally so many of the ancient metaphors. Meteors—shooting stars—as blood, as tears, as semen. Meteorites as the stony gods. Versions of ourselves.

That my own life has changed drastically as I've researched meteorites has only sharpened these connections. In one year-long span, I had fallen in love with Kathe; confronted my shame and silence about sexuality; left my marriage; helped scatter my mother's ashes; watched as my new lover flew away under a double rainbow to China, then, not long after her return, I had held her when she learned of her father's death, just months before we moved to Northern Utah so I could start a new job.

Days before leaving Utah for the Southern Hemisphere, rolling my long johns in tight bundles, placing books of poetry in among jeans and setting aside sweaters I'd decided against, I felt the exhaustion of moving again. A stray cat we'd just adopted—we named him Shackleton—snuggled in my shirts. But this would be a *trip*—a three-month geological immersion in New Zealand, Australia, and Antarctica—not a *move*. I would come back to a life better than any I had before. Still, this felt like loss again. When Kathe and I had left the apartment in Kansas to move to Utah, I stared at the white walls and thought of all that she and I had talked of there, all the silences we had broken, and I didn't want to leave a space that had been so crucial to us. Before leaving town, I had walked the prairie trail with its blue false indigo and big bluestem—a landscape I had loved for years—and I cried. Now I had to go again, this time leaving Kathe behind. This, I thought, *this* is adventure?

So the harder answer to the question of how I ended up in Antarctica was this: I was searching a different sort of landscape, that of obsession. I was trying out my Lao Tzu against my Richard Byrd.

We had pitched our four Scott tents in a line on hard snow, near the dimpled blue ice of LaPaz, surrounded by low rolls and swells and levels of ice, of snow; this was an Antarctic prairie that reminded me of the Smoky Hills of Kansas. The wind-shaped snow extended to the horizon in sastrugi, furrows of hard-packed snow that metaphor can make into hundreds of shapes: fish hooks, mesas, ploughshares. Wind gave some sastrugi the aspect of tears.

Where the snow gave out the blue ice began, not smooth but pockmarked, scalloped, and blistered. Compacted snow inside the blue ice, beneath it, and crevasses filled with snow on the surface cross such blue like a Cubist rendering of crazed kelp.

The ice itself was the color of blue eyes with cataracts.

It was at blue ice fields—stranding surfaces—like the one where we were camped that meteorites could be found. We drove snowmobiles out to the ice and lined up in ragged V-formations to hunt for the stones. At LaPaz, an eight-person team stayed for some six weeks, systematically searching for meteorites, while a four-person team, which I would later join, moved along the Transantarctic Mountains in a "recce," a reconnaissance, to scout possible future sites for thorough collection.

At LaPaz, we searched for meteorites in places we kept straight with subdivision names: Kozy Katabatic Kove or Terrapin Landing Royale. At LaPaz, we were lucky. Anything dark was either a meteorite or a shadow.

Though I didn't see *The Simpsons* while at LaPaz, Ralph played several songs from different episodes stored on his computer, we did more imitations, and we watched an episode of the comedy series *Ripping Yarns* called "Crossing the Andes by Frog," a perfect little send-up of adventurers trying to, well, cross the Andes by frog.

Sometimes it seemed as though there were more chores than meteorites, more camp work than searches. Each day there was chipping ice, bringing it back to the tent, melting it for drinking water; fishing out supplies—frozen veggies, frozen chicken patties, frozen steaks—from the thick cardboard boxes in rows in front of our tents or from between the double walls of our tent; searching for utensils and spices inside one of the wooden boxes kept inside the tent (one such box was labeled "Bedlam"); cooking; wiping down pots with paper towels (much faster than actually washing them); fueling snowmobiles; fueling the small stoves we kept burning when we were awake in the tent; snapping and unsnapping covers from the snowmobiles. Going to the bathroom also proved to be a chore, and in the poo tent one had to squat over a very cold bucket. My thighs have never looked so pale.

Usually the Antarctic veterans let us novices know when we aren't quite getting the jobs done right. Once, after a morning search for meteorites, I changed into dry socks and leaned into my small camp chair in the Scott tent I shared with Ralph, which improved my mood considerably, until he interrupted my reverie with a comment about the stoves. I don't recall what it was. Perhaps I'd spilled some fuel earlier. Perhaps I'd let a stove run out of fuel, which made the temperature in the tent drop noticeably and a gas stink pervade the air. He didn't say anything until lunch. I responded testily, "I can't read your mind, Ralph."

"Maybe you should try harder," he replied.

"Maybe your brainwaves aren't strong enough," I countered.

Smiling, Ralph eased the tension, "Good, good comeback."

I went out to chip ice. It was at times such as these that I felt the curious mixture of long-forgotten memories and desire for the ease of home and the tingly strangeness, not unwelcome, of learning how to live on the polar plateau. Perhaps then I thought of the tiny half-bath off the bedroom in the house I had shared for years with my ex-wife, where I stood once, a long time ago, hearing her throw the word "stupid" into the gulf between us. Or of the kitchen in the house Kathe and I had renovated in the months before my departure, a kitchen where one could merely *turn* a tap for water. Or of the trickle of water from mountain streams I'd pumped through a filter when I backpacked. The longest time I'd ever spent on the trail in a tent had been my last backpacking trip with my ex, just three nights in the Wind River Range in Wyoming. Now I'm to live in a tent on the ice for weeks.

*

Early in my LaPaz stint, I had bustled into the tent with a bucket of ice.

"Your next Antarctic lesson," Ralph told me, "will be how to chip out perfectly square blocks of ice so they nestle up against each other in the pot." I sighed. I learned that lesson quickly, however, and sometimes relished chipping ice as a break from the tent. We kept water going constantly to refill bottles and to have on hand for hot drinks and soups. At the top of the tall tents we hung socks and boots, which I finally deduced was the origin of the linty debris that kept appearing in the bottom of our water pots.

Water and heat. Elements of survival. Creating them became an unceasing inconvenience. But there was more to it than inconvenience.

For example, Ralph had characterized my attitude about refueling stoves as "trauma." This was overstatement, but it did take several days before I mastered the process, reducing my time to refuel the stove from thirty minutes (in snowy wind— Ralph timed me) to a matter of seconds. Refueling involved several steps, most dangerously moving an unlit though very hot stove through the tent's cumbersome double-tubed fabric entrance then refueling the stove while one's body was half-inside, half-outside. There were caps, funnels, fuel cans, wooden planks on which to set the stove, burn paste to light if the stove had cooled, a pump. Only once did I catch a bit of spilled fuel on fire, which Ralph patted out. The worst, he said, was when someone lit their crotch on fire…then their sleeping bag…then their sleep pad. The first time I refueled and relit my stove quickly, without using burn paste, Ralph and I exchanged satisfied looks.

Never a handy person, I worried a lot about looking foolish when it came to manual labor. During a brief trip near McMurdo Station—a "shakedown" for the team, in order to practice winter camping and crevasse-rescue techniques prior to leaving for the field—I publicly demonstrated my inability to tie even the simplest knots, making it clear to everyone that they would die if their lives depended on my remembering the story of Mr. Ropey, a wee narrative that helps one tie a figure-eight-on-a-bight. But, at the end of the shakedown, as we drove our snowmobiles back to the station, Ralph had attached a rope from my machine to a sledge in front of me, while, in the lead, he pulled the sledge with his snowmobile. This stabilized the sledge when we hit tiny pressure ridges and hummocks. My task was simple: keep the rope between me and the sledge from becoming too slack and too taut. "Nice job," he said, upon our return to McMurdo. I needed the compliment, he knew it, but this sense of being tested never left me, because, deep down, I felt unworthy of a continent that had attracted explorers who could sew the rotten bottoms of their feet back on.

After four days of weather-delimited traverses, I spotted a meteorite—it would be assigned field number 16706—and exulted. I had seen two black chunks cut in the middle by snow. No mistaking it! Revving the snowmobile, standing up as we often did to see better, I squinted and hoped and yelled and sped to the spot, my words lost in the din of the engine and the clattery-smacks of snowmobile skis on uneven ice. The ordinary chondrite—the size of a gourd you put out as countertop decoration in the fall—sat behind some snow, making it appear to be two rocks. When I got off my snowmobile, I peered at the meteorite, disbelieving and thrilled, then stood up, waving briskly, people converging. I forgot about the persistent pain of "throttle thumb" in my right hand and, absurdly gloved, smacked the cargo box mounted behind my seat, saying, "Hot damn!" Andrew Dombard, one of the scientists, pulled up and asked, "Is this your first?" I responded with an enthused, "Oh yay!"

Throwing my thick gloves down as kneepads, I worked with others to collect the rock. Ralph pulled up in his GPS-equipped snowmobile and took a location and jotted field notes as we measured the rock and how much "fusion crust" covered the stone. (Fusion crust is the melted skin of a meteorite that's left after its fiery plunge through the atmosphere.) Photographs were taken, then we used tongs and plastic bags to collect the stone. And we avoided touching the meteorite or dripping snot on it—this was not always successful—and made damn certain to leave a lead on the white tape we used to secure the folded baggie. One or two others chipped a hole in the ice for the bamboo flagpoles we carried on our snowmobiles. Someone wrote the field number on the pole then plunged it into the ground, as if claiming a new planet for NASA. If we needed to return to retake a GPS, we could locate the flagpole, then, later, when we were done with a particular ice field, we'd drive back and "harvest" the flags for re-use.

I stood up, walked back to my snowmobile, then suddenly worried that by finding the meteorite I had cut into another team member's lane. A no-no. How typical—even in success I had to find reason to feel chagrined. I was starting over to apologize to Barb Cohen when...I spotted my second meteorite! I waved again, then took some good-natured ribbing for the size of my second discovery. But I was happy. I had found what I believed I had come for.

✳

I thought: I am Erik Kramer. I am Bobby Douglass. I am…*Doug Flutie.*

I pulled away from the line of scrimmage, lurching back to heave a throw into the crowded end zone, a Hail Mary pass of my glove stuffed with a frozen box of juice. It would later burst. It didn't matter. A perfect loft, a perfect fade. Botta scores!

The day before I was to leave the LaPaz team and join "recce," we played five-step football on the snow. (After the ball is snapped, each player is allowed only five steps. You can take them all at once or stop-and-start.) My love of the Chicago Bears and scientist Oliver Botta's admiration of Green Bay's Brett Favre had led to jokes, but now we found ourselves on the same team. Taller than me, he was a natural at quarterback. He deferred. Having played soccer—real football to him—he didn't feel confident throwing the ball. Though I felt a bit ragged, I was having fun that afternoon, and the touchdown pass the highlight of my football career, which I thought had ended the day I walked off the Fulton Junior High practice field, my despised coach swearing after me. What if Coach Bertalon could see me now, I thought, throwing a touchdown pass in a place that made the frozen tundra of the Packers' Lambeau Field look like a tropical beach?

Our two teams tied—fitting, given the good feeling of our camp.

Ralph made certain we engaged in play—five-step football, Bad Samurai Theater, French cricket—in order to stay warm, to stay active, to let us sweat out the frustrations any prolonged camping experience incites.

So on another day when we needed to "muscle fuck" fuel drums that had been air-dropped two miles from camp before we arrived, I gladly went. Anything to minimize sitting in the tent. I snowmobiled out to the drop site along with Andrew and meteoriticist Tim Swindle and field safety leader Bill McCormick. We were to bring the drums back to camp on sleds hitched to our snowmobiles. It was then that I told Bill some of how I'd been feeling, how, even before I left Utah, I felt homesick. He sounded intrigued: "How can you be homesick before you've left home?" I wasn't sure how to compress autobiography and exhaustion into a coherent response, so I simply said, "Well, we had only been in the house for a few months." After Bill responded, "Oh," which sounded unsure, so I added, "And it's just all the chaos of the past two or three years." I wasn't sure how much more to say.

Despite some poor nights of little sleep; despite thinking of home and reading of Odysseus's quest for Ithaca (I kept Homer in a tent pocket); despite that awkward silence after talking with Bill by the fuel drums; despite the seeming eternity just after I'd press a button on the satellite phone, ending my latest conversation with Kathe or my father and stepmother or my sister; despite frustrations with stoves; despite all this, I felt, frequently, sudden surges of adrenal amazement. *Here I was.*

Here I was standing next to fuel drums, cutting ties to the pallets, talking about poet Richard Hugo with Bill, a man who, while working at the South Pole once, took his breaks in a heated hut where he'd read short stories by Alice Munro. Here I was, seeing a wall of wind-blown snow rising in the distance and coming closer, the sun shining through the scrim. And here, killing my engine and then stopped suddenly by a new sound, a tinkling like chimes hanging over a porch—ah, the wind blowing bits of ice my treads just cut. And here, content, sipping cocoa, surrounded by my temporary domestic life in the tent in the evenings, leaning in my camp chair, my bulky outdoor clothes shoved at the foot of my sleeping bag, the tent pockets beside me stuffed with goggles, gloves, books, a Walkman, CDs. Clothespins attached to tent pockets held pictures of Kathe, our house and the Blacksmith Fork River.

Then, here, crossing pinnacles, the most prominent topography at LaPaz: smooth humps of ice, frozen rollers whose formation is a mystery, a rising-and-falling of ice that we would travel through while looking for meteorites.

Then, here, kneeling beside a meteorite that looked for all the world like a chunk of dried, overcooked meatloaf or maybe a piece of partially melted Mexican chocolate, a wee nubbin of genesis.

Once, on an early traverse at LaPaz, all of us heading back to camp over the swells of ice, the furrows of snow, the world in hues of blue, silver, gray and white, one of the Twin Otter airplanes that flies in support of the field camps came in low behind us and raced overhead, buzzing us. It was a hoot-n-holler moment, and I didn't feel one bit of the gauntlets and exhaustion I'd been fighting. A plane strafed us! I'd seen meteorites! This is fucking Antarctica, man! The plane banked, dipped, circled and landed. I loved it.

I had been at LaPaz for two weeks and at McMurdo Station the week before, with a stop in-between at the South Pole. With meteoriticist Gretchen Benedix, I now had to leave LaPaz—beyond which, Ralph had joked, "There be dragons"—to swap out with two other expedition members on the recce team.

Hauling crammed orange duffel bags onboard the ski-equipped Twin Otter parked near our tents, Gretchen and I climbed in, strapped into our tiny seats and looked out our tiny windows. The plane whined and shuddered on its rough ice runway, then jumped into the air.

Later, I would remember something Ralph said—big, booming, occasionally gruff, football-player-sized Ralph, who sometimes called himself "Mongo" and "Primitive Man." As we talked once about the sense of connection and dislocation one felt when traveling across the ice prairies of LaPaz, Ralph told me: "You see what's in your heart, not just what's around you." On some traverses, the sunlight just right, I could see my eyes reflected on the inside of my goggles, so I stared at myself staring at the sterile sublime.

I am crying. I am counting. Behind my ski mask, I am crying.

This morning we set out under a sky glittering with crystals and refraction: tangential arcs, halos, parhelia, shimmering opacities gifting me on this, my forty-first birthday. We collect meteorites beneath lovely chances of light, but I am stolid with the deadness of the polar plateau, with the quietness of camp life, with the creeping consequences of insomnia.

I am at the Otway Massif—the last of my four field camps...LaPaz, Davis Nunataks, Scott Icefalls, now here—and I have been counting since even before leaving home.

Each day of the trip I keep track of numbers of days till weekends, till Wednesdays, till day-after-tomorrows, till new destinations, till coming home. I keep score of how many changes of underwear I have left, how many satellite calls to Kathe, how many nights might be left in the tent, how many search days. I say things to myself like, on a Monday, "The day after tomorrow is hump day, and then you can say the day after tomorrow is the end of the week."

When the LaPaz team found, after my departure, a headless skua, I felt a surge of envy—a bird! Had it been wandering the interior only to encounter the moving propeller of a Twin Otter? I longed to see its body, this evidence of life. I had not been prepared for how unnerved I was by the lack of visible life on the polar plateau. There was nothing green to see, to touch, to smell.

It doesn't help that with recce leader Johnny Schutt we work faster—as a smaller team, just four of us, we have to—and we work in harsher conditions than at LaPaz. Once we collected in winds gusting to 30 knots, in wind-chill of -20°F to -25°F. Not exactly Hillary on Everest but the wind seared a portion of my forehead, and I felt cold and singular.

And now even the traverses themselves have begun to feel oddly routine. Each morning, before we head out, Johnny, Gretchen, Monika Kress and I gather outside while John fills us in on the day's plans. At one briefing, he actually said, "We'll have some tedious searching followed by some tedious collecting." This frankness surprised me, and, sensing our flagging spirits, he took us off the blue ice and into some low hills bouldered with weathered red dolerite. Gretchen pulled out an inflatable TV character toy and took his picture: "Mr. Krabs on Mars!"

Suffering from a massive sugar crash—having eaten a startling amount of thawed raspberries that morning—I wandered off alone and, while noting abstractly the alien beauty of the place, also dug into the thought that these were not my mountains. A few minutes later, John started back to his snowmobile—a sign to regather—and he asked us all, "Didn't you always want to walk on Mars?" On the traverse that day, a productive search, we found thirty-seven meteorites, and Frost's line ran in my head: "Earth's the right place for love. I don't know where it's likely to go better." Yet—I *had* always wanted to walk on Mars.

Always prone to depression when I've not gotten enough sleep, I find myself struggling each morning as I wait for my stove to boil water for coffee, and later, on the snowmobile—when I'm not fussing with my headgear to keep my glasses from steaming up—I plan careful rearrangements of blankets, clothes and pillow to find ways to cover myself against the cold without getting too confined in the sleeping bag. At night, I take Benadryl and melatonin and aspirin. "That's quite a cocktail," Johnny told me once. I mask my eyes against the light. I put in earplugs against the sounds of my tentmate, the sounds of the Coleman fuel can and the ice sheet expanding or contracting, the sounds of wind or silence.

Inside the tent, I can feel high winds vibrating my skin, and the wind sounds, as explorer Carsten Borchgrevink wrote, like "centuries of heaped-up solitude." That heaped-up solitude is the reason Scott tents don't have floors. If the tent blows away, you don't go with it.

The afternoon of my birthday, having found meteorites under all that morning crystalline light and having taken a tent break, we head out again just to drive up a glacier to the top of the Otway Massif. A joyride. At 10,000 feet, we walk about, talk some, look off into distances, take pictures, take in the silence. For a time, I stand alone, gratefully apart, at the edge, watching the mounded snowy ridge touched by cloud shadow go on and on, then the polar plateau below go on and on. This is the lonely top of the world, I think—peaks and snow and clouds and ice—and when I look at my friends, I see that in our red parkas we are like a bunch of puffy, vermillion Buddhas.

On the way back to camp, I can't stop thinking about my dead mother and I shed tears again, as I have in the poo tent, when through with a satellite phone call. (The poo tent is the only place for real privacy.) I have sobbed the way I did on the day I left Utah for the first flights that would eventually drop me here, at the end of the Earth. On the way back to camp, we look for meteorites and for the first time this makes me very, very angry. I am like two people: that one, the angry, tear-stained one, and the other, the one who felt more blessed than any person alive to be there, at the top of the massif.

One evening at the Otway, I write, "Savor: No wind!" I read Arthur Waley's translation of the *Tao te Ching.* As always, John keeps the radio on, so voices call from McMurdo, the field camps, the South Pole. "Moody camp, Moody camp, Mac Ops on 7995." "South Pole, South Pole…" "This is Moody Camp, Mac Ops, go ahead." I read: *As good sight means seeing what is very small/so strength means holding on to what is weak.*

Thursday, Jan. 15, 2004, Overcast, 4 degrees.

A fairly fitful night. It became especially cold, chilling my face and keeping me awake. I hate this place now. I'm going to write a to-do list again for the sake of focus. I'm a failure as an explorer. I've decided to call Medical and ask for sleeping pills and anti-depressants to be sent on the next flight, when we're to move to another location. I close my eyes from 10 A.M. to noon and never really sleep then sit up, my arms on my knees, my head hanging down. I simply can't patch together enough rest. I tell Johnny I feel shaky.

"Flu?"

"No, depression."

I find myself telling him how I felt the trip was a mistake, the whole three months—traveling with geologists in New Zealand and Australia before meeting up with the ANSMET team in Christchurch—because I'd only just then started settling into my new life with Kathe. I admit my crying and obsessive counting. I tell him I haven't had a full night's sleep for a long time; even the "good" ones here are terrible. John leaves the tent and comes in with a large plastic box full of medical supplies. He rummages then hands me some sedatives. He calls Medical at McMurdo but it's lunch hour so we wait. I say that I am ashamed I'm not strong enough to stave off this depression anymore.

John taps my leg and says, "Don't worry about it."

I reach Medical. The doctor asks if I am feeling suicidal, and I pause. My thoughts are moving slowly, like my speech. I can't say no but it's not exactly yes. "Maybe," I say, "A little."

There was a weekend after I had left my wife when, following a phone call from her, listening to her body wrenched with sobbing, I crawled into bed. I knew that if I went back she would be better. I knew that if I went back I would not be happy. I knew that if I went back I would hurt Kathe. What to do? And could I tell Kathe I felt this way? I stayed in bed for two days, thinking. The ceiling was my empty map. I knew that if I kept staring at that map I could not make it, that to be trapped beneath such emptiness was untenable. I understood then, in a kind of abstracted way, that one means to end such entrapment was suicide.

The doctor and I agree: I should be pulled from the field.

Massif. A "mountainous mass broken up into separate peaks and forming the backbone of a mountain range." From the French for "solid" and "massive." Greek and Latin roots lead to Indo-European, *-mag-*, "whence MAKE."

At the Otway Massif, I think in all but words that I am an unmaking.

Friday, Jan. 16, 2004 M. sunny, then cloudy, 10 degrees calm.

Godawful waiting to see if a plane will come. Weather is better, flyable, John says. Drugged, I slept more soundly, but still feel edgy, exhausted, depressed. I don't belong here. Funny, if I knew we were pulling out tomorrow I could have made it, I tell myself—but the prospect of another week here is an eternity, a terrible slowness I cannot withstand. I nearly cried when Mac Ops said the Twin Otter wasn't "off-deck."

8:41 call from Mac Ops. The Twin Otter called "KBH" has taken off. I sigh a quiet "thank God" and now such relief mingles with shame. Then Ralph calls. John tells him, "Chris decided to pull himself out of the field." I want to protest—not just me, the doctor, too. I get on the phone and Ralph tells me, "You have to take care of yourself first."

Later, waiting for the plane to show up, suited up in all my Extreme Cold Weather gear, I wander aimlessly in camp. Sit on a box. Lean on a snowmobile. Clouds hang onto dusted Otway. Overcast now. Poor horizon. Poor surface.

Food no longer appeals, and Gretchen says, "That's not a good sign." I crawl into the tent, not meeting anyone's gaze and sit on a wooden box. *Please land*, I whisper. I look at the unbearable yellow walls of the tent. I go outside when we hear the Twin Otter come closer now.

John: "He has his landing lights on." John had put out jerry cans and bundles of our bamboo-pole flags to mark surface and runway. KBH seems to be coming right at me. I whisper, "His flaps are down." He's low, nose up, skis suddenly scraping snow, and I feel my body rise up as I whisper, "Thank God." Suddenly the plane has taxied up, opened its door.

Erika Escholz clambers out, ecstatic, for very few support

staff at McMurdo ever have a chance to come out to the deep field. Erika works in expedition support at McMurdo and she's taking my place for the last few days of the expedition. She is grinning.

"Great people, great people," I say to Erika. "You'll love it."

"So, flu?" Erika asks me.

I pause, "Ah—no—a...depression thing."

I'm a gutless, sleepless loser, you beautiful blonde adventurer. I turn to ask John to let Medical know that I'll stop by tonight. "Do you need more pills?" he asks.

"That would be a good idea."

We walk to a box on the cargo line. I say to him, emphatically, "John, I'm so sorry..."

"You're doing the right thing," John says, as he finds the right baggie and puts two pills in my hand. I shove them in my wallet.

"Besides," he says, "look at my new roommate." I manage a smile.

When I hug Gretchen and Monika, I say, "I'm sorry. Thank you." I shake John's hand.

We lift up my bags. I thank the pilots, Trevor and Scotty, for landing. Suddenly I'm getting seated. The plane taxis, bumpity bump, across ice. I'm waving. The women wave back.

The plane bites into the air and lifts, and I watch the Otway, the same mountain I had watched one lovely evening of sun and little wind when I listened to Tippet's Second Symphony in my headphones. I feel the sweeping relief I felt when I pulled out of my driveway, when I left my wife.

I watch the massif until I can watch no more.

I am flying over Antarctica.

I am dazzled by wraiths of white at the Cloudmaker, abject grandeur.

I am listening to the pilots, their mics left on: "Did you see? He had tears in his eyes."

Today's cargo on flight "KBH": two boxes of meteorites, me, garbage, and human waste.

Over the Queen Elizabeth Range, I see fans of crevasses gaping like the open gills of some impossible white shark. I see sharp peaks hidden by vast mounds of snow, a range that snakes beyond my understanding and perhaps beyond my desire to understand.

So easily does the clarity of Antarctica trick you. What seems near here is almost always farther than you think.

Back home in Northern Utah, I listen as a therapist asks me if I thought things would have turned out differently had I gone to Antarctica at another time, if I had gone later, after feeling more at home. I don't hesitate. Oh yes, I say. But I applied when I did, went when I did, and now have years to reflect on what happened. I lived in a tent in the middle of Antarctica for five weeks. All told, the two teams found 1,358 meteorites—including one Martian and a higher-than-usual proportion of achondrites, carbonaceous chondrites, and odd ordinary chondrites. I'm, well, I'm proud of having been a part of that. I left in a way that I'll always regret, thankful that I had not slowed the recce team, thankful, too, that I didn't have to spend several more days at the Otway, which the team had to when the weather turned to shit.

In an email, Oliver Botta tells me to think of what happened as I would think of a physical injury. This is yet another act of kindness visited upon me by my compatriots.

During the past few months, I have read a good deal,

discovering that sleep disturbance and depression are commonplace in extreme and/or confined quarters, such as polar environments, submarines and long-duration space flights. One researcher who had been to Antarctica years before tells me of struggles with depression while there, above and beyond the so-called "third-quarter blues" that affect nearly everyone on missions of one kind or another. Apart from causes one would suspect, such as bad news from home, depression can be triggered or accentuated by, for example, high winds. I think of how wind-crazed pioneers in the American West would sometimes cut off their limbs.

Ralph tells me that "…only a few scary people seem to eat the whole season up like candy; the rest of us need to work at it. I think virtually everyone has gone through periods of depression while out in the field, and I mean everyone.… To me, depression is something always there, always lurking.… The difference is that yours was pushed off the chart by the intense isolation that is unavoidable in Antarctica."

For Ralph—who once experienced a deep melancholy because he was in the field and not with his newborn son back in Ohio—making phone calls home has helped stave off the worst feelings. "I fear those calls," he admits, "and long desperately for them. I may get the worst news, I may get the best, but I call home and conquer that fear.… And because people I love are on the other side of that phone, I never ever use it to vent and I never soft-pedal my feelings." He joshes, "I save the venting and soft-pedaling for my tentmate."

In *The White Continent*, Thomas R. Henry notes that Robert Scott "was a sentimentalist who would burst into tears" upon hearing songs or stories. His rival, Roald Amundsen, "was a thwarted, unhappy man," despite having won the South Pole. Both were moody, both devoted to "adventure, wild beauty in action." But it's not all wild beauty, as they knew. The great American explorer Robert Byrd once wrote of living in Antarctica: "You are hemmed in on every side by your own inadequacies and the crowding pressure of your associates. The ones who survive with a measure of happiness are those who live profoundly of their intellectual resources, as hibernating animals live off their fat." Byrd wintered alone at a weather station for months before being rescued due to carbon monoxide poisoning. Me, I arrived too lean.

More directly relevant to my experience is a study included in the book *From Antarctica to Outer Space*. In an article called "The International Biomedical Expedition to the Antarctic: Psychological Evaluations of the Field Party," the researchers report that one member of the team "had to be evacuated…" Fellow team members wrote in their journals that this individual was "preoccupied, strained, sad, tired, and lacking enthusiasm for work. He did not like the food, felt cold, slept badly; he got depressed, felt homesick, had difficulty in accepting separation from his family and friends, and reported feeling that 'he has fallen into a trap.'"

What Ralph tells others suffering from the blues—or worse—is to take stock of where they are, to let Antarctica "in under your skin and stay there," because they likely will never be back. What the researchers studying the psychological effects of the IBEA tell readers is that psychological screening "is an absolute necessity." Perhaps so. And yet had I been screened prior to ANSMET 2003-2004 (and I admit some surprise that I was not) I likely would not have been allowed to go. I would not now be making art out of loss and frontiers.

The Antarctic is a place of romance, but spending a honeymoon on the Ice takes that idea one step further. The notion of beautiful scenery and adventures is, for Kristan Hutchison, quickly replaced with endless hours of editorial work in the small busy office of the Antarctic Sun. Newspapers hold an important place in polar exploration—Scott's men published the South Polar Times, and the Sun continues in that tradition, setting science next to human interest stories. News while in the Antarctic, where the "real world" seems far away, becomes vital and these days is easy to access—breakfast in the galley in McMurdo is served with a print out from The New York Times online. But the Sun is the only publication that lets people know what is happening on the continent. (Follow along at antarcticsun.usap.gov)

After that first year as the editor of the Sun, Kristan spent four more seasons in McMurdo Station before returning to her home in Alaska. A journalist with an interest in the edges of the world, she has followed stories to the Arctic tundra, the melting shores of Greenland, and the southern tip of Chile. She's been published in The Juneau Empire, The Anchorage Daily News, The London Times, USA Today, Alaska Fisherman's Journal, Spaceref.com, and numerous other publications. Though her Antarctic adventure and her marriage both have ended, she remembers them fondly, with a touch of amnesia.

Antarctic Honeymoon

⋆ * ⋆

KRISTAN HUTCHISON

AT FIRST, I DID NOT SEE THE BIRD WAS DEAD. DREAMS still clouded my morning eyes and I thought the skua was sleeping, too, there in the road, blending into the Antarctic dirt. But when it came fully into the tunnel of my vision, into the circle of space I could see from within a fur-lined hood, I knew he would not wake up. The right wing spread across the dirt, as if preparing to fly. But blood, not yet frozen, soaked into the ground where the wing met the body. His head and beak extended flat. The black eye reflected gray clouds.

I'd known this skua. We all had. He returned each year when we did, flying south from some unknown point to scavenge a living from a land that is 98 percent ice and 100 percent unforgiving. We shared this island of volcanic dirt, something once hot and flowing now crushed to dust. The back entrance of the cafeteria had been his hunting ground.

I walked a bit beyond the corpse, to the building entrance, when another skua landed, ten feet from the dead. I wondered then, how far will the brutality of nature go? Skua chicks will kill and eat each other while the parents watch. Would the same be true of adults, hunger overcoming fidelity? So I watched.

The second skua approached slowly with the stilted gait common to ravens, crows, and gulls. When it stood over the other, the skua bent her head, beak closed, and lightly touched the soft feathers at the throat of her dead mate. Once, twice, three times, as if nudging him. Wake up. Wake up.

Then she took three steps back, spread her wings and flew, circling once at roof level before flying away, toward the hillside, the glacier, the volcano, perhaps her nest where chicks were waiting.

Left with only one parent, the chicks would starve. It takes two to survive and raise chicks when winds blow and the temperature drops to -30°F. Skuas mate for life, sometimes thirty years, nesting further south than any other flying bird. Unlike penguins, who trade sexual favors for stones and switch mates easily if the old one doesn't return to the colony in time, skuas are faithful. Together, skua pairs defend their territory, hunt for food, and migrate from the Arctic to the Antarctic, just as we had.

We'd met on the northern end of the skua migration, working for a newspaper in Alaska's rainforest. On my first day the reporter two cubicles down spun his chair to look out the window at the layers of water, trees, mountains and fog. He clapped his hands with the unfiltered joy of a child, applauding the world, and I was caught by Mark's grin.

Both new to town, both drawn to the mountains, both borderline workaholics driven by deadline, we became hiking partners. On our first hike in the Juneau rain I asked Mark where in the world he'd most like to go.

"Antarctica," he answered and I paused to look more closely at the man who'd just voiced my childhood dream. His brown curls and lean, six-foot frame led the way up the hillside.

I fell in love with the way his rumpled shirts couldn't stay tucked in and his collar always needed to be straightened; with the stick figure cartoons he left on my desk, his willingness to follow me onto a dance floor and the irreverent humor he brought to the political beat.

"No matter how you look at it, the legislature is still mostly a bunch of white guys," he started one story.

Over the next four years we hiked every trail in Juneau, cuddled together on the rooftop to watch the northern lights and won the costume contest at the Halloween dance. Sometimes when my short fingers intertwined with his long ones, I caught myself thinking in clichés like "forever," "always," and "happily ever after."

Eventually came the question and answer: "Yes. And our honeymoon will be in Antarctica."

If there is a mythical place left, an edge to the world, it is the white hole at the bottom of the globe. It's a blank spot waiting to be written on, white as a wedding dress. Together we had flipped through *National Geographic* magazines, craving the jagged peaks jutting from ice, the comedic penguins arching over their eggs. I imagined us walking in swirling snow, warming each other's cold lips so our breath rose as one cloud. Where better to share mugs of hot chocolate and long hours beneath the covers, without worrying about cooking or cleaning or driving to work?

Unable to afford an Antarctic cruise, and wanting to stay longer than a few days, we applied for jobs at the only newspaper on the continent, *The Antarctic Sun*. In the tradition of many family businesses, we'd be working side-by-side, two-thirds of the three-person staff. We tossed ideas for new sections back and forth as we packed and later sketched possible page designs on the planes from Alaska to New Zealand to Antarctica.

Landing on floating ice ten feet thick, we blinked against the interrogating light of the sun. In a dorm room half the size of a school bus, we pushed our single beds together and padded the gap. Then we started work.

Our Antarctica had orange carpet patched with duct tape, computers set on folding tables and one window overlooking a row of trash bins in a dusty lot where the skua sometimes sat. When the wind blew against the building, our feet grew cold and I draped my down parka over my lap while I typed. Mark ate at his desk, writing stories that would be black-lined by scientists, bureaucrats, and corporate public relations before finally being printed. Favorite phrases and humorous snippets were replaced with the dry language of science. The paper wouldn't mention the baskets of condoms in the bathrooms or the quantity of alcohol sold in the station store. The photos of a penguin wearing an instrument pack on its back and a polar adventurer draped in his country's flag had to be replaced.

Somewhere outside the office was the Antarctica we'd dreamed of. I glimpsed it on the walk to and from the office each day, the bluish white triangles of the Transantarctic Mountains wavering on the horizon. We interviewed people who had seen penguins, miles away where the water met the ice. We took notes as scientists described hiking through the Mars-like landscape of the Dry Valleys.

I knew Mark and I slept in the same room, because his pile of dirty clothes grew and shrank alongside mine. The covers on his side of the bed had changed shape each morning, but he was gone by 4 A.M., already at his desk. We said good morning in the office, aware there was a third person in the room. Aware too that the community was watching.

Our moments alone outside the office were rare. On

Christmas morning, while the rest of the station slept off the previous night's party, we followed a line of frayed green flags across the glacier behind the station. Nothing stirred. Even the wind was still. The flags hung limp, casting short shadows in the twenty-four-hour sunshine.

I stopped to look around, waiting for Mark to catch up, his footsteps crunching slowly on the packed snow. The world sparkled, as if created from layers of reflected light rather than ice, less solid than the deep blue of the sky above.

"Are you O.K.?" I asked.

"Yeah. Just tired," he said.

A rock bridged the ice and sky, fortress-like. We scaled the side of Castle Rock and found the top empty, emanating warmth stored in the red-brown volcanic rock. Warm enough to sit for hours, leaning against each other and talking of nothing. Warm enough to take off my shoes and wiggle bare toes. Warm enough to melt away the layers of stress and frustration. From that height we could see the blue edge on the horizon, where the ice ended and the sea began, and everything seemed possible again.

When red dots approached across the white, growing into tiny people in parkas, we descended, surrendering Castle Rock to them. The wind picked up, pushing us back toward the station.

In January someone decided to celebrate Mardi Gras. We'd all be gone by the time the true holiday arrived in March and since Halloween and Thanksgiving celebrations were always moved to the weekend so as not to disturb the six-day work week, why not move Mardi Gras as well. I cut masks for Mark and myself from cardboard, covered with colored paper scraps and held on with rubber bands. My dancing feet were itching to go, but Mark had work still.

"You don't need me," he said. "Go have fun on your own. Maybe I'll come later."

I stepped into the bar alone, scanning it through the holes cut in my cardboard mask. Forks impaled dollar bills into the low ceiling and the posts were painstakingly wrapped in rope, knotted nautically. It had the well-worn comfort of a torn but favorite pair of jeans, the patina of age that makes antiques so valuable. Men lined the wooden bar, and a few stood around the bare linoleum, where the pool table had been pushed aside to open up a dance floor.

Men will lead charges into battle or climb alone up mountains, but turn on music and offer them a bare floor and suddenly they are like a flock of penguins, each standing back and trying to push someone else into the drink. Getting a dance started is one of those primary contradictions in life, like needing job experience to get your first job. Most people won't step onto the floor until a certain magic number of people are already dancing. A brave few dancers will enter the dance floor when there is only one out there already. But someone has to be the sacrificial first dancer.

I'm usually that someone. Years ago I decided it would be one of my smaller roles in life to be first on the dance floor. So I walked past the guys and their beers without a glance. Like jumping into cold water, I took a deep breath, closed my eyes and spun myself onto the floor. The world blurred into streaks of colored light. I let my hips play the drums, caught the sinuous melody passing through my spine, stretched my arms and moved in any way that felt good. The music became like a river and I was the streambed it ran through.

As if I'd conjured them, others began to move onto the floor. Then I felt limbs like shadows behind my own, tracing the same electric currents through the air.

"You came," I said, and turned to face him. But it was not Mark. This man had straight, sandy hair and blue eyes that looked directly into mine. And his body moved smoothly in sync, limbs weaving in and out as if they were attached to the same string. A string that was pulling them closer. I felt the heat from his legs, the feathery touch of his fingers passing across my back, my waist, reading my curves like Braille. We were like seals underwater, skin slipping across skin. The pull between us stronger than gravity, until I was afraid I wouldn't escape this whirlpool.

He leaned into my ear, so close I could feel his lips as he spoke over the music.

"You are beautiful.... I noticed you at the Halloween party."

"I'm married," I said, expecting him to step back, expecting the waters to part. But our bodies kept moving in rhythm.

"I know. Where's your husband?"

"In the office."

"May I kiss you?"

"No," I said.

"Just once?"

"No."

"On your cheek?"

"No."

"Your neck?"

"No."

"Just your nose?"

"My nose?" I laughed.

"Yes," he said, still serious.

"I guess." It seemed so ridiculous it had to be harmless.

He leaned forward, lips just above my own, closing over the tip of my nose. Then slowly pulling back, hesitating with his face so close to my own that we were releasing and inhaling the same warm air. I closed my eyes and pictured Mark, wanting to lean forward into a kiss and find my husband's chocolate eyes on the other side.

I stepped back abruptly.

"I've got to go. Now. I'm sorry." And then again, quietly, "I'm sorry."

Stepping outside, the sun and cold were like an alarm clock back to reality. Steam rose from my damp arms as I jogged between buildings. Mark was where I'd left him, facing the computer screen. I laid my hands on his shoulders.

"Hey, ready for a break?"

He didn't turn. "No, I'm not in the mood."

"The music's great. Everyone's dancing."

"That's fine, you have a good time."

"It would be nice if you were there. I keep getting hit on."

"I'm just really tired."

"It's late, maybe I should go home," I said.

"O.K."

"Will you come?"

"Maybe later."

In our room I stared at our bed, which seemed as vast and lonely as the Antarctic plateau. I lay awake for hours and woke to find my eyes still stinging and the other side of the bed still empty. He was in the office when I arrived.

A few days later Mark was sent to the South Pole to research some stories. The trip from McMurdo to Pole takes three hours, flying 300 mph over the TransAntarctic Mountains and the plateau, the equivalent of going over the Rocky Mountains and the plains states if all were coated in snow. Stepping from the plane the air is sharp and thin, so cold it burns the throat and nose lining. Painful as it was, he gasped for more. The Pole is at 9,300 feet above sea level, but because of the vagaries of the Earth's spin and barometric pressures, the effective altitude is usually higher. Arriving from sea level was like going from the beach to nearly halfway up Everest without acclimatizing.

Mark threw himself into his work, as usual, walking around in forty pounds of fleece, down, and insulated boots. Wanting to fit in, he stayed up late helping with dinner dishes in the station kitchen. He figured he'd sleep off the headache pulsing through his temples and be better by morning.

His room was in one of a row of canvas-and-wood military tents on the far side of the station, away from the silver dome covering the main buildings. The bathroom was in another building, so when he woke at 2 A.M. he had to stumble outside in his long underwear.

I could see this part better even than he remembered it. How he slumped suddenly over the sink in the bathroom, his oxygen-deprived brain shutting off. He bumped his head against the mirror and jolted awake enough to make it out the door again. One, two, ten steps until he was between the buildings. Then swaying briefly before falling like the last tree in a clearcut. His right shoulder hit the cement-hard ice, opening a gash three inches long and half an inch wide. The tin of mints in his pocket crushed beneath his hip, denting both. Limbs splayed out, he didn't notice any of it. In my mind, I watch him lie there without a coat, right cheek and ear pressed to the ice. Nothing moves except the cold, which creeps in on his still body, his gloveless fingers, his hatless head. Each time I think of it I scan the scene desperately for something to move, someone to walk up and wake him. But everybody is sleeping. Nothing moves but the plume of steam rising from the generator a half mile away.

At −20°F it takes minutes for hypothermia to set in. The body's core temperature drops, blood is drawn to the center, the heart, head, and lungs, in an effort to save them.

Mark doesn't know how long he lay there. His hands and feet were numb when some survival alarm went off in his brain and woke him. He crawled inside and collapsed again just inside the door. A while later he woke, pulled himself under the covers, and shivered until he passed out.

By the time I heard the story, he was telling it in our room, half unpacked. I tried to take my breath in even measures as he spoke. He pulled off his shirt to show where his shoulder had split open like some overripe fruit, revealing a red pulp. I touched it so softly I couldn't feel it before he pulled away in pain.

"Oww."

Then I was the one gasping for breath, shaking, my mind frozen with what-ifs.

"What's wrong?" he asked.

"What if…what if you hadn't…woken?" I said, tears sliding down my cheeks. "What if you just lay there?"

"But I didn't. I'm here. I'm O.K."

I thought of this as I watched the still figure of the skua in the road. Our last week, after packing our bags, we walked up that road hand in gloved hand and talked about our future. Wind blew bits of dust into my eyes, my mouth, the gritty taste of reality.

Forget the fairy tale. It was time to rub the dreams from my eyes. Antarctica is not about penguins cavorting. Marriage is not a romantic comedy. But I keep coming back to both, propelled by a brand of stubbornness called love. The skuas are right. We need each other, more so than ever now that the honeymoon is over.

Freezing to death must be a queer business. Sometimes you feel simply great. The numbness gives way to an utter absence of feeling. You are as lost to pain as a man under opium. But at other times, in the enfolding cold, your anguish is the anguish of a man drowning slowly in fiery chemicals.

—ADMIRAL RICHARD E. BYRD, *ALONE*

Leaving Antarctica is excruciating. As I sat knee to knee in the cargo plane leaving the Ice I looked around at the tears rolling down the cheeks of the men and women surrounding me. I cried too because the chance of returning was slim; I was leaving forever.

McMurdo, which has all the charm of a remote industrial town, does have several quirky, poetic details—the library, for one. Another is a poem engraved, one word per step, on a small wooden pedestrian bridge that spans some above-ground pipes. This was one of the first things that I was shown (by contributor Karen Joyce) when I arrived in McMurdo and as he leaves the ice, William L. Fox weaves his poetic tribute to the continent around this poem.

Bill has published ten books about cognition and landscape, fourteen collections of poetry in three countries, and numerous essays in exhibition catalogs, photography monographs, and journals. He has received awards from the Guggenheim Foundation, National Science Foundation, National Endowment for the Humanities, and been a visiting scholar at the Getty Research Institute and the Clark Art Institute. Fox has led treks in Nepal, taught both climbing and the writing of art criticism at the University of Nevada, Reno, and worked in both the Antarctic and Canadian High Arctic. He is a fellow of both the Royal Geographical Society and the Explorer's Club.

Leaving the Ice

*   *   *

WILLIAM L. FOX

McMurdo, Antarctica: January

walking

IT'S EIGHT O'CLOCK AT NIGHT AND WE'RE SHIVERING, despite the sunlight glinting in a golden haze off the sea ice. The sun, elevated only a couple of hand-widths above the horizon, is unable to warm us. Two weeks ago on New Year's Eve it was 51°F here, the warmest temperature ever recorded at McMurdo. Dozens of us sat out on a deck at midnight, faces tilted into the sun and watching as the low light burnished the glaciers in the Transantarctic Mountains into rivers of molten brass. We took off our boots and socks, rolled up our pant legs, and drank red wine. It could have been Malibu Beach, except for the thirty miles of frozen ocean separating us from the mountains on the coast opposite.

The height of summer has passed within a week, and this evening the wind chill is far below zero. At this time of year there might be as many as five thousand people on a continent the size of the United States and Canada combined, and roughly twelve hundred of them are stationed in and work out of McMurdo, the southernmost port in the world. The "town" covers a hundred square acres, the largest station on the ice, but its metal-clad buildings on pylons and heavy equipment make it feel more like the backside of a mining operation in Alaska. When it's warm enough to allow a sense of smell, the odor of aircraft fuel hangs faintly everywhere. It gave the wine on New Year's, an Australian Shiraz, a bouquet akin to diesel.

across

The three of us working on the Bridge of Size get cold-soaked every half hour or so, and take turns going into Crary Laboratory or Building 155, the buildings at either end, to get warm. Crary is the central working facility for the American scientists working on the ice, which is to say almost anywhere in the Antarctic. The Antarctic is famously the coldest, windiest, highest, driest, most remote continent on Earth, and McMurdo's buildings are designed to cope with those superlatives. The doors into the lab are the kind you find on freezers in meat packing plants, but they are used here to keep out the cold. The lab walls are a foot thick, the atmosphere warm and humidified, and the building is heavily anchored on concrete footings underneath which snow is supposed to blow through, as opposed to accumulate in drifts. The design was worked out by an architectural firm in Hawaii. Crews spend weeks patiently chipping out the ice that builds up underneath the buildings.

Building 155 contains the cafeteria, barbershop, and local radio station, two Wells Fargo automatic teller machines, and public computer terminals used for e-mailing people back home. It's insulated as heavily as the lab and its windowless dorm rooms are notoriously too warm at times. In a place where it gets so cold during the six-month night that hammers shatter and screwdrivers snap like twigs, it's difficult for a species that evolved in the temperate zones to get it right.

a

Melissa Iszard, her tongue poking out between her teeth as she concentrates, carefully letters the words of a poem in pencil on the front of each step of the wooden bridge that crosses the pipes running in between Crary and 155. Twenty-four-hour sunlight at this time of year means that people routinely work until midnight, and traffic between the two busiest buildings is brisk, even at this time of day. Or night. It doesn't really matter what you call it, the sun orbiting around the horizon at all hours.

poem

The bridge is nine feet high, twenty-five feet long, eleven steps up, eleven steps down. One word per tread. Risk Miller, who has a Bachelor of Fine Arts degree from the Cleveland Institute of Art, but who works as an ironworker here, manages to put several of his many skills to use as he carves the words with an electric router. Our source of power is the power pole they plug the trucks into to keep the engine blocks from freezing.

When Melissa asked me for a poem to add to the bridge, I envisioned a trope for the strangers who create a community here every year. I wanted a text about the meeting and greeting and leavetaking that occur on the bridge that you would both read and walk upon as you engaged in those very acts.

Melissa draws, Risk carves, and I talk to pedestrians as they cross the bridge—geologists and astrophysicists, heavy equipment operators and cooks, helicopter pilots and visiting dignitaries. Most people who work here nod in appreciation of the poem, but a couple of visiting military personnel mock the idea of poetry in the Antarctic. Everyone keeps walking, however, no matter how they feel about it. The top of the bridge is just high enough to catch the wind.

today

I've been here for almost three months, working as a visiting writer both in the Crary library and out in the field, and this is my last night in the Antarctic. I'm heartbroken to be flying out in two hours on a National Guard cargo plane to Christchurch. It does that to everyone, leaving here. I've never met anyone who has worked in the Antarctic who didn't want to go back. Unlike Melissa and Rick, who expect to return next season, I have no reason to suspect that I will be able to return. Visiting writers and artists are usually given only one trip per lifetime.

Just offshore a red-and-white U.S. Coast Guard icebreaker churns a circle in the sea ice, keeping open the channel it's made for the annual delivery of food and supplies that will soon arrive on a freighter. Across the sound the mountains stand 14,000 feet high. I've spent much of the last three months looking at them, either while out on the sea ice or from the top floor of the lab. Every time I'd take a break from writing on my laptop, I'd go prop my elbows on the deep window casements to stare out at the peaks and glaciers. Most mornings, when the air had warmed enough above the sea ice, a fata morgana would appear; impossible cliffs would flicker into existence for an hour or two, slowly changing shape as the thermal discontinuity between surface and air shifted slightly.

The Antarctic is like that, throwing up extravagant

promises before you and then melting them away. The Bridge of Size is a pun on the Bridge of Sighs in Italy, and tonight both wind and emotion cut through me, singing a duet of loss, which is what the poem is about.

two

Melissa comes to the ice every austral summer to work, as do many of the town's hundreds of seasonal residents. There are no permanent settlers here, and no mammals live on the continent. The seals haul out only to sun themselves and to whelp their pups, and even penguins hop out of the water only to incubate their eggs. People will sometimes winter-over—Melissa has—but this year she's down just for the summer to work as one of the senior administrators at Crary. No one is allowed to spend more than eighteen continuous months here, a precaution based on the psychological experiences of early explorers.

During the other half of the year Melissa lives in a cabin on her property in Maine, a place she helped build by hand. When she comes to the Ice, she brings fabric with which to drape the walls in the two-person dorm room that she shares with another woman, a carpenter who works in the Arctic during the summer. Books of poetry and cross-country skis are also part of her personal kit, the latter so she can glide out from Ross Island and onto the sea ice, inscribing a brief trace of her own on the landscape.

The ice—geologists here consider it a mineral, and when they drill or cut into it, the tools they use are those of hard-rock mining. The ice is on the sea, on the ground, in the air. In places it is almost three miles thick and has depressed the bedrock below sea level, making the Antarctic simultaneously the highest and the lowest continent. It reflects back more than eighty percent of the light falling upon it, and bends the sun into improbable arcs and circles. You walk on it, drive across it, breathe it in.

strangers

Like most people who work on the Ice, Melissa is anchored to two places. She looks forward to returning north next month, yet is already regretting it. In Maine there's an orchard that needs pruning, an arbor to be rebuilt, and trails around the boundary of her wooded acreage that need to be cleared of deadfall from this winter's storms. But within a week of returning to Maine, she'll be on the phone to Raytheon, the defense contractor that currently runs polar logistics for the National Science Foundation from its offices in Denver. She'll be looking for work for the next season on the Ice, so she can resume work on her natural history of Hut Point Peninsula, this part of Ross Island.

Ice people say that you have to say goodbye to your family twice a year if you work in the Antarctic. You bid the folks at home farewell when you head south; then you have to say goodbye to everyone at McMurdo when you go north. It wears on you, but you adapt. Some support people have been commuting for two decades, spending a cumulative total of more than seven years on the Ice. That makes them as close to residents as you can become here.

speak

Risk is a compactly built, affable fellow in his mid-thirties. He'll depart this year on the same schedule as Melissa, and along with a bunch of other people spend a few weeks decompressing on the coast of New Zealand. Afterwards, he'll take advantage of the round-the-world airfares that are among the perks of working on the Ice. His end-of-season bonus will be large enough to keep him in Europe during spring before he has to show up for work in Alaska, where he drives a tour bus in Denali National Park during the northern summer.

Risk remains deeply unsure about what to do with his bipolar life. Unmarried, wandering, unsettled, he's an artist talented enough to have been offered a solo exhibition at one of the better galleries in the western United States, but he blew it off to come to the Ice this year. Many artists would kill for an invitation to exhibit in that venue—but not someone bound for the Antarctic.

each

Uphill from us is a chain of hands about ten feet long that Risk cut out of some scrap steel last year. It forms what could perhaps be justified as a safety railing downhill from the carpentry shop. In theory it might prevent people from slipping on ice or mud into the path of the red pickups and vans, the yellow graders, and other equipment plying the road. The reality is that people here, like any other tribe living on the edge of the possible, will use whatever material they can find in order to make something that symbolizes who and where they are—part of the process of converting land into landscape, space into place.

Next to one of the pale green metal buildings in town is a twenty-foot-long orca made from scrap rebar. It stands on steel runners welded to its torso so it can be dragged on the snow. Orcas swim in the sound just offshore scouting for penguins and seals, and they are the emblematic top of the food chain here. The sculpture is as much a totem as anything else, and many of us think it should be dragged back into the middle of town, which consists of a dirt square hosting the bus stop for the shuttles that ply the road between McMurdo and the nearby New Zealand base. A small sign identifies the square as Derelict Junction.

other's

The wooden Bridge of Size is a sturdy assemblage of two-by-fours and other assorted sizes of lumber. Its purpose is to allow people passage over six thickly insulated pipes and conduits, part of the network that winds its way around town bearing water, power, sewage, and glycol. The latter, a chemical cousin of the antifreeze that flows in the blood of the Antarctic cod swimming offshore in McMurdo Sound's 29°F waters, heats the radiators in the buildings. In a sense, we're injecting a poem into the town's circulatory system.

Originally there was supposed to be another course of pipes stacked above the present one, and the bridge was built high enough to accommodate them. Its "size" is a reminder of how often things here don't fit as planned, although they work well enough. Much human presence in the Antarctic is like that: jury-rigged to accommodate available materials to circumstances.

Karen Joyce, the woman who runs Internet Services at Crary, has been adding embellishments to the bridge. She collects items from around McMurdo—small plastic dinosaurs, for example, and unusual rocks brought in from elsewhere on the continent—and glues them onto the wood. At first she just placed them on the railings, but people insisted on taking them, so she's taken to fixing them down permanently with increasingly stronger bonding agents. It's not that people are stealing her additions. Perhaps appropriating is the more accurate term—finding yet another context in which the items would be valued. People have also been donating new items to the bridge, including words on magnetic pieces shuffled into poems, and a metal cube by Risk that asks to be turned over, then displays the words "Thank you" on the other side.

tongue

Melissa has worked her way over the top of the bridge and is about to start on the far side, but she's beginning to shiver, even inside the huge parka that I've lent her. She nods and takes off for the galley in 155 to warm up. Risk keeps carving away, still on the first side; his task is the slower of the two. He stops to warm his hands from time to time. I stand and watch, keep talking to people as they pass over the bridge. The station manager comes out of 155 and casts a glance in our direction. I flinch. Carving up U.S. government property, much less with government-issue tools and without authorization, isn't considered a legitimate science project. People have been banned for life from the Ice for lesser offenses. He turns and walks the other way.

climbing

The original Bridge of Sighs was built in Venice in 1600 and connected the palace of the Doge to the prison across a narrow canal. Its interior is so cramped you have to hunch down to make your way. Thomas Hood used the phrase in a poem written in 1875 about a young woman committing suicide, but it was Lord Byron who first applied it to the bridge in Venice. In his poem he speculated upon the melancholy that prisoners might have felt as they crossed on their way to internment, seeing, perhaps for the last time, the lagoon and the freedom it represented.

In attaching keepsakes to the bridge, Karen and her cohorts were playing consciously off Byron's notion of loss.

When you leave the Ice it is a potential exile because you never know if you'll be hired to return. You might not pass the rigorous physical exam the next year, or your job could be eliminated. The most horrible fate that can be meted out by the authorities in the Antarctic is to banish you deliberately from the continent. It's a simple matter to do so—they just put you on a plane and won't rehire you. Even if you were rich enough to return as a tourist on one of the infrequent ships that manages to visit this far south, you'd be able to stay only for a few hours. You'd never again be able to cross-country ski across the frozen ocean, or be part of the McMurdo community.

The exile is much more than geographical. Scientists who come to the Antarctic are here for their work; Ross Island could be Venezuela for all they care. But the support people come mostly because they want specifically and in the worst way to be on the Ice. The guy who runs the mechanical shop is a former Fulbright scholar specializing in Antarctic history. The woman who this season drives a grader along the main road in town—mockingly referred to as "Antarctic 1"—has skied to the South Pole. Ask a bus driver what he does, and you're likely to find out that he's climbed Mount Everest. Twice. On a per capita basis they are the most accomplished, curious, self-sufficient, and dependable people I've ever met. To be cast out from such a highly motivated community against your will is the worst divorce imaginable.

a

Melissa returns and now it's Risk's turn to take a break inside. He puts down the router and trots off, while she goes back to lettering. Melissa did her master's thesis in biology on alpine plants, and she's expert at locating the smallest scraps of life. As part of her research for the book about the natural history here, she monitors the growth of moss on the peninsula. I had told her that the scientists insisted that no moss grows this far south—farther north on the island, up near the Adélie penguin rookery at Cape Royds, yes, but not down here. Melissa smiled, shook her head, and one late November morning took me for a walk out past Scott's *Discovery* hut. After climbing up the nearby ridge, we found a thumbnail-sized piece of moss growing near a trickle of water flowing from a glacial remnant.

A month later we returned, when the snow cover had retreated from around McMurdo, and clumps of moss were visible almost anywhere there was flowing water, which during this unusually warm summer was all over the ridge. "Life wants to live," she reminded me.

bridge

Across tiny Winter Quarter's Bay, which is visible between the dorms on the other side of Derelict Junction, I can glimpse Scott's Hut from his *Discovery* expedition. It's one of the oldest standing structures in the Antarctic, a protected historical site, and a testament to the changes in our relationship to the continent. Scott bought the Australian outback building before sailing from Hobart. It featured deep eaves all around, and was designed to shed heat, not collect and retain it—at the very least a dubious choice. It was bitterly cold inside, even during summer, and still smells of the seal blubber burned in the stoves, soot from which coats the walls. It was so miserable that it was used mostly for storage; the explorers chose to live instead in the much more familiar and cozy berths aboard the ship.

Take a photograph from the far side of the hut and looking

toward the dorms and Crary Lab—the construction punch list for which was just finished this year—and you capture the entire history of McMurdo in a single frame. To survive on the Ice at the beginning of the twentieth century, human beings had very much to want to live. No glycol flowed through radiators to keep them warm. No hot showers awaited them after the long hours of taking observations in the wind. What kept them going was a sense of common purpose and community, feelings abetted by the presence of the ship, their link to England.

of

Now it's ten o'clock and Risk has worked his way over to the other side of the bridge, where Melissa has finished the lettering. I'm beginning to think that we won't get all the words carved before I have to walk uphill to catch my ride on the Terra Bus, a Canadian vehicle with tires as tall as I am that's made for traversing the roads plowed on the sea ice. I've made more friends here in three months than I have in the last ten years, and the thought of not working alongside them within sight of ice—sea ice, glacial ice, the ice shelf, icebergs—it's as if someone were stealing the light from me.

You're not officially allowed on the plane if you're drunk, and like many first timers I'm almost tempted to hit one of the three local bars hard and fast. Almost. It's a tactic that's been tried before. They put you on the plane anyway, or just sober you up until the flight the next day.

words

On the other side of town from Scott's Hut is Observation Hill, a steep 750-foot-high mound of volcanic rock that veers in color from red and orange through brown and black. Its summit is the most frequented hiking destination near town, one often sought by people within twenty-four hours of arriving, as they instinctively seek high ground from which to orient themselves. This was my favorite time of day to hike its abrupt switchbacks, pausing at the ledge halfway up where the early explorers took their meteorological readings. The rocks there offer shelter from the wind, and it's a place to collect your breath before continuing up the second and steeper half of the trail, which tends to collect more snow and ice. Slip on the lower half, and you might roll downhill a few yards; take a tumble up above and the consequences could be fatal.

At the summit stands the famous wooden cross commemorating Scott and his four companions who died with him when returning from their attempt to be the first to reach the South Pole. The Norwegian Amundsen, who adopted travel methods from the Arctic Inuit, had beaten them by a month and survived the trip in good shape. Scott and his men, in part through lack of planning, starved and froze to death only eleven miles from a food cache and less than ninety miles from "Ob Hill."

The cross quotes Scott, who was in turn quoting Tennyson's *Ulysses*: "To strive, to seek, to find, and not to yield." People trudge up the hill and touch the cross, metaphorically clasping hands with that earlier generation—but there's a sense of irony in the gesture, too. When something goes wrong at McMurdo or in the field, Ice people are likely to intone, with a less-than-straight face: "It's a harsh continent." It's a way of acknowledging not only the reality of the place, but the inevitable incompetence that we drag around behind us as we attempt to turn parts of an extreme land into a human landscape.

two

The view from the top of Ob Hill is a lesson in such extremities. When you arrive at the top your back is to McMurdo Sound, which stretches away to the north. To your right stand the Transantarctic Mountains, which for 1,370 miles separate the archipelago of West Antarctica from the barren ice plateau of East Antarctica. To your left is Mount Erebus, the southernmost active volcano in the world, and at 13,000 feet the most prominent vertical landmark for McMurdo residents. In front of you is the white tabula rasa of the Ross Ice Shelf, where Scott and his companions perished.

Mount Erebus is, simply, mythical. A constant plume of ash and steam reminds us that it holds a live lava lake in its crater, one of perhaps only three in the world. If you're fortunate enough to climb the mountain in the company of the vulcanologists camped on its upper slopes, you can lean gingerly over the rim and observe the constant venting process. Peering into the crater through clouds of steam to glimpse the lake is to take the pulse of the planet.

lovers

If Erebus is the dominant vertical element from the top of Ob Hill, then the great unbroken flat expanse of the Ross Ice Shelf, which stretches out over the horizon in front of you, is the corresponding horizontal feature. Formed by the confluence of the glaciers that flow down through the Transantarctics from the plateau, its surface area is the size of France, and it's the single largest piece of ice on the planet. Pieces of it as large as Rhode Island have been breaking off during the last year; if the shelf were to melt, several American cities would find themselves treading water, an idea that seemed entirely within the realm of the possible on New Year's Eve, as we basked in midnight sun.

Turning in a circle, keeping one hand on the cross for balance on the icy crown of the hill, you gaze out over what seems to be the purest landscape you can imagine—a white page bordered by peaks, the air so clear that you can see individual ridges and gullies a hundred miles away. Even the industrial detritus of McMurdo is attractive in its own way, in the same way that the everyday clutter of a living room signals that it's home.

I look up at Ob Hill from my station next to the bridge and stamp my feet on the ground, which produces no warming effect whatsoever. Two people are walking up the trail in their red government-issue parkas. Despite the wind and cold, they'll be sweating from the exertion. They'll find a nook in the rocks below the cross, and settle in to watch the icebreaker, its circular wake a slow wave of slurry in the dark waters.

parted

We're not going to finish the poem before I have to leave, and Risk takes a break to say goodbye. The words he has carved into the front of the steps will see this scene repeated many times over the years. Melissa gives me back my parka, then walks with me uphill to the bus. She's on the verge of passing beyond shivers and into hypothermia, but stops long enough to give me a strong hug, then turns and runs downhill to the warm galley.

from

On the airplane we're strapped into the webbing on both sides of trash pallets headed to recycling in Christchurch. The ice runway flashes beneath us, the white page of an exam booklet left blank with our ignorance in the face of some obscure question. I'm lucky to have a small window nearby, and see the summit plume of Mount Erebus steaming straight up for a thousand feet before it drifts gently toward the South Pole, 850 miles south. As we fly north the ice gives way to a blue-black sea patterned with tabular icebergs, the cleavered remains of glaciers.

We're all wearing, per Antarctic flight regulations, our Extreme Cold Weather parkas, the huge red down-stuffed garments so warm and commodious that, should you get into trouble in the field, you often can just settle into them as if they were a sleeping bag and wait for help. We're all warm enough to unzip the bulky jackets and use them to pad the webbing, creating one long continuous bed. I curl up next to Mary Miller, a science writer who's been producing live web-casts from the Ice for the Exploratorium in San Francisco. We're both desolate.

one

Three hours later I suddenly wake up, knowing that something is very wrong. I look outside where it's unexpectedly dark and wonder what maelstrom it is that we're flying into, and if we'll have to turn around. Weather often forces flights from Christchurch to McMurdo to boomerang, and I suppose it could happen going in the opposite direction.

Then I realize: it's just night.

I haven't seen the sun go down in three months. I'd forgotten.

another

Eleven months later, while sitting at my desk in the West Texas town of Marfa, yet another temporary residence, I receive an e-mail from Melissa at McMurdo. It's snowing, she says, and the words of the poem are filled with snow. She thought I'd like to know, and I do.

walking　　　　*climbing*
across　　　　*a*
a　　　　*bridge*
poem　　　　*of*
today　　　　*words*
two　　　　*two*
strangers　　　　*lovers*
speak　　　　*parted*
each　　　　*from*
other's　　　　*one*
tongue　　　　*another*

If there is a contemporary literature about the Antarctic it is thanks to the National Science Foundation. The Foundation, which Congress created to award public funds for basic science research at universities, came to add artists and writers to the select list of people it was willing to sponsor in its scientist-oriented Antarctica program. But adding writers and artists was neither obvious nor easy, and they needed a champion. That man is Guy G. Guthridge. For thirty-five years Guy nudged the NSF toward supporting the humanities in Antarctica so that now it is a thriving program sending four or five artists every year. Four contributors to this anthology were awarded these special grants, which sends writers and artists to Antarctica; while there, they are clothed, fed, housed, and shuttled about the continent. The story behind the creation of this anthology rests, in other words, on Guy's story.

In this essay about his journey we see the forces of science and writing that shaped Guy. Those forces are still at play in his life. Since Guy retired in 2005, he has lived aboard a boat and writes about the intersection of science and societal issues regarding the Chesapeake Bay and its watershed.

Maverick Among Scientists

✷ ✷ ✷

GUY G. GUTHRIDGE

I WAS GOING TO BE A MAN OF LETTERS. AS A YOUTH IN Arlington, Virginia, I romantically figured writing was to be my likely career because my hero, author Jack London, had written extensively about hopping freight trains and I hopped freight trains—on the Washington & Old Dominion Railroad, whose tracks were near my house. Only later would I understand that the apparent simplicity of Jack London's writing masked a storytelling genius and years of experiment.

College did not move me in the direction of literary greatness. Enrolled in 1959 for reasons of heritage in the School of Engineering at the University of Virginia, I fell in with other misfits. We mocked the straight-up engineers, referred to the enterprise as the Tool School, and dubbed a dreaded professor The Wedge because he was the Simplest Tool Known To Man. We believed the rumor that, over in the College of Arts and Sciences, English majors were allowed to take final exams with bottles of whiskey on their desks. William Faulkner had taught here, written here. Afternoons I read Jack Kerouac, sitting under a Southern Railroad trestle.

After two years of load diagrams and leveling circuits I decamped to Paris, France, for a semester of exuberant liberation from the Tool School. Just forty years before, an impoverished Ernest Hemingway had sat on park benches there and trapped pigeons as dinner for his wife and infant son. I practiced diligently my one flawless sentence, and for years after accepted any opportunity to toss off, *"J'ai passé six mois à la Sorbonne dans le cours de civilisation française pour les étrangers."*

Broke and in New York, in 1963 I got work surveying in Staten Island, Brooklyn, and Queens for a pipeline under the streets to pump jet fuel from the tank farm in Elizabeth, New Jersey, to what is now JFK Airport. When done, the project would take countless fuel trucks off the road. The Wedge, back at U.Va., had made sense. I enthusiastically visualized threading fourteen-inch-diameter pipes underground through intersections crammed with utility lines. The city assigned our potentially toxic project to the lowest position, even lower than the sewers. Deep meant expensive, so we planned cleverly (we thought) to stay as shallow as we could. My writing aspiration had morphed into mechanical drawing.

After two years in The Big Apple, reading mainly the *Village Voice* and a Henry Miller volume smuggled from France, I decompressed back to Virginia to finish in English. I received the gentlemanly C in the one course in creative writing I dared take, was good at literary criticism, debating, and the Rhetoric of Aristotle.

Graduated in 1967 and by then with wife and infant son just like Hemingway, I dodged eating pigeon. Instead, in Washington, D.C., I got paid to edit technical manuscripts for companies of the kind Washingtonians called Beltway Bandits. One report, issued earnestly by the nuclear utilities company I worked for, recommended the Coast Guard power its new icebreakers with nuclear reactors. The Coast Guard ignored it, designing diesels and gas turbines into plans for the coming new Polar class. But my role was enough to land a job in 1970 with the National Science Foundation's Office of Polar Programs.

I found myself editor of *Antarctic Journal of the United States* and soon in love with scientists' insistence on having incontrovertible data to back up assertions they made in print. The mail brought manuscripts for the *Journal*—rough sculptures wanting editing, sometimes badly. The literary career faded further as, instead, my pencil honed the ideas of others. The effort earned thanks from some researchers, indifference from more, enmity from a few. The intellectually challenging work was an education in science. And it was a step toward digesting the potential presented by NSF's—and my—involvement with the amazing continent of Antarctica.

Because by then I was astraddle—one foot in the logic and beauty of words, the other in the wonder of scientific discovery.

Four seminal events during my NSF career shaped how the fledgling Antarctic Artists and Writers Program came to hold what now seems (I hope) a permanent place among the programs the Foundation supports.

The first was an early assignment to consider requests, should any actually arrive, from writers or artists hoping to spend time in the Antarctic at National Science Foundation expense. Before I arrived, a poet—Donald Finkel—had published a book, *Adequate Earth*, after somehow getting NSF to sponsor such a visit. Of my colleagues only Philip M. Smith seemed to care about these nonscientists, and Phil gave me the Office of Polar Programs copy of Finkel's slim volume as his way of passing the torch, or perhaps hot potato. "Whelped in

the time of ice, we adapt to anything," jumped from a page of
the poet's book,

> even
> this continent: five and a half
> million square miles of glorious
> unconditional ice, asleep
> in the farthest sea like a godmother's gift,
> bewitched so only the brave might find her,
> or the lost…

Could I have written that?

But NSF wasn't paying me to write poetry. More compelling anyway was that in 1970, the same year I got my
Antarctic job, the President had signed a memorandum telling
NSF to "support the range of U.S. Antarctic interests." The
range had to include the arts and letters! Around the Office
of Polar Programs I made the point tentatively, earning yawns
and the occasional arched eyebrow.

As junior member of the team I focused on my *Antarctic
Journal* editing, building sentiment, I hoped, for keeping
someone without a science degree on the payroll.

The second seminal event came after four dry years in
Antarctica for artists and writers. Our National Bicentennial
was coming, and not being in an arts agency I asked the
National Endowment for the Arts to help NSF bring
Antarctica to the table for the country's two-hundredth birthday party. We got two winners: landscape painter Daniel Lang
and one of the twentieth century's celebrated color photographers, Eliot Porter.

Word got around that the Science Foundation had an
Antarctic arts program, even though the Arts Endowment
collaboration was little more than a one-time thing. But

NSF's own nascent Antarctic Artists and Writers Program was still informal, known only by word of mouth, and driven by criteria that were unwritten. No way to run a program, but the polar office was not yet willing to buck the NSF culture by suggesting that scholars in the humanities receive the same status as scientists. I sent "regret negative" letters to applicants who were accomplished practitioners of the arts, unwittingly setting myself up for the third seminal event.

A letter saying no went to Charles Neider of Princeton, New Jersey, after spirited internal discussion at NSF that weighed literary achievement versus organizational ego. Mr. Neider had published extensively including the screenplay for a Marlon Brando movie. His latest book had come out in 1974, based on an earlier Antarctic trip the Navy had sponsored and a second that NSF supported, and it portrayed a support unit in the U.S. Antarctic Program unflatteringly. Senator Harrison Williams of New Jersey, hearing from Charles about NSF's negative decision for a third trip, phoned Foundation director H. Guyford Stever and told him to reverse it.

Down in the polar office, I quickly found out that NSF directors don't like to get such calls. It was no fun being overruled by an outsider, even a United States Senator. And my little program for artists and writers was generating more than its share of water-cooler talk.

Looking back over the record, I'm saddened to see that five more dry years followed Charles Neider's 1977 Antarctic visit. His resulting book was published in 1980, was well received critically, and did not offend NSF. His Antarctic trips more than thirty years ago resulted in three worthy books, and all three still are in print; one—an anthology—belongs on any Antarctican's shelf. Charles died, after a long and generous life, in 2001 on the Fourth of July. I try never to forget about the impact of an NSF decision.

In 1982, now with an officially approved Antarctic Artists and Writers Program patterned after the NSF procedure for vetting science proposals, I was able to send earth science historian Stephen J. Pyne to the Antarctic. His magnificent book *The Ice: A Journey to Antarctica*, which took another five years to research and write, was a 1987 *New York Times* best book; in 1988 Pyne won a MacArthur Fellowship (the "genius award"). A paragraph from his book became iconic:

> Ice is the beginning and ice is the end of Antarctica. To enter Greater Antarctica is to be drawn into a maelstrom of ice. Antarctica contains 90 percent of the planet's glacial ice, and during the winter when the seas around it congeal into a frozen pack, the size of the Antarctic ice field doubles. Antarctica is literally fused together, as a continent, by ice. The magnitude of the Antarctic ice sheet is enough to deform the planet. The scale of its ice field affects global climate. The dimensions of Antarctic ice control the level of the world ocean. Antarctica—the Ice—is the Earth's sink for heat and water, a cold fusion that absorbs rather than emanates, a geophysical underworld. The Ice is organized, like Dante's Inferno, into concentric rings. There is a gradient to the terranes—loose, information-rich, dynamic on the perimeter; fixed, information-poor, invariant at the core. To journey to its source region is to pass through an increasingly ice-dominated landscape until land itself vanishes into exclusionary ice. The reductionism of The Ice is relentless. Ice replaces everything that is not ice. Ice confines ice. Ice defines

ice. A continent is reduced to a single mineral. In Antarctica more is less.

I never found a better statement about why the arts are important than the 1965 legislation (still in effect: see nea.gov) by which the Congress of the United States establishes the National Foundation on the Arts and the Humanities. Here is an excerpt:

An advanced civilization must not limit its efforts to science and technology alone, but must give full value and support to the other great branches of scholarly and cultural activity in order to achieve a better understanding of the past, a better analysis of the present, and a better view of the future… The practice of art and the study of the humanities require constant dedication and devotion. While no government can call a great artist or scholar into existence, it is necessary and appropriate for the Federal Government to help create and sustain not only a climate encouraging freedom of thought, imagination, and inquiry but also the material conditions facilitating the release of this creative talent… The world leadership which has come to the United States cannot rest solely upon superior power, wealth, and technology, but must be solidly founded upon worldwide respect and admiration for the Nation's high qualities as a leader in the realm of ideas and of the spirit.

Still, at NSF and in its Office of Polar Programs, not everyone was clear on the concept. Several more years, and one more seminal event, were needed before the Antarctic Artists and Writers Program was to flourish.

Peter E. Wilkniss headed the Office of Polar Programs from 1984 to 1993. He was so strong and alive that it's hard to accept his death in 2005 at the age of seventy. He brought huge, innovative, and welcome change to the U.S. Antarctic Program. He was hierarchical in outlook and a warrior, wielding power instinctively and decisively. In personal contact with a higher authority, though, he was deferential almost to the point of timidity.

Peter was heavy-handed and had fired several managers. Those of us still around wondered if we were next. Early in his reign he was indifferent to some of my projects, if he had bothered to find out about them at all, so when he assembled the staff after returning from an important trip to the Ice in late 1988 I wondered if it was my last day on the job when he started to talk about the Antarctic Artists and Writers Program.

Here is what had happened in Antarctica.

Barry Lopez and Michael Parfit were that season's Antarctic Artists and Writers Program participants. Barry, one of the nation's most prominent writers, especially concerning the relationship between the physical landscape and human culture, had written *Arctic Dreams* (1986), which won the National Book Award. Michael Parfit was on his second trip and had published his first major Antarctic work, the book *South Light*. Peter traveled to Antarctica this particular time to escort Senator Al Gore and others on an inspection and fact-finding visit.

On the trip down in the plane Peter was stunned to see his powerful guests reading the Parfit and Lopez books instead of the information packets they had been issued. In the chow line at McMurdo Station, Senator Gore met Mike Parfit, whose first two chapters describe some startling operations during the preseason LC-130 flights to McMurdo called

Winfly. Mr. Gore said something like, "So you're the one who scared the hell out of us on the way down." Mike introduced the Senator to a senior scientist studying the West Antarctic Ice Sheet.

In the TransAntarctic Mountains, where Barry Lopez was visiting a glacial geology research team, Gore maneuvered a private conversation with Barry in addition to receiving NSF's planned briefing about the science project from the principal investigator. Lopez writes on his web site, "Gore impressed us as someone unusually well-informed about the scientific questions involved, and he struck us as the model of a public servant. He was smart, courteous, a determined questioner, and a keen listener. It was -5°F and he'd had to hike a half mile uphill to the drill site from the spot where the helicopter set him down. He didn't complain and never struck a pose. He was a man on a mission. Gore refers to this visit to our Newell Glacier camp in his documentary, *An Inconvenient Truth*.

Back at McMurdo that evening in 1988, I heard from colleagues that Al Gore said to Peter something like, "I was impressed by the work and the scientists. But what really impressed me was that you can get writers like this."

And back at NSF at the staff meeting with Peter Wilkniss, the Antarctic Artists and Writers Program had a good day. "Whatever you're doing back there," he said, "keep it up."

It wasn't just Peter who bought in. The Foundation as a whole began insisting that the programs it was funding get "broader impact." Investigators and others were to reach past the communities of science to people who don't read the primary scientific literature. In the Foundation's presentations to Congress and the public, Antarctica with its inherent appeal became even more visible than before.

After 1988 the Antarctic Artists and Writers Program fielded no less than two participants each season. In the last decade or so of my tenure the typical annual number was five or six. Other Antarctic nations set up artist-writer programs patterned more or less on the NSF one. The Antarctic Treaty System, whose forty-six member nations represent two-thirds of the world's population, noted that Antarctica had been the subject of significant works of art, literature, and music. The international body adopted a resolution in 1996 promoting understanding of the values of the Antarctic through the contributions of writers, artists, and musicians.

I retired from NSF in 2005, having managed ninety-three projects in the Antarctic Artists and Writers Program (some contained more than one participant, and some artists and writers went to the Antarctic more than once). Looking back, I like to think it inevitable that sooner or later the folks in charge would realize, with or without my being there, that painters and photographers, poets and essayists and novelists and musicians and sculptors should take their rightful place in the national program for Antarctica just as they have in other walks of American life.

But, sometimes, I'm not so sure the Antarctic humanities program was a slam dunk. The financial pressures on NSF are great, cuts invariably have to be made, and the Foundation's middle name is Science. What was my effect? Two quotes come to mind. One is from Winston Churchill's famous 1941 speech: "Never give in. Never give in. Never, never, never, never—in nothing, great or small, large or petty—never give in, except to convictions of honor and good sense." The other is the last line of Richard E. Byrd's 1938 book *Alone*: "A man doesn't begin to attain wisdom until he recognizes that he is no longer indispensable."

Somewhere between the two became my focus the last few years I was at NSF. I worked to make the process of administering the Antarctic Artists and Writers Program so indistinguishable from the regular science programs that stopping it (not that anyone wanted to anymore) would be harder than letting it keep rolling along. I stopped arguing that the program was unique and could never tolerate using the automated proposal system called FastLane that the scientists have to use. Now the artists and writers use FastLane, too (and complain about it, as the scientists used to). The internal evaluation procedures were made as much like those for science projects as they could be. The program attained an institutional routine and momentum, and I figured it would outlast me, and so far that's been the case.

Artists show us what we see, and they remind us what is important. Peter Nisbet, a painter, and Jody Forster, a photographer, worked side by side for a week at the Barne Glacier. Back at McMurdo the painter told a Sunday night audience, "One of Jody's photographs showed me something I had completely overlooked while we were there." Maybe some hue of light, or structure. I don't remember. But the comment seared into my memory.

Neelon Crawford, a photographer, made five trips to the Antarctic, including a winter, and observed, "Antarctica's most significant influences will reach far beyond the important scientific discoveries made here. Antarctica is central to our understanding of both the physical systems of our planet and the psychological forces struggling to direct our future path. The United States Antarctic Program is the experiment." Painter Alan Campbell: "I have no choice but to be a listener here." Painter Lucia deLeiris, "having to constantly remind myself that this was actually part of the earth I knew." Photographer

Stuart Klipper: "We whistle anthems of nations near where whiteness blanches all hope of domain and distinction." Barry Lopez: "Antarctica—where there is no war, no famine, no inflation, no polluting industry, no dictator, no bunkered ghetto—allows us to think hard, and with little distraction, upon our biology. To confront the tenuousness of it. Underneath persistent questions about the effects of ozone fluctuation or the perturbed chemistry of the atmosphere lurks a question we'd rather not hear: Is our biology promising? In an era of catastrophic loss of species, the suspicion of some is that we ourselves are not exempt." Author Sara Wheeler: "The landscape was intact, complete and larger than my imagination could grasp.... It was sufficient unto itself, untainted by the inevitable tragedy of the human condition.... I had glimpsed a world in which everything made sense." Charles Neider: "Let me stress one resource which isn't spoken of and which in our utilitarian and pragmatic age is insufficiently valued, and that is Antarctica's remarkable beauty." Michael Parfit: "These pieces of memory seem unaccountably valuable, as if the assembling of them will somehow reveal why, after spending months or years being cold, uncomfortable, and lonely, so many human beings persist in thinking that their time here was a gift."

Back to the dreams of childhood, for the most part I long ago accommodated to the reality that I won't be a literary great. I got some excellent writing done, after all. Just not mine. It was a gift.

Index

Acknowledgments

Thanks goes first to the National Science Foundation for granting me a trip to the Ice and to those who directly made that possible: Guy Guthridge and Elaine Hood. Philip Roth, Leon Botstein, and Bard College all supported this grant, for which I will always be grateful. I'd like to thank all of the scientists and camp managers who welcomed me to their camps: David Ainley and Jennifer Blum who shared penguins, some wine, and their list of favorite books while waiting out a storm at Cape Royds; Rae Spain who made extraordinary meals at Camp Hoare; the carpenters at New Harbor, especially Solar Joe and BK; Jeb Barrett at Lake Fryxell; hilarious Phil Allen, Melissa Hage, and Kaycie Ann Billmark for their pudding pie at Garwood Valley; Paul for the tour of South Pole station and for allowing me to go skiing onto the polar plateau; our Kiwi neighbors performing archaeological work at Scott's Hut at Cape Evans who let me chip ice from the south side of the hut. Monika Gablowski made the logistics of my travel by helicopter both easy and fun. Thanks to my sister Rebecca and her family and to many friends who supported my trip to the Ice and listened to my stories. John Cronin and Donna Steiner were both patient and extraordinary readers. Wendy Strothman pushed this collection forward and Travelers' Tales welcomed me into their world of travel narratives. Thanks above all to the writers in this collection who have offered their stories.

298 Antarctica: Life on the Ice

"In This Dream" by Joe Mastroianni published with permission from the author. Copyright © 2007 by Joe Mastroianni.

"The Day It Rained Chickens" by Karen Joyce published with permission from the author. Copyright © 2007 by Karen Joyce.

"Lost in the Storm" by Jim Mastro published with permission from the author. Copyright © 2007 by Jim Mastro.

"Sunrise at 90 South" by Katy M. Jensen published with permission from the author. Copyright © 2007 by Katy M. Jensen.

"The Ultimate Risky Business" by Jon Bowermaster published with permission from the author. Copyright © 2007 by Jon Bowermaster.

"The Secret of Silence" by Susan Fox Rogers published with permission from the author. Copyright © 2007 by Susan Fox Rogers.

"AGO 1" by Jason Anthony published with permission from the author. Copyright © 2007 by Jason Anthony.

"The Big Chill" by Phil Jacobsen published with permission from the author. Copyright © 2007 by Phil Jacobsen.

"True Point of Beginning" by Jules Uberuaga, published with permission from the author. Copyright © 2007 by Jules Uberuaga.

"Seeing Mount Erebus" by Beth Bartel, published with permission from the author. Copyright © 2007 by Beth Bartel.

"Food for Thought, Foods as Fuel" by Mark Lehman published with permission from the author. Copyright © 2007 by Mark Lehman.

"Shrink Rap" by Glenn Grant published with permission from the author. Copyright © 2007 by Glenn Grant.

"How to Find a Dinosaur" by Lucy Jane Bledsoe published with permission from the author. Copyright © 2007 by Lucy Jane Bledsoe.

"We Ate No Turkey: A Holiday on Ice" by Traci J. MacNamara published with permission from the author. Copyright © 2007 by Traci J. MacNamara.

"Toast on Ice: Wintering in Antarctica" by Nicholas Johnson published with permission from the author. Copyright © 2007 by Nicholas Johnson.

"A Letter from Cape Royds: Of Penguins and Men" by David Ainley published with permission from the author. Copyright © 2007 by David Ainley.

About the Editor

Susan Fox Rogers is the editor of ten book anthologies including *Solo: On Her Own Adventure* and *Going Alone: Women's Adventures in the Wild*. In the austral summer of 2004-05 she spent six weeks on an NSF grant in McMurdo. From there she traveled to various remote camps and to the South Pole. She lives in the Hudson River Valley and teaches creative writing and First Year Seminar at Bard College.